RAYMOND WILLIAMS is now best known as [...] materialist' approach in cultural studies. Duri[...] life, Williams succeeded in recasting the r[...] especially literature, was analysed and discussed. Working with a broad and generous conception of culture as a 'structure of feeling', Williams consistently sought to place aspects of culture in the context of a process of cultural 'production' which was itself rooted in historically specific social relations. In these pages, Williams demonstrates the fertility of this method through his careful analysis of phenomena as diverse as English naturalist theatre, the Bloomsbury Group, advertising, science fiction, and the Welsh industrial novel.

Williams was temperamentally inclined never to take theoretical categories and tools as given, but rather sharpened his case studies by continually reflecting on notions such as materialism, social relations and forces of production and their relevance to the cultural sphere. Thus, in these essays one can observe Williams's penetrating insight at work as he considers these concepts both at a high level of abstraction (different notions of nature, the growth of Social Darwinism, and the relationship between biological and historical materialism), and as directly applied to his specialised field (the sociology of literature, the usefulness of the 'base and superstructure' metaphor, and the means of communication seen as means of production). Despite his enormous impact in the sphere of cultural studies Raymond Williams was not merely a Marxist academic, but a committed and passionate socialist activist, and this is reflected in the final two essays in this collection, in which he discusses the legacy and future of socialism in Britain and internationally.

RAYMOND WILLIAMS was born in Wales in 1921 and died in 1988. Until his retirement in 1983, he was Professor of Drama at the University of Cambridge. During the 1960s and 1970s, Raymond Williams was a leading figure in the New Left, and his political writings include *The Long Revolution* (1961) and *Towards 2000* (1983), as well as, with Verso, the collected interviews in *Politics and Letters: Interviews with New Left Review* (1979) and *Resources of Hope: Culture, Democracy, Socialism* (1989). Amongst his other publications were, *Culture and Society* (1958), *Modern Tragedy* (1966), *Drama from Ibsen to Brecht* (1968), *The Country and the City* (1973), *Keywords* (1976), *Marxism and Literature* (1977) and, with Verso, *Writing in Society* (1983) and *The Politics of Modernism: Against the New Conformists* (1989; reissued as a Verso Classic, 1996). Williams was also the author of a number of novels, including *Border Country* (1960), *The Volunteers* (1978), and the two volumes of *People of the Black Mountains* (1989; 1990).

VERSO
CLASSICS

The last few decades have seen an immense outpouring of works of theory and criticism, but, as the number of titles has increased dramatically, it has become more and more difficult to find one's way round this vast body of literature and to distinguish between those works of real and enduring value and those of a more ephemeral nature. The Verso Classics series will rise to the challenge by taking stock of the last few decades of contemporary critical thought and reissuing, in an elegant paperback format and at affordable prices, those books which genuinely constitute original and important intellectual contributions.

Many of these works are currently out of print or difficult to obtain; Verso Classics will bring them back into the public domain, building a collection which will become the 'essential left library'.

Problems in Materialism and Culture

Selected Essays

RAYMOND WILLIAMS

VERSO

London · New York

First published by Verso 1980
This edition published by Verso 1997
© Raymond Williams 1980
All rights reserved

Verso
UK: 6 Meard Street, London W1V 3HR
USA: 180 Varick Street, New York, NY 10014–4606

Verso is the imprint of New Left Books

ISBN 1–85984–113–9

British Library Cataloguing in Publication Data
A catalogue record for this book is available from the British Library

Library of Congress Cataloging-in-Publication Data
A catalog record for this book is available from the Library of Congress

Printed in Great Britain by Creative Print and Design (Wales), Ebbw Vale

Contents

Publisher's Note

'Selected essays' are not uncommon in English-language culture, but their rationale as a form of publication is notably variable, and often indefinite. It may be pertinent, therefore, briefly to indicate our purpose in compiling *Problems in Materialism and Culture*.

Raymond Williams's many books – from *Reading and Criticism* to *Marxism and Literature* – are well known and, with very few exceptions, widely available. What are less generally known and, for evident material reasons, not nearly so accessible, are the numerous essays that have accompanied them. Anticipating or developing the themes of the major works, augmenting them with more detailed studies or extending their methods into new areas of research, these essays are a crucial component of Williams's writing as a whole, and it was in order to make them available to the wider readership of his full-length books that this volume was conceived.

The fourteen texts included here were chosen and arranged in the light of a related consideration. Many thousands of readers have encountered Williams's major works as they appeared, in an intellectual acquaintanceship going back twenty years and more. But there is an increasing number for whom, inevitably, this is not the case. So large and complex a body of work can pose problems of access, for anyone – teacher or student, specialist or general reader – approaching it for the first time. It seemed important, therefore, that any selection of essays should aim to cover its entire range (apart from the novels), to compose a volume at once compact and representative.

Problems in Materialism and Culture has been designed to meet these requirements. The earliest of the essays dates from the period of *The Long Revolution*, having been written in 1958-59, the most recent from

New Year, 1980. Their occasions are lectures and book-reviews as well as relatively independent and long-standing contexts of research. In mode the volume ranges from wholly abstract theoretical exposition to concrete historical analysis, from specialist research through collaborative dissent to engaged polemic. The subjects of discussion include literature and drama; theories of culture and of nature; dominant and subordinate, celebrated and marginal, forms of cultural production; structural features of late capitalist society and of the socialist order beyond it; the related political problems of contesting the one and constructing the other. The central theme – and practice – of the volume, already given in its title, is the elaboration within Marxist theory and socialist politics of a 'cultural materialism'.

A Hundred Years of Culture and Anarchy, the opening essay of the book, looks back to illuminate a decisive and profoundly ambivalent moment in the emergence of English cultural criticism: Arnold's response to the popular agitation of the late 1860s. Then follow a group of three studies in cultural theory: a tribute to Lucien Goldmann that discusses his work and meditates on its complex relations with received intellectual traditions in England; a re-examination of the concept of 'base and superstructure'; and a theoretical analysis of means of communication. The next group of three essays is devoted to the problem of 'nature', as represented in the dominant humanist tradition; in the ideological formations, past and present, of Social Darwinism; and in the writings of the Italian Marxist Sebastiano Timpanaro. A fourth section brings together five concrete studies dealing successively with English naturalist theatre; the Bloomsbury group; advertising; utopianism and science fiction; and the Welsh industrial novelists. These exemplify the analytic programme of cultural theory.

Politics is the keynote of the fifth and last section of the volume. Here Williams reflects on the problematic history of Marxism in post-war Britain and on his own relation to it, and then, in a concluding essay on Rudolf Bahro's *Alternative*, turns to consider the state of 'actually existing socialism' – the comparable blockages of the instituted social order in the East and of the movement in the West – and to project a course beyond it, through the theory and practice of 'cultural revolution'.

NLB

Acknowledgments

The essays now collected in this volume were first published as follows: *A Hundred Years of Culture and Anarchy* in *The Spokesman*, 8, December 1970, based on a lecture given in Manchester in April 1969; *Literature and Sociology: in Memory of Lucien Goldmann* in *New Left Review*, 67, May-June 1971, based on a lecture given in Cambridge in April 1971; *Base and Superstructure in Marxist Cultural Theory* in *New Left Review*, 82, November-December 1973, based on a lecture given in Montreal in April 1973; *Means of Communication as Means of Production* in *Prilozi*: *Drustvenost Komunikacije*, Zagreb, 1978; *Ideas of Nature* in *Ecology: the Shaping Inquiry* (ed. J. Benthall), Longman, 1972, based on a lecture given at the Institute of Contemporary Arts, London, in 1971; *Social Darwinism* in *The Limits of Human Nature* (ed. J. Benthall), Allen Lane, 1973, based on a lecture given at the Institute of Contemporary Arts, London, in 1972; *Problems of Materialism* in *New Left Review*, 109, May-June 1978; *Social Environment and Theatrical Environment* in *English Drama: Forms and Development* (ed. M. Axton and R. Williams), Cambridge University Press, 1977; *The Bloomsbury Fraction* in *Keynes and the Bloomsbury Group* (ed. D. Crabtree and A.P. Thirlwall), Macmillan, 1980, based on a lecture given in Canterbury in 1978; *Advertising: the Magic System*, originally written as a chapter in *The Long Revolution* (1961), withdrawn from that book for inclusion in a collective book on advertising which in the event was not published, then published in part in *New Left Review*, 4, July-August 1960 (the *Afterword* to this essay was published in *The Listener*, 31 July, 1969); *Utopia and Science Fiction* in *Science Fiction Studies*, Vol. 5 (1978), Montreal, and in *Science Fiction: a Critical Guide* (ed. P. Parrinder), Longman, 1979; *The Welsh Industrial Novel*, University College Press, Cardiff, 1979, based on the inaugural Gwyn Jones lecture given in Cardiff, April 1978; *Notes on Marxism in Britain since 1945* in *New Left Review*, 100, November 1976-January 1977; *Beyond Actually Existing Socialism* in *New Left Review*, 120, March-April 1980. I have taken the opportunity to revise all the essays for this volume.

R.W.

1

A Hundred Years of
Culture and Anarchy

In the late sixties several issues came together. Issues and controversies. About parliament, about law and the trade unions, about demonstrations and public order, about education and its expansion. In the late eighteen-sixties, I mean. In the years when George Eliot began *Middlemarch*, when Marx published the first volume of *Capital*, when Carlyle wrote *Shooting Niagara*, and Matthew Arnold wrote the lectures and articles which became *Culture and Anarchy*.

In our own late sixties the spirit of Arnold is often invoked, especially in the universities. He has been taken as a kind of patron of things like the *Black Papers*: in some ways astonishingly, for all his working life he was a hardworking inspector of education and the most effective exponent of the need for a new system of secondary schooling. Nevertheless, the invocation is neither accidental nor wholly misguided. Arnold's emphasis on culture—his kind of emphasis—was a direct response to the social crisis of those years, and what he saw as opposed to culture was *anarchy*, in a sense very similar to many recent public descriptions of demonstrations and the protest movement. He did not see or present himself as a reactionary, but as a guardian of excellence and of humane values. That, then as now, was the strength of his appeal.

What then was the actual crisis? In immediate terms it was an argument about the franchise: that the right to vote should be extended to working-class men in the towns. Not, it now seems, so very radical a proposal. Just a hundred years later that hard-won right is part of our 'immemorial' democratic traditions. But at the time it was critical. In 1866 the first form of the bill was defeated and the Liberal government fell. The campaign was taken to the country by the Reform League. The meetings in London were especially large. The only suitable places for such large

Arnold argued—very quickly abstracting and simplifying—was a symptom of the general anarchy. He did not want revolution, though he would like his own class to rule, just as the aristocracy and the middle class prefer their own forms of domination. In 'our paradisical centres of industrialism and individualism' many people were taking the bread out of one another's mouths, for there was no real social order, no idea of the State as the collective and corporate character of the nation. So, having not yet quite settled to his place in the system, the rioter—he becomes suddenly 'the rough'—

> is just asserting his personal liberty a little, going where he likes, assembling where he likes, bawling as he likes, hustling as he likes.

The temperature, it will be noticed, is rising.

> His right to march where he likes, meet where he likes, enter where he likes, hoot as he likes, threaten as he likes, smash as he likes. All this, I say, tends to anarchy.

It certainly does. Nothing is stranger, in Arnold's often scrupulous, often self-consciously charming and delicate prose, than the escalation, the coarseness, of these Hyde Park verbs. Then, writing while the argument was still going on in parliament, he went suddenly much further. He restated his general position:

> For us, who believe in right reason, in the duty and possibility of extricating our best self, in the progress of humanity towards perfection, for us the framework of society, that theatre on which this august drama has to unroll itself, is sacred; and whoever administers it, and however we may seek to remove them from their tenure of administration, yet, while they administer, we steadily and with undivided heart support them in repressing anarchy and disorder; because without order there can be no society; and without society there can be no human perfection.

It is a point of view. Certainly it contrives to forget the start of the disorder: the defeat of the reform legislation, the locking of the gates against the reform meeting (for which, as it happens, there were no legal grounds). As so often, it picks up the story at a convenient point: at the point of response, sometimes violent, to repression; not at the repression itself. Even so, it is a point of view, and a familiar one.

But then Arnold again goes on:

> I remember my father ... when the political and social state of the

country was gloomy and troubled [in *the 1820s*—RW] and there were riots in many places, goes on, after strongly insisting on the badness and foolishness of the government ... and ends thus: *As for rioting, the old Roman way of dealing with that is always the right one; flog the rank and file, and fling the ringleaders from the Tarpeian Rock!* And this opinion we can never forsake, however our Liberal friends may think a little rioting, and what they call popular demonstrations, useful sometimes to their own interests and to the interests of the valuable practical operations they have in hand.

Even if it is to abolish the slave-trade

—still we say no, and that monster processions in the streets and forcible irruptions into the parks, even in professed support of this good design, ought to be unflinchingly forbidden and repressed.

In a later edition Arnold left this out. We must give him the credit of his second thoughts. But it is still very remarkable that the humane argument of the initial position should approach, let alone reach, this degree of anger and desire for repression.

Yet the conjunction may be significant, at some level quite difficult to define. The hostile reaction to demonstrations and sit-ins, in our own period, is easy to understand when it comes from the traditional right. But there is now also a New Right, talking of excellence and humane values and discipline, in the same breath; seeing minor demonstrations as 'anarchy' and 'chaos' and opposing them in the name of reason and culture and education.

Arnold is a source for this group, though it is significant that many of them have dropped much of his actual social criticism and especially his untiring advocacy of extended popular education. That part of Arnold, indeed, is now seen as a main symptom of the 'disease' they believe they are fighting. But that is often how names and reputations are invoked from the past.

There are others they might have chosen. I can't agree with all Mill did, in those months, but if you want liberal reason in action, Mill then embodies it: the emphasis on law and moderation but also the emphasis on change and reform (he had introduced a bill giving the vote to women, a measure well beyond the thoughts of the majority of the Reform League; it was derisively defeated). Mill, one could say, shows how a traditional intellectual can respond at his best: acting through the values of reason at the points where it mattered. I would differ from him in my belief that the second Hyde Park meeting ought to have been held and supported; there was no law or reason to prevent it, and any provocation or violence would have come only from the authorities. But Mill was anxious. He mediated and moderated. He kept to his own values.

Arnold is different, and so are our own little Arnolds. Excellence and humane values on the one hand; discipline and where necessary repression on the other. This, then as now, is a dangerous position: a culmination of the wrong kind of liberalism, just as Mill, as far as he went, was a culmination of liberalism of the most honest kind. The issues continue: the law and the unions; new education acts; the ins and outs of two dominant and competing parliamentary parties. As we think and act through very comparable events, a hundred years later, it is of some real help to know how the 'culture and anarchy' argument started.

But what is even more important is to identify and prevent that short-circuit in thought which Arnold represents. The attachment to reason, to informed argument, to considered public decisions, and indeed, in Arnold's terms, to learning from all the best that has been thought and said in the world, requires something more than an easy rhetorical contrast with the practices of demonstration and of direct action. For these, in the eighteen-sixties as in the nineteen-sixties, were entered into at just those points where truth and reason and argument were systematically blocked, and where 'authorized' force was invoked not to clear the barriers but to erect and defend them.

It then matters very much whether those who believe in reason and in informed argument are able, within the noise of confrontation, to go on making the necessary distinctions. It matters also whether, in the inevitable tensions of new kinds of argument and new kinds of claim, the defenders of reason and education become open to new and unfamiliar relationships, or instead relapse to their existing habits and privileges and then—as is now happening, but as significantly didn't happen in Arnold —manoeuvre and combine to restrict, to purge, to impoverish education itself. For the culture which is then being defended is not excellence but familiarity, not the knowable but only the known values. And while people like that dominate and multiply, it will always be necessary to go again to Hyde Park.

2

Literature and Sociology

In Memory of Lucien Goldmann

Last spring* Lucien Goldmann came to Cambridge and gave two lectures. It was an opportunity for many of us to hear a man whose work we had welcomed and respected. And he said that he liked Cambridge: to have trees and fields this near to lecture-rooms. I invited him and he agreed to come back again this year. More particularly we agreed to exchange our current work directly, for we were both aware of the irony that the short physical distance between England and France converts, too often, to a great cultural distance, and especially at the level of detail. And then, in the autumn, he died, at the age of 57. The beginning of a project had to revert to print, as must perhaps always finally happen. But first I want to remember him directly, as an act of respect and as an active acknowledgment of what I believe is now necessary: a bringing together and a discussion of work and ideas occurring in very different traditions but nevertheless sharing many common positions and concerns. My regret, of course, is that he cannot be here to take part in the dialogue. For the manner of his lectures in Cambridge was precisely dialogue: in a sense to my surprise, having read only his published writings, which are marked by a certain defining and systematic rigour.

I think many people have now noticed the long-term effects of the specific social situation of British intellectuals: a situation which is changing but with certain continuing effects. In humane studies, at least, and with mixed results, British thinkers and writers are continually pulled back towards ordinary language: not only in certain rhythms and in choices of words, but also in a manner of exposition which can be called unsystematic but which also represents an unusual consciousness

*1970

of an immediate audience: a sharing and equal-standing community, to which it is equally possible to defer or to reach out. I believe that there are many positive aspects of this habitual manner, but I am just as sure that the negative aspects are serious: a willingness to share, or at least not too explicitly to challenge, the consciousness of the group of which the thinker and writer—his description as intellectual raises the precise point —is willingly or unwillingly but still practically a member. And while this group, for so long, and of course especially in places like Cambridge, was in effect and in detail a privileged and at times a ruling class, this pull towards ordinary language was often, is often, a pull towards current consciousness: a framing of ideas within certain polite but definite limits.

It is not at all surprising to me, having observed this process, to see so many students, since the early sixties, choosing to go instead to intellectuals of a different kind. In sociology, where we have been very backward —indeed in many respects an undeveloped country—there are, of course, other reasons. But the same thing has happened in literary studies, where for half a century, and in Cambridge more clearly than anywhere, there has been notable and powerful work. A sense of certain absolute restrictions in English thought, restrictions which seemed to link very closely with certain restrictions and deadlocks in the larger society, made the search for alternative traditions, alternative methods, imperative. Of course all the time there was American work: in what appeared the same language but outside this particular English consensus. Theory, or at least system, seemed attractively available. And most American intellectuals, for good or ill, seemed not to have shared this particular integration with a non-intellectual governing class. Complaints that a man explaining his life's work, in as precise a way as he could, was not instantly comprehensible, in a clubbable way, to someone who had just happened to drop in from his labour or leisure elsewhere, seemed less often to arise.

And it was then noticeable that in certain kinds of study the alternative manner became attractive and was imitated: at times substantially, in the long reach for theory; at times more superficially, in certain habits of procedural abstraction: the numbered heads and sub-heads of an argument; definitions attaining the sudden extra precision of italics; the highly specialized and internal vocabulary. Everybody except the English, it suddenly seemed, thought or at least wrote in this way. To rely on other kinds of order and emphasis was a provincial foible. A break with the English bourgeoisie, in particular, seemed to demand these alternative procedures and styles, as one of the few practical affiliations that could be made at once and by an act of will.

But really the situation was more complicated. It needed Chomsky, in his specialist work a very rigorous thinker, to remind us how easily the abstract methods and vocabulary of a particular social science could be used to achieve another kind of consensus, with a governing class that had learned to talk, in public, not of power and influence, but of operational strategies and global scenarios: not human rule but an administration. As in one of Chomsky's examples, the bombing of refugee peasants in Vietnam could be described, in a show of procedure, as accelerated urbanization. Very aware of this danger, which does not have to be but can be called dehumanizing and mystifying, English thinkers could easily, too easily, fall back on their older habits, professing not to understand abstractions like a power structure though they could traditionally understand a microcosm, or not to understand reification though they could understand the objective correlative, or not to know mediation although they knew catharsis. Certain received habits of mind, a very particular and operative selection of traditional and pre-democratic concepts and adjustments, acquired, by what one has to call alchemy, the status of concrete, or of minute particulars. Yet the more clearly one saw this happening, the more clearly one had also to see the genuinely mixed results of a social situation in which intellectuals had little choice but to define themselves as a separate profession: able then to see more clearly into the society which would appoint but not embrace them, acquiring a separate and self-defining language and manner which at least was not limited by the more immediate prejudices and encouragements, but was nevertheless a language and a manner of the monograph and the rostrum: a blackboard numbering, a dictated emphasis, a pedagogic insistence on repeatable definitions: habits which interacted strangely with the genuine rigour of new and bold inquiries and terms.

Problems of Theory

Lucien Goldmann, a thinker trained in this major continental tradition, born in Bucharest and moving to Vienna, to Geneva, to Brussels, to Paris, had at once this separated mobility and this impersonality: very clearly in the style of his work. But it was then interesting to me, having read his work presented in those familiar ways, to hear the voice of a different mind: mobility in that other sense—the quick emotional flexibility, the varying stares at his audience, the pacing up and down of this smiling man in his open-necked shirt, more concerned with a cigarette than with notes but concerned above all with the challenge of his argument, a challenge that evidently included himself. There was a sense of paradox: of amused but absolute seriousness, of provisional but passionate conviction; a kind of self-deprecating and self-asserting boldness. Perhaps the paradox was Goldmann in Cambridge, but it may be more.

For I think we cannot doubt that in sociology and in literary studies we are living through a paradox, and this presents itself to us in many different ways but most evidently as a problem of style. The basic form of the paradox is this: that we need theory, but that certain limits of existence and consciousness prevent us from getting it, or at least making certain of it; and yet the need for theory keeps pressing on our minds and half-persuading us to accept kinds of pseudo-theory which as a matter of fact not only fail to satisfy us but often encourage us to go on looking in the wrong place and in the wrong way. An idea of theory suggests laws and methods, indeed a methodology. But the most available concept of laws, and from it the most available organized methods, come in fact, as Goldmann reminded us, from studies that are wholly different in kind: from the physical sciences, where the matter to be studied can be held to be objective, where value-free observations can then be held to be possible, as a foundation for disinterested research, and so where the practice of hard, rigorous, factual disciplines can seem—indeed can impressively be—feasible.

And then I think it is clear that the existence, in works of literature, of material so laden with values that if we do not deal directly with them we have literally nothing to deal with, leads to an obvious crisis in the whole context of a university which defines itself, more and more, in terms of rigorous, specialist, disinterested disciplines. It is hardly surprising that in England it has been literary critics, and above all Leavis, who have led the opposition to what Goldmann calls 'scientism'. The record in sociology has been less clear and, I would say, less honourable. For of course it is possible in social studies, by acts of delimitation, isolation, definition, to produce or project certain kinds of objective material which can be held to be value-free because none of the connections to the rest of experience or to other kinds of relationship are made. Even values themselves can be studied in this way, as in a more or less sophisticated opinion polling: that while a percentage believes this another percentage believes that, and this result, until the next time, is the end of the research. And I wouldn't want to say that the results of these kinds of work mightn't contribute, very valuably, to the central business of social studies, which because they must deal with men in social relationships and in history must, whether they know it or not, deal with active values and with choices, including the values and choices of the observers. All I am saying is that in the end it is this centre that is absent, or is insufficiently present; and that from this very default, compounded by the historical failure to develop British social studies in any adequate way (and we remember the difficulty of getting them established in Cambridge at all), the claim began to be made that in literature, in English, where values and their discussion were explicit, a real centre, a humane centre, might be found.

But this is where the central problem of the relation between literature and social studies at once arises. We must not think, by the way, that in literary as in social studies the pursuit of the falsely objective wasn't undertaken. The classical languages, and by a hasty derivation their literatures, could be studied by a rigorous internal textual methodology, which has had its effect on nearly all literary studies. The study of other languages in the same spirit, by isolated set texts and the like, has similarly been inserted into the process of literary study, often explicitly as a way of providing at least some rigorous discipline. In our own studies of the very rich and important English medieval literature, such internal methodologies, and a relative isolation from active questions of value and of history, have made considerable headway. Everything is again justifiable, in its own immediate terms; it is the connection of those terms to the central inquiry that has become problematic or, more graciously, ultimate.

The outstanding difference between physical and humane studies is not only a matter of inevitable questions of expressed and active values. It is also a matter of the nature of change: that societies and literatures have active and conflicting human histories, which are always inseparable from active values. But in literary as in some social, historical and anthropological studies these facts of change can be projected into an apparent totality which has the advantage of containing them and thus of making them at last, like the rocks, stand still. Except, of course, that in the actual physical sciences we soon learn, even against everyday experience, that only some rocks stand still, and that even these are the products of change: the continuing history of the earth. It is not really from science, but from certain philosophical and ideological systems, and I suppose ultimately from religions, that these apparent totalities, which contain, override or rationalize change, are projected.

In literature the most common of these false totalities is 'tradition', which is seen not as it is, an active and continuous selection and reselection, which even at its latest point in time is always a set of specific choices, but now more conveniently as an object, a projected reality, with which we have to come to terms on its terms, even though those terms are always and must be the valuations, the selections and omissions, of other men. The idea of a fixed syllabus is the most ordinary methodological product of just this assumption. And of course, given this kind of totality, the facts of change can then be admitted, but in particular ways. We can be positively invited to study the history of literature: only now not as change but as variation, a series of variations within a static totality: the characteristics of this period and the characteristics of that other; just as in empirical history we come to know this period and that, but the 'and' is not stressed, or is in any case understood as temporal variation rather than as qualitative change.

Similar false totalities have been very widely projected in economics, in political theory, in anthropology and even in contemporary sociology, where variation is seen as a fact but as only a fact, which does not necessarily involve us with the disturbing process of active values and choices. Certainly, as is so often said, we cannot do without the facts, and it is a hard, long effort to get them. But this persuasive empiricism is founded, from the beginning, on the assumption that the facts can be made to stand still, and to be, as we are, disinterested. Theory, we are told, can come later, but the important point is that it is there, tacitly, from the beginning, in the methodological assumption of a static, passive and therefore empirically available totality. The most obvious example, from literary studies, is the methodology of the study of 'kinds' or 'genres'. There, making all the empirical work possible, is the prior assumption of the existence, within the 'body' of literature, of such 'permanent forms' as epic, tragedy, or romance, and then all our active study is of variations within them, variations that may be admitted to have proximate causes, even a social history, but that in their essential features are taken in practice as autonomous, with internal laws: an *a priori* and idealist assumption which prevents us not only from seeing the important history of the generation of such forms—which whatever might be said are never in fact timeless—but also from seeing those radical and qualitative changes, within the nominal continuity of the forms, which are often of surpassing importance in themselves, and which indeed, at times, make a quite different method of study, a method not depending on that kind of general classification, imperative.

The Limits of 'Practical Criticism'

Yet it is on none of these methods, with their apparent objectivity, that the claim of literature to be the central human study has rested. It has been on 'practical criticism', which deserves attention both in itself and because it is from this, paradoxically, that much of the English work in literary sociology has come. I know Goldmann would have been surprised—every visitor is surprised—to meet the full intensity, the extraordinary human commitment, of this particular and local allegiance. In his attack on 'scientism' he might for a moment have assumed that there were Cambridge allies, who had attacked the same thing in the same word. But this wouldn't have lasted long. Goldmann's attack on scientism—the uncritical transfer of method from the physical to the human sciences—was above all in the name of a critical sociology; whereas that word 'sociology' has only to be mentioned, in practical-critical circles, to provoke the last sad look at the voluntarily damned. And I would give it about fifteen minutes, as Goldmann began to describe his own methodology, for that crushing quotation to be brought out from Lawrence: 'We judge a work of art by its effect on our sincere and vital emotions and nothing else. All the critical twiddle-twaddle about style and form, all this pseudo-scientific classifying and analysing of books in an imitation-botanical fashion, is mere impertinence and mostly dull jargon.' So no methodology here, thank you; only sincere and vital emotion. But who decides the sincerity and vitality? If you need to ask that you couldn't begin to understand the answer. People decide it, in themselves and in an active and collaborative critical process.

But which people, in what social relationships, with each other and with others? That, at whatever risk of damnation, is the necessary question of the sociologist. Practical criticism is vulnerable at several points: in its hardening into an apparently objective method which is based, even defiantly, on subjective principles; in its isolation of texts from contexts; in its contemplative aspects, which have often made it hostile to new literary work. But all these weaknesses are most apparent, we say, when it is badly done: well or badly being again an internal criterion. In fact, however, all these weaknesses, or potential weaknesses, follow from the specific social situation of its practitioners. The real answer to that question—which people, in what social relationships?—was, as we know, precise and even principled: the informed critical minority. What began as the most general kind of claim, a visibly human process centred on the apparently absolute qualities of sincerity and vitality, ended, under real pressures, as a self-defining group. But then, because the critical activity was real, very different social relations—a sense of isolation from the main currents of a civilization in which sincerity and vitality were being limited or destroyed, an implacable opposition to all agents of this limitation or destruction—emerged and forced a generalization of the original position. English literary sociology began, in effect, from this need of a radical critical group to locate and justify its own activity and identity: the practical distinction of good literature from the mediocre and the bad extending to studies of the cultural conditions underlying these differences of value—a critical history of literature and of culture; and then further extending, from its starting-point in critical activity, to one major element of these conditions, the nature of the reading public. The particular interpretation then given was of course one of cultural decline; the radical isolation of the critical minority was in that sense both starting-point and conclusion. But any theory of cultural decline, or to put it more neutrally, of cultural crisis—and the practical critics had little difficulty in establishing *that*—acquires, inevitably, wider social explanation: in this case the destruction of an organic society by industrialism and by mass civilization.

In the 1930s this kind of diagnosis overlapped, or seemed to overlap, with other radical interpretations, and especially perhaps, with the Marxist interpretation of the effects of capitalism. Yet almost at once there was a fundamental hostility between these two groups: a critical engagement between *Scrutiny* and the English Marxists, which we can have little doubt, looking back, *Scrutiny* won. But why was this so? That the *Scrutiny* critics were much closer to literature, were not just fitting it in, rather hastily, to a theory conceived from other kinds, mainly economic kinds, of evidence? I believe this was so, but the real reason was more fundamental. Marxism, as then commonly understood, was weak in just the decisive area where practical criticism was strong: in its capacity to give precise and detailed and reasonably adequate accounts of actual consciousness: not just a scheme or a generalization but actual works, full of rich and significant and specific experience. And the reason for the corresponding weakness in Marxism is not difficult to find: it lay in the received formula of base and superstructure, which in ordinary hands converted very quickly to an interpretation of superstructure as simple reflection, representation, ideological expression—simplicities which just will not survive any prolonged experience of actual works. It was the theory and practice of reductionism—the specific human experiences and acts of creation converted so quickly and mechanically into classifications which always found their ultimate reality and significance elsewhere— which in practice left the field open to anybody who could give an account of art which in its closeness and intensity at all corresponded to the real human dimension in which works of art are made and valued.

I have said there was a victory, and it was indeed so crushing that in England, for a generation, even the original questions could hardly be raised. Teachers and students already knew, or thought they knew, the answers. Still today, I have no doubt, the work of Lukács or of Goldmann can be quickly referred to that abandoned battlefield. What have these neo-Marxists got, after all, but a slightly updated vocabulary and a new political lease of life? I think they have more, much more, but I am sure we must remember that decisive engagement, for certain real things were learned in it, which make the specifically English contribution to the continuing inquiry still relevant, still active, however much any of us might want to join in the run from the English consensus to a quite other consciousness and vocabulary.

The Social Totality

It was above all, as I have said, the received formula of base and superstructure which made Marxist accounts of literature and thought often weak in practice. Yet to many people, still, this formula is near the centre of Marxism, and indicates its appropriate methodology for cultural history and criticism, and then of course for the relation between social and cultural studies. The economic base determines the social relations which determine consciousness which determines actual ideas and works. There can be endless debate about each of these terms, but unless something very like that is believed, Marxism appears to have lost its most specific challenging position.

Now for my own part I have always opposed the formula of base and superstructure: not primarily because of its methodological weaknesses but because of its rigid, abstract and static character. Further, from my work on the nineteenth century, I came to view it as essentially a bourgeois formula; more specifically, a central position of utilitarian thought. I did not want to give up my sense of the commanding importance of economic activity and history. My inquiry in *Culture and Society* had begun from just that sense of a transforming change. But in theory and practice I came to believe that I had to give up, or at least to leave aside, what I knew as the Marxist tradition: to attempt to develop a different kind of theory of social totality; to see the study of culture as the study of relations between elements in a whole way of life; to find ways of studying structure, in particular works and periods, which could stay in touch with and illuminate particular art-works and forms, but also forms and relations of more general social life; to replace the formula of base and superstructure with the more active idea of a field of mutually if also unevenly determining forces. That was the project of *The Long Revolution*, and it seems to me extraordinary, looking back, that I did not then know the work of Lukács or of Goldmann, which would have been highly relevant to it, and especially as they were working within a more conscious tradition and in less radical an isolation. I did not even then know, or had forgotten, Marx's analysis of the theory of utility, in *The German Ideology*, in which—as I now find often happens in reading and re-reading Marx—what I had felt about the reductionism of the base-superstructure formula was given a very precise historical and analytic focus.

This being so, it is easy to imagine my feelings when I discovered an active and developed Marxist theory, in the work of Lukács and Goldmann, which was exploring many of the same areas with many of the same concepts, but also with others in a quite different range. The fact that I learned simultaneously that it had been denounced as heretical, that it was a return to Left Hegelianism, left-bourgeois idealism, and so on, did not, I am afraid, detain me. If you're not in a church you're not worried about heresies; it is only (but it is often) the most routinized Marxism, or the most idealist revolutionism, which projects that kind of authoritative, believing, formation. The only serious criterion was actual theory and practice.

What both Lukács and, following him, Goldmann had to say about reification seemed to me the real advance. For here the dominance of economic activity over all other forms of human activity, the dominance of its values over all other values, was given a precise historical explanation: that this dominance, this deformation, was the specific characteristic of capitalist society, and that in modern organized capitalism this dominance—as indeed one can observe—was increasing, so that this reification, this false objectivity, was more thoroughly penetrating every other kind of life and consciousness. The idea of totality was then a critical weapon against this precise deformation; indeed, against capitalism itself. And yet this was not idealism—as assertion of the primacy of other values. On the contrary, just as the deformation could be understood, at its roots, only by historical analysis of a particular kind of economy, so the attempt to overcome and surpass it lay not in isolated witness or in separated activity but in practical work to find, to assert and to establish more human social ends in more human political and economic means.

At the most practical level it was easy for me to agree. But then the whole point of thinking in terms of a totality is the realization that we are part of it; that our own consciousness, our work, our methods, are then critically at stake. And in the particular field of literary analysis there was this obvious difficulty: that most of the work we had to look at was the product of just this epoch of reified consciousness, so that what looked like the theoretical breakthrough might become, quite quickly, the methodological trap. I cannot yet say this finally about Lukács, since I still don't have access to all his work; but in some of it, at least, the major insights of *History and Class-Consciousness*, which he has now partly disavowed, do not get translated into critical practice, and certain cruder operations—essentially still those of base and superstructure—keep reappearing. I still read Goldmann collaboratively and critically asking the same question, for I am sure the practice of totality is still for any of us, at any time, profoundly and even obviously difficult.

Yet advances have been made, and I want to acknowledge them. In particular Goldmann's concepts of structure, and his distinctions of kinds of consciousness—based on but developed from Lukács—seem to me very important. And they are important above all for the relation between literary and social studies. At a simpler level, many points of contact between literature and sociology can be worked on: studies of the reading public, for example, where literary analysis of the works being read and sociological analysis of the real formations of the public have hardly yet at all been combined. Or the actual history of writers, as changing historical groups, in any full critical relation to the substance of their works. Or the social history of literary forms, in their full particularity and variety but also in the complex of their relation with other formations. I attempted each of these kinds of analysis in a preliminary way in *The Long Revolution*, but I felt then and have felt ever since a crucial absence of collaborators, and especially of people who did not say or have to say, as we approached the most difficult central problems, that there, unfortunately, was the limit of their field.

Goldmann, of course, did not accept these limits. He spoke now as sociologist, now as critic, now as cultural historian; but also, in his own intellectual tradition, a philosophy and a sociology were there from the beginning; the patient literary studies began from that fact. Thus, when he spoke of structures, he was consciously applying a term and a method which did not so much cross as underlie the apparently separate disciplines. It is a term and a method of consciousness, and so the relation between literature and sociology is not a relation between, on the one hand, various individual works and on the other hand various empirical facts. The real relation is within a totality of consciousness: a relation that is assumed and then revealed rather than apprehended and then expounded. Much that has to be proved, in our own tradition—and especially the very existence of significant primary relations between literature and society—can there be surpassed, in general philosophical and sociological terms, before the particular analyses begin. Looking at our work it could be said that we lacked a centre, in any developed philosophy or sociology. Looking at his work—and for all his differences he was representative of the whole other tradition—it could be said that he had a received centre, at the level of reasoning, before the full contact with substance began.

Structures of Feeling

I think the subsequent argument, if it can be developed, has this necessary tension and even contradiction of method. I will give a central example. I found in my own work that I had to develop the idea of a structure of feeling. This was to indicate certain common characteristics in a group of writers but also of others, in a particular historical situation. I will come back to its precise application later. But then I found Goldmann beginning, very interestingly, from a concept of structure which contained, in itself, a relation between social and literary facts.

This relation, he insisted, was not a matter of content, but of mental structures: 'the categories which simultaneously organize the empirical consciousness of a particular social group and the imaginative world created by the writer'. By definition, these structures are not individually but collectively created. Again, in an almost untranslatable term, this was a genetic structuralism necessarily concerned not only with the analysis of structures but with their historical formation and process: the ways in which they change as well as the ways in which they are constituted. The foundation of this approach is the belief that all human activity is an attempt to make a significant response to a particular objective situation. Who makes this response? According to Goldmann, neither the individual nor any abstract group, but individuals in real and collective social relations. The significant response is a particular view of the world: an organizing view. And it is just this element of organization that is, in literature, the significant social fact. A correspondence of content between a writer and his world is less significant than this correspondence of organization, of structure. A relation of content may be mere reflection, but a relation of structure, often occurring where there is no apparent relation of content, can show us the organizing principle by which a particular view of the world, and from that the coherence of the social group which maintains it, really operates in consciousness.

To make this more critical, Goldmann, following Lukács, distinguishes between actual consciousness and possible consciousness: the actual, with its rich but incoherent multiplicity; the possible, with its maximum degree of adequacy and coherence. A social group is ordinarily limited to its actual consciousness, and this wil! include many kinds of misunderstanding and illusion: elements of false consciousness which are often, of course, used and reflected in ordinary literature. But there is also a maximum of possible consciousness: that view of the world raised to its highest and most coherent level, limited only by the fact that to go further would mean that the group would have to surpass itself, to change into or be replaced by a new social group.

Most sociology of literature, Goldmann then argues, is concerned with the relatively apparent relations between ordinary literature and actual consciousness: relations which show themselves at the level of content, or in conventional elaboration of its common illusions. The new sociology of literature—that of genetic structuralism—will be concerned with the more fundamental relations of possible consciousness, for it is at the centre of his case that the greatest literary works are precisely those which realize a world-view at its most coherent and most adequate, its highest possible level. We should not then mainly study peripheral relations: correspondences of content and background; overt social relations between writers and readers. We should study, in the greatest literature, the organizing categories, the essential structures, which give such works their unity, their specific aesthetic character, their strictly literary quality; and which at the same time reveal to us the maximum possible consciousness of the social group—in real terms, the social class—which finally created them, in and through their individual authors.

Now this is, I believe, a powerful argument, and I make my observations on it within that sense. The idea of a world-view, a particular and organized way of seeing the world, is of course familiar to us in our own studies. Indeed I myself had to spend many years getting away from it, in the ordinary form in which I found it presented. The Elizabethan world-picture, I came to believe, was a thing fascinating in itself, but then it was often more of a hindrance than a help in seeing the full substance of Elizabethan drama. Again, I learned the Greek world-picture and was then baffled by Greek drama; the Victorian world-picture and found the English nineteenth-century novel amazing. I think Goldmann's distinction might help us here. He would say that what we were being given was actual consciousness, in a summary form, whereas what we found in the literature was the often very different possible consciousness. I have no doubt this is sometimes true, but it is as often the case that we need to reconsider the idea of consciousness itself. What is ordinarily extracted as a world-view is, in practice, a summary of doctrines: more organized, more coherent, than most people of the time would have been able to make them. And then I am not sure that I can in practice always distinguish this from the kind of evidence Goldmann himself adduces as possible consciousness, when he is engaged in an analysis. Moreover I think either version is often some distance away from the real structures and processes of literature. I developed my own idea of structures of feeling in response to just this sense of a distance. There were real social and natural relationships, and there were relatively organized, relatively coherent formations of these relationships, in contemporary institutions and beliefs. But what seemed to me to happen, in some of the greatest literature, was a simultaneous realization of and response to these underlying and formative structures. Indeed, that constituted, for me, the specific literary phenomenon: the dramatization of a process, the making of a fiction, in which the constituting elements, of real social life and beliefs, were simultaneously actualized and in an important way differently experienced, the difference residing in the imaginative act, the imaginative method, the specific and genuinely unprecedented imaginative organization.

We can feel the effect, in all this, of major individual talents, and indeed I believe that there are discoverable specific reasons, of a social kind, in the immediate histories of writers, why this imaginative alternative was sought. But I am also sure that these creative acts compose, within a historical period, a specific community: a community visible in the structure of feeling and demonstrable, above all, in fundamental choices of form. I have tried to show this in actual cases, in the late nineteenth- and twentieth-century European drama, and in the development and crisis of the nineteenth- and twentieth-century English novel. And what seems to me especially important in these changing structures of feeling is that they often precede those more recognizable changes of formal idea and belief which make up the ordinary history of consciousness, and that while they correspond very closely to a real social history, of men living in actual and changing social relations, they again often precede the more recognizable changes of formal institution and relationship, which are the more accessible, indeed the more normal, history. This is what I mean when I say that art is one of the primary human activities, and that it can succeed in articulating not just the imposed or constitutive social or intellectual system, but at once this and an experience of it, its lived consequence, in ways very close to many other kinds of active response, in new social activity and in what we know as personal life, but of course often more accessibly, just because it is specifically formed and because when it is made it is in its own way complete, even autonomous, and being the kind of work it is can be transmitted and communicated beyond its original situation and circumstances.

Now if this is so, it is easy to see why we must reject those versions of consciousness which relate it directly, or with mere lags and complications, to a determining base. The stress on an active consciousness made by Lukács and Goldmann gives us a real way beyond that. And it might be possible to say that the relation I have tried to describe—between formal consciousness and new creative practice—might be better, more precisely, described in their terms: actual consciousness and possible consciousness. Indeed I hope it may be so, but I see one major difficulty. This relation, though subtle, is still in some ways static. Possible consciousness is the objective limit that can be reached by a class before it turns into another class, or is replaced. But I think this leads, rather evidently, to a kind of macro-history: in many ways adequate but in relation to actual literature, with its continuity of change, often too large in its categories to come very close, except at certain significant points when there is a radical and fundamental moment of replacement of one class by another. As I read Goldmann, I find him very conscious of just this difficulty, but then I am not sure that it is accidental that he is much more convincing on Racine and Pascal, at a point of evident crisis between a feudal and a bourgeois world, than he is on the nineteenth- and indeed twentieth-century novel, where apparently small but no less significant changes within a bourgeois society have to be given what can be called micro-structural analysis. To say, following Lukács, that the novel is the form in which, in a degraded society, an individual tries and fails to surpass an objectively limited society and destiny—the novel, that is to say, of the problematic hero—is at once illuminating and partial; indeed, the evidence presented for it is so extremely selective that we are almost at once on our guard. No English novels are considered at all: the other side of that enclosure of which we are usually, on our side of the channel, so conscious. But while one can offer, willingly, *Great Expectations, Born in Exile, Jude the Obscure*, and in a more complicated but still relevant way *Middlemarch*, one is left to face a different phenomenon in, for example, *Little Dorrit*. And I think this is not only an argument about particular cases. The most exciting experience for me, in reading Lukács and Goldmann, was the stress on forms. I had become convinced in my own work that the most penetrating analysis would always be of forms, specifically literary forms, where changes of viewpoint, changes of known and knowable relationships, changes of possible and actual resolutions, could be directly demonstrated, as forms of literary organization, and then, just because they involved more than individual solutions, could be reasonably related to a real social history, itself considered analytically in terms of basic relationships and failures and limits of relationship. This is what I attempted, for example, in *Modern Tragedy*, and I then have to say that I have since learned a good deal, theoretically, from the developed sociology of Lukács and Goldmann and others, in just this respect. But much of the necessary analysis of forms seems to me barely to have begun, and this is not only, I think, a matter of time for development.

Perhaps I can put the reason most sharply by saying that form, in Lukács and Goldmann, translates too often as genre or as kind; that we stay, too often, within a received academic and ultimately idealist tradition in which 'epic' and 'drama', 'novel' and 'tragedy', have inherent and permanent properties, from which the analysis begins and to which selected examples are related. I am very willing to agree that certain general correlations of this kind, between a form and a world-view, can be shown. But we have then to face the fact, above all in the last hundred years, that tragedy and the novel, for example, exist, inextricably, within the same culture, and are used by identical or very similar social groups. Or the fact that within modern tragedy, and even more within the novel, there are radically significant changes of form in which many of the changes in literature and society—changes in the pace of a life, an experience, rather than of a whole historical epoch—can be quite directly apprehended. Certainly this is recognized in practice. Goldmann has an interesting contrast between the traditional bourgeois novel and the new novel of Sarraute or Robbe-Grillet, which he relates to a more completely reified world. Lukács makes similar distinctions, from Balzac through Mann and Kafka to Solzhenitsyn. But the full theoretical issue, of what is meant by form, is still in my view confused, and perhaps especially by the fact that there is this undiscarded ballast of form in a more abstract, more supra-historical sense. Thus even a Goldmann can say, as if he were an ordinary idealist and academic critic, that Sophocles is the only one of the Greek dramatists who can be called tragic 'in the now accepted sense of the word'. The prepotence of inherited categories is then striking and saddening.

Past Victories, Present Penalties

But then limitations of this kind are organically related to the strengths of this alternative tradition. The habitual and as it were inevitable relation of structure to doctrine, or the application of formal categories, is a characteristic of the developed philosophical position which in most other respects is a source of real strength. That is why it is so important, now, to go beyond the kind of argument which developed in English in the 1930s, for while particular refutations of this or that reading, this or that method, have an immediate significance, in our whole situation they can hide the fact that behind our local English practicalities is a set of unexamined general ideas, which then suddenly materialize on quite another plane as a sort of social theory: from the critical minority to minority culture and minority education; or from the richness of past literature to a use of the past against the present, as if the past, and never the future, the sense of a future, were the only source of values. The local victory of the thirties was bought at a price we have all since paid: the most active relations between literary and social studies, and the most fundamental and continuing relations between literature and real societies, including present society, have in effect been pushed away from attention, because in theory and in practice any critical examination of them would disturb, often radically, our existing social relations and the division of interests and specialisms which both expresses and protects them.

I want to end by emphasizing two concepts used by Goldmann, which we ought to try to clarify, theoretically, and which we ought to be trying, collaboratively, to test in practice. The first is the idea of the 'collective subject': obviously a difficult idea, but one of great potential importance. Literary studies in fact use a related idea again and again. We not only refer, confidently, to 'the Jacobean dramatists' 'the Romantic poets' and 'the early Victorian novelists', but also we often use these descriptions in a quite singular sense, to indicate a way of looking at the world, a literary method, a particular use of language, and so on. In practice we are often concerned with breaking down these generalizations, and that is right: to know the difference between Jonson and Webster, or Blake and Coleridge, or Dickens and Emily Brontë, is in that real sense necessary. Yet beyond this we do come to see certain real communities, when we have taken all the individual differences into account. To see only the differences between Blake and Coleridge, but not also the differences between a Romantic poem and a Jacobean play and an early Victorian novel, is to be quite wilfully limited and indeed quite unpractical. And then to be able to give an account of this precise community, a community of form which is also a specific general way of seeing other people and nature, is to approach the problem of social groups in a quite new way. For it is no longer the reduction of individuals to a group, by some process of averaging; it is a way of seeing a group in and through individual differences: that specificity of individuals, and of their individual creations, which does not deny but is the necessary way of affirming their real social identities, in language, in conventions, in certain characteristic situations, experiences, interpretations, ideas. Indeed the importance for social studies may well be this: that we can find ways of describing significant groups which include, in a fundamental way, those personal realities which will otherwise be relegated to a quite separate area. To have a sociology concerned only with abstract groups, and a literary criticism concerned only with separated individuals and works, is more than a division of labour; it is a way of avoiding the reality of the interpenetration, in a final sense the unity, of the most individual and the most social forms of actual life.

The problem is always one of method, and this is where the second idea, of the structures of the genesis of consciousness, must be taken seriously. We are weakest, in social studies, in just this area: in what is called the sociology of knowledge but is always much more than that, for it is not only knowledge we are concerned with but all the active processes of learning, imagination, creation, performance. And there is very rich material, within a discipline we already have, for the detailed description of just these processes, in so many individual works. To find ways of extending this, not simply to a background of social history or of the history of ideas, but to other active processes through which social groups form and define themselves, will be very difficult but is now centrally necessary. For relating literary process to the social product, or the social process to the literary product—which is what now we mostly do—in the end breaks down, and people retire, with that by now professional expression of resigned intelligence and virtue, to the teaching of the day before yesterday. But if in every case we try, by varying forms of analysis, to go beyond the particular and isolated product—'the text'—to its real process —its most active and specific formation—I believe we can find points of connection that answer, as our separated studies so often do not, to our closest sense of our own living process.

On each of these points—the idea of the collective subject, and the idea of the structures of the genesis of consciousness—Lucien Goldmann's contribution, though unfinished, was significant. Locked as he was in much immediate controversy, he seems often to have been limited to restating his most general positions; yet even here, in ways that in summary I have not been able to indicate, he produced refinements and further definitions, in so complex a field, from which we can all learn. We can dissent, as I often do, from particular formulations and applications, and still recognize the emphasis, the exceptionally valuable emphasis, which he gave, theoretically and practically, to the development of literary and social studies.

And this is more than a professional concern. Beyond the arguments, as listening to him last spring in Cambridge it was not difficult to see, there is a social crisis, a human crisis, in which, in just these ways, we are ourselves involved. For the achievement of clarity and significance, in these most human studies, is directly connected with the struggle for human means and ends in a world that will permit no reserved areas, no safe subjects, no neutral activities. Now and here, in respecting his memory, I take the sense he gave: of a continuing inquiry, a continuing argument, a continuing concern; of a man who made, in our time, a significant response, and with whom we can find, as I think he would have said, a significant community, a way of seeing and being and acting in the world.

Base and Superstructure in Marxist Cultural Theory

Any modern approach to a Marxist theory of culture must begin by considering the proposition of a determining base and a determined superstructure. From a strictly theoretical point of view this is not, in fact, where we might choose to begin. It would be in many ways preferable if we could begin from a proposition which originally was equally central, equally authentic: namely the proposition that social being determines consciousness. It is not that the two propositions necessarily deny each other or are in contradiction. But the proposition of base and superstructure, with its figurative element, with its suggestion of a fixed and definite spatial relationship, constitutes, at least in certain hands, a very specialized and at times unacceptable version of the other proposition. Yet in the transition from Marx to Marxism, and in the development of mainstream Marxism itself, the proposition of the determining base and the determined superstructure has been commonly held to be the key to Marxist cultural analysis.

It is important, as we try to analyse this proposition, to be aware that the term of relationship which is involved, that is to say 'determines', is of great linguistic and theoretical complexity. The language of determination and even more of determinism was inherited from idealist and especially theological accounts of the world and man. It is significant that it is in one of his familiar inversions, his contradictions of received propositions, that Marx uses the word which becomes, in English translation, 'determines' (the usual but not invariable German word is *bestimmen*). He is opposing an ideology that had been insistent on the power of certain forces outside man, or, in its secular version, on an abstract determining consciousness. Marx's own proposition explicitly denies this, and puts the origin of determination in men's own activities. Nevertheless, the particular history and continuity of the term serves to remind us that there are, within ordinary use—and this is true of most of the major European languages—quite different possible meanings and implications of the word 'determine'. There is, on the one hand, from its theological inheritance, the notion of an external cause which totally predicts or prefigures, indeed totally controls a subsequent activity. But there is also, from the experience of social practice, a notion of determination as setting limits, exerting pressures.*

Now there is clearly a difference between a process of setting limits and exerting pressures, whether by some external force or by the internal laws of a particular development, and that other process in which a subsequent content is essentially prefigured, predicted and controlled by a pre-existing external force. Yet it is fair to say, looking at many applications of Marxist cultural analysis, that it is the second sense, the notion of prefiguration, prediction or control, which has often explicitly or implicitly been used.

Superstructure: Qualifications and Amendments

The term of relationship is then the first thing that we have to examine in this proposition, but we have to do this by going on to look at the related terms themselves. 'Superstructure' (*Überbau*) has had most attention. In common usage, after Marx, it acquired a main sense of a unitary 'area' within which all cultural and ideological activities could be placed. But already in Marx himself, in the later correspondence of Engels, and at many points in the subsequent Marxist tradition, qualifications were made about the determined character of certain superstructural activities. The first kind of qualification had to do with delays in time, with complications, and with certain indirect or relatively distant relationships. The simplest notion of a superstructure, which is still by no means entirely abandoned, had been the reflection, the imitation or the reproduction of the reality of the base in the superstructure in a more or less direct way. Positivist notions of reflection and reproduction of course directly supported this. But since in many real cultural activities this relationship cannot be found, or cannot be found without effort or even violence to the material or practice being studied, the notion was

* For a further discussion of the range of meanings in 'determine' see *Keywords*, London 1976, pp. 87-91.

introduced of delays in time, the famous lags; of various technical complications; and of indirectness, in which certain kinds of activity in the
cultural sphere—philosophy, for example—were situated at a greater
distance from the primary economic activities. That was the first stage of
qualification of the notion of superstructure: in effect, an operational
qualification. The second stage was related but more fundamental, in
that the process of the relationship itself was more substantially looked at.
This was the kind of reconsideration which gave rise to the modern
notion of 'mediation', in which something more than simple reflection or
reproduction—indeed something radically different from either reflection or reproduction—actively occurs. In the later twentieth century
there is the notion of 'homologous structures', where there may be no
direct or easily apparent similarity, and certainly nothing like reflection
or reproduction, between the superstructural process and the reality of
the base, but in which there is an essential homology or correspondence
of structures, which can be discovered by analysis. This is not the same
notion as 'mediation', but it is the same kind of amendment in that the
relationship between the base and the superstructure is not supposed to
be direct, nor simply operationally subject to lags and complications and
indirectnesses, but that of its nature it is not direct reproduction.

These qualifications and amendments are important. But it seems to
me that what has not been looked at with equal care is the received notion
of the 'base' (*Basis, Grundlage*). And indeed I would argue that the base is
the more important concept to look at if we are to understand the realities
of cultural process. In many uses of the proposition of base and superstructure, as a matter of verbal habit, 'the base' has come to be considered
virtually as an object, or in less crude cases, it has been considered in
essentially uniform and usually static ways. 'The base' is the real social
existence of man. 'The base' is the real relations of production corresponding to a stage of development of the material productive forces. 'The
base' is a mode of production at a particular stage of its development. We
make and repeat propositions of this kind, but the usage is then very
different from Marx's emphasis on productive activities, in particular
structural relations, constituting the foundation of all other activities.
For while a particular stage of the development of production can be
discovered and made precise by analysis, it is never in practice either
uniform or static. It is indeed one of the central propositions of Marx's
sense of history that there are deep contradictions in the relationships of

production and in the consequent social relationships. There is therefore the continual possibility of the dynamic variation of these forces. More-ovr, when these forces are considered, as Marx always considers them, as the specific activities and relationships of real men, they mean something very much more active, more complicated and more contradictory than the developed metaphorical notion of 'the base' could possibly allow us to realize.

The Base and the Productive Forces

So we have to say that when we talk of 'the base', we are talking of a process and not a state. And we cannot ascribe to that process certain fixed properties for subsequent translation to the variable processes of the superstructure. Most people who have wanted to make the ordinary proposition more reasonable have concentrated on refining the notion of superstructure. But I would say that each term of the proposition has to be revalued in a particular direction. We have to revalue 'determination' towards the setting of limits and the exertion of pressure, and away from a predicted, prefigured and controlled content. We have to revalue 'super-structure' towards a related range of cultural practices, and away from a reflected, reproduced or specifically dependent content. And, crucially, we have to revalue 'the base' away from the notion of a fixed economic or technological abstraction, and towards the specific activities of men in real social and economic relationships, containing fundamental contra-dictions and variations and therefore always in a state of dynamic process.

It is worth observing one further implication behind the customary definitions. 'The base' has come to include, especially in certain twentieth-century developments, a strong and limiting sense of basic industry. The emphasis on heavy industry, even, has played a certain cultural role. And this raises a more general problem, for we find ourselves forced to look again at the ordinary notion of 'productive forces'. Clearly what we are examining in the base is primary productive forces. Yet some very crucial distinctions have to be made here. It is true that in his analysis of capitalist production Marx considered 'productive work' in a very particular and specialized sense corresponding to that mode of production. There is a difficult passage in the *Grundrisse* in which he argues that while the man who makes a piano is a productive worker, there is a real question whether the man who distributes the piano is also a productive worker; but he probably is, since he contributes to the realization of surplus value. Yet when it comes to the man who plays the piano, whether to himself or to others, there is no question: he is not a productive worker at all. So piano-maker is base, but pianist superstructure. As a way of considering cultural activity, and incidentally the economics of modern cultural activity, this is very clearly a dead-end. But for any theoretical clarification it is crucial to recognize that Marx was there engaged in an analysis of a particular kind of production, that is capitalist commodity production. Within his analysis of this mode, he had to give to the notion of 'productive labour' and 'productive forces' a specialized sense of primary work on materials in a form which produced commodities. But this has narrowed remarkably, and in a cultural context very damagingly, from his more central notion of *productive forces*, in which, to give just brief reminders, the most important thing a worker ever produces is himself, himself in the fact of that kind of labour, or the broader historical emphasis of men producing themselves, themselves and their history. Now when we talk of the base, and of primary productive forces, it matters very much whether we are referring, as in one degenerate form of this proposition became habitual, to primary production within the terms of capitalist economic relationships, or to the primary production of society itself, and of men themselves, the material production and reproduction of real life. If we have the broad sense of productive forces, we look at the whole question of the base differently, and we are then less tempted to dismiss as superstructural, and in that sense as merely secondary, certain vital productive social forces, which are in the broad sense, from the beginning, basic.

Uses of Totality

Yet, because of the difficulties of the ordinary proposition of base and superstructure, there was an alternative and very important development, an emphasis primarily associated with Lukács, on a social 'totality'. The totality of social practices was opposed to this layered notion of base and a consequent superstructure. This concept of a totality of practices is compatible with the notion of social being determining consciousness, but it does not necessarily interpret this process in terms of a base and a superstructure. Now the language of totality has become common, and it is indeed in many ways more acceptable than the notion of base and superstructure. But with one very important reservation. It is very easy for the notion of totality to empty of its essential content the original Marxist proposition. For if we come to say that society is composed of a large number of social practices which form a concrete social whole, and if we give to each practice a certain specific recognition, adding only that they interact, relate and combine in very complicated ways, we are at one level much more obviously talking about reality, but we are at another level withdrawing from the claim that there is any process of determination. And this I, for one, would be very unwilling to do. Indeed, the key question to ask about any notion of totality in cultural theory is this: whether the notion of totality includes the notion of intention.

If totality is simply concrete, if it is simply the recognition of a large variety of miscellaneous and contemporaneous practices, then it is essentially empty of any content that could be called Marxist. Intention, the notion of intention, restores the key question, or rather the key emphasis. For while it is true that any society is a complex whole of such practices, it is also true that any society has a specific organization, a specific structure, and that the principles of this organization and structure can be seen as directly related to certain social intentions, intentions by which we define the society, intentions which in all our experience have been the rule of a particular class. One of the unexpected consequences of the crudeness of the base/superstructure model has been the too easy acceptance of models which appear less crude—models of totality or of a complex whole—but which exclude the facts of social intention, the class character of a particular society and so on. And this reminds us of how much we lose if we abandon the superstructural emphasis altogether. Thus I have great difficulty in seeing processes of art and thought as superstructural in the sense of the formula as it is commonly used. But in many areas of social and political thought—certain kinds of ratifying theory, certain kinds of law, certain kinds of institution, which after all in Marx's original formulations were very much part of the superstructure —in all that kind of social apparatus, and in a decisive area of political and ideological activity and construction, if we fail to see a superstructural element we fail to recognize reality at all. These laws, constitutions, theories, ideologies, which are so often claimed as natural, or as having universal validity or significance, simply have to be seen as expressing and ratifying the domination of a particular class. Indeed the difficulty of revising the formula of base and superstructure has had much to do with the perception of many militants—who have to fight such institutions and notions as well as fighting economic battles—that if these institutions and their ideologies are not perceived as having that kind of dependent and ratifying relationship, if their claims to universal validity or legitimacy are not denied and fought, then the class character of the society can no longer be seen. And this has been the effect of some versions of totality as the description of cultural process. Indeed I think we can properly use the notion of totality only when we combine it with that other crucial Marxist concept of 'hegemony'.

The Complexity of Hegemony

It is Gramsci's great contribution to have emphasized hegemony, and also to have understood it at a depth which is, I think, rare. For hegemony supposes the existence of something which is truly total, which is not merely secondary or superstructural, like the weak sense of ideology, but which is lived at such a depth, which saturates the society to such an extent, and which, as Gramsci put it, even constitutes the substance and limit of common sense for most people under its sway, that it corresponds to the reality of social experience very much more clearly than any notions derived from the formula of base and superstructure. For if ideology were merely some abstract, imposed set of notions, if our social and political and cultural ideas and assumptions and habits were merely the result of specific manipulation, of a kind of overt training which might be simply ended or withdrawn, then the society would be very much easier to move and to change than in practice it has ever been or is. This notion of hegemony as deeply saturating the consciousness of a society seems to me to be fundamental. And hegemony has the advantage over general notions of totality, that it at the same time emphasizes the facts of domination.

Yet there are times when I hear discussions of hegemony and feel that it too, as a concept, is being dragged back to the relatively simple, uniform and static notion which 'superstructure' in ordinary use had become. Indeed I think that we have to give a very complex account of hegemony if we are talking about any real social formation. Above all we have to give an account which allows for its elements of real and constant change. We have to emphasize that hegemony is not singular; indeed that its own internal structures are highly complex, and have continually to be renewed, recreated and defended; and by the same token, that they can be continually challenged and in certain respects modified. That is why instead of speaking simply of 'the hegemony', 'a hegemony', I would propose a model which allows for this kind of variation and contradiction, its sets of alternatives and its processes of change.

For one thing that is evident in some of the best Marxist cultural analysis is that it is very much more at home in what one might call *epochal* questions than in what one has to call *historical* questions. That is to say, it is usually very much better at distinguishing the large features of different epochs of society, as commonly between feudal and bourgeois, than at distinguishing between different phases of bourgeois society, and different moments within these phases: that true historical process which demands a much greater precision and delicacy of analysis than the always striking epochal analysis which is concerned with main lineaments and features.

The theoretical model which I have been trying to work with is this. I would say first that in any society, in any particular period, there is a central system of practices, meanings and values, which we can properly call dominant and effective. This implies no presumption about its value. All I am saying is that it is central. Indeed I would call it a corporate system, but this might be confusing, since Gramsci uses 'corporate' to mean the subordinate as opposed to the general and dominant elements of hegemony. In any case what I have in mind is the central, effective and dominant system of meanings and values, which are not merely abstract but which are organized and lived. That is why hegemony is not to be understood at the level of mere opinion or mere manipulation. It is a whole body of practices and expectations; our assignments of energy, our ordinary understanding of the nature of man and of his world. It is a set of meanings and values which as they are experienced as practices appear as reciprocally confirming. It thus constitutes a sense of reality for most people in the society, a sense of absolute because experienced reality beyond which it is very difficult for most members of the society to move, in most areas of their lives. But this is not, except in the operation of a moment of abstract analysis, in any sense a static system. On the contrary we can only understand an effective and dominant culture if we understand the real social process on which it depends: I mean the process of incorporation. The modes of incorporation are of great social significance. The educational institutions are usually the main agencies of the transmission of an effective dominant culture, and this is now a major economic as well as a cultural activity; indeed it is both in the same moment. Moreover, at a philosophical level, at the true level of theory and at the level of the history of various practices, there is a process which I call the *selective tradition*: that which, within the terms of an effective dominant culture, is always passed off as '*the* tradition', '*the* significant past'. But always the selectivity is the point; the way in which from a whole possible area of past and present, certain meanings and practices are chosen for emphasis, certain other meanings and practices are neglected and excluded. Even more crucially, some of these meanings and practices are reinterpreted, diluted, or put into forms which support or at least do not contradict other elements within the effective dominant culture. The processes of education; the processes of a much wider social training within institutions like the family; the practical definitions and organization of work; the selective tradition at an intellectual and theoretical level: all these forces are involved in a continual making and remaking of an effective dominant culture, and on them, as experienced, as built into our living, its reality depends. If what we learn there were merely an imposed ideology, or if it were only the isolable meanings and practices of the ruling class, or of a section of the ruling class, which gets imposed on others, occupying merely the top of our minds, it would be—and one would be glad—a very much easier thing to overthrow.

It is not only the depths to which this process reaches, selecting and organizing and interpreting our experience. It is also that it is continually active and adjusting; it isn't just the past, the dry husks of ideology which we can more easily discard. And this can only be so, in a complex society, if it is something more substantial and more flexible than any abstract imposed ideology. Thus we have to recognize the alternative meanings and values, the alternative opinions and attitudes, even some alternative senses of the world, which can be accommodated and tolerated within a particular effective and dominant culture. This has been much under-emphasized in our notions of a superstructure, and even in some notions of hegemony. And the under-emphasis opens the way for retreat to an indifferent complexity. In the practice of politics, for example, there are certain truly incorporated modes of what are nevertheless, within those terms, real oppositions, that are felt and fought out. Their existence within the incorporation is recognizable by the fact that, whatever the degree of internal conflict or internal variation, they do not in practice go beyond the limits of the central effective and dominant definitions. This is true, for example, of the practice of parliamentary politics, though its internal oppositions are real. It is true about a whole range of practices and arguments, in any real society, which can by no means be reduced to an ideological cover, but which can nevertheless be properly analysed as in my sense corporate, if we find that, whatever the degree of internal controversy and variation, they do not in the end exceed the limits of the central corporate definitions.

But if we are to say this, we have to think again about the sources of that which is not corporate; of those practices, experiences, meanings, values which are not part of the effective dominant culture. We can express this in two ways. There is clearly something that we can call alternative to the effective dominant culture, and there is something else that we can call oppositional, in a true sense. The degree of existence of these alternative and oppositional forms is itself a matter of constant historical variation in real circumstances. In certain societies it is possible to find areas of social life in which quite real alternatives are at least left alone. (If they are made available, of course, they are part of the corporate organization.) The existence of the possibility of opposition, and of its articulation, its degree of openness, and so on, again depends on very precise social and political forces. The facts of alternative and oppositional forms of social life and culture, in relation to the effective and dominant culture, have then to be recognized as subject to historical variation, and as having sources which are very significant as a fact about the dominant culture itself.

Residual and Emergent Cultures

I have next to introduce a further distinction, between *residual* and *emergent* forms, both of alternative and of oppositional culture. By 'residual' I mean that some experiences, meanings and values, which cannot be verified or cannot be expressed in terms of the dominant culture, are nevertheless lived and practised on the basis of the residue—cultural as well as social—of some previous social formation. There is a real case of this in certain religious values, by contrast with the very evident incorporation of most religious meanings and values into the dominant system. The same is true, in a culture like Britain, of certain notions derived from a rural past, which have a very significant popularity. A residual culture is usually at some distance from the effective dominant culture, but one has to recognize that, in real cultural activities, it may get incorporated into it. This is because some part of it, some version of it—and especially if the residue is from some major area of the past—will in many cases have had to be incorporated if the effective dominant culture is to make sense in those areas. It is also because at certain points a dominant culture cannot allow too much of this kind of practice and experience outside itself, at least without risk. Thus the pressures are real, but certain genuinely residual meanings and practices in some important cases survive.

By 'emergent' I mean, first, that new meanings and values, new practices, new significances and experiences, are continually being created. But there is then a much earlier attempt to incorporate them, just because they are part—and yet not a defined part—of effective contemporary practice. Indeed it is significant in our own period how very early this attempt is, how alert the dominant culture now is to anything that can be seen as emergent. We have then to see, first, as it were a temporal relation between a dominant culture and on the one hand a residual and on the other hand an emergent culture. But we can only understand this if we can make distinctions, that usually require very precise analysis, between residual-incorporated and residual not incorporated, and between emergent-incorporated and emergent not incorporated. It is an important fact about any particular society, how far it reaches into the whole range of human practices and experiences in an attempt at incorporation.. It may be true of some earlier phases of bourgeois society, for example, that there were some areas of experience which it was willing to dispense with, which it was prepared to assign as the sphere of private or artistic life, and as being no particular business of society or the state. This went along with certain kinds of political tolerance, even if the reality of that tolerance was malign neglect. But I am sure it is true of the society that has come into existence since the last war, that progressively, because of developments in the social character of labour, in the social character of communications, and in the social character of decision, it extends much further than ever before in capitalist society into certain hitherto resigned areas of experience and practice and meaning. Thus the effective decision, as to whether a practice is alternative or oppositional, is often now made within a very much narrower scope. There is a simple theoretical distinction between alternative and oppositional, that is to say between someone who simply finds a different way to live and wishes to be left alone with it, and someone who finds a different way to live and wants to change the society in its light. This is usually the difference between individual and small-group solutions to social crisis and those solutions which properly belong to political and ultimately revolutionary practice. But it is often a very narrow line, in reality, between alternative and oppositional. A meaning or a practice may be tolerated as a deviation, and yet still be seen only as another particular way to live. But as the necessary area of effective dominance extends, the same meanings and practices can be seen by the dominant culture, not merely as disregarding or despising it, but as challenging it.

Now it is crucial to any Marxist theory of culture that it can give an adequate explanation of the sources of these practices and meanings. We can understand, from an ordinary historical approach, at least some of the sources of residual meanings and practices. These are the results of earlier social formations, in which certain real meanings and values were generated. In the subsequent default of a particular phase of a dominant culture, there is then a reaching back to those meanings and values which were created in real societies in the past, and which still seem to have some significance because they represent areas of human experience, aspiration and achievement, which the dominant culture under-values or opposes, or even cannot recognise. But our hardest task, theoretically, is to find a non-metaphysical and non-subjectivist explanation of emergent cultural practice. Moreover, part of our answer to this question bears on the process of persistence of residual practices.

Class and Human Practice

We have indeed one source to hand from the central body of Marxist theory. We have the formation of a new class, the coming to consciousness of a new class. This remains, without doubt, quite centrally important. Of course, in itself, this process of formation complicates any simple model of base and superstructure. It also complicates some of the ordinary versions of hegemony, although it was Gramsci's whole purpose to see and to create by organization that hegemony of a proletarian kind which would be capable of challenging the bourgeois hegemony. We have then one central source of new practice, in the emergence of a new class. But we have also to recognize certain other kinds of source, and in cultural practice some of these are very important. I would say that we can recognize them on the basis of this proposition: that no mode of production, and therefore no dominant society or order of society, and therefore no dominant culture, in reality exhausts the full range of human practice, human energy, human intention (this range is not the inventory of some original 'human nature' but, on the contrary, is that extraordinary range of variations, both practised and imagined, of which human beings are and have shown themselves to be capable). Indeed it seems to me that this emphasis is not merely a negative proposition, allowing us to account for certain things which happen outside the dominant mode. On the contrary, it is a fact about the modes of domination that they select from and consequently exclude the full range of actual and possible human practice. The difficulties of human practice outside or against the dominant mode are, of course, real. It depends very much whether it is in an area in which the dominant class and the dominant culture have an interest and a stake. If the interest and the stake are explicit, many new practices will be reached for, and if possible incorporated, or else extirpated with extraordinary vigour. But in certain areas, there will be in certain periods practices and meanings which are not reached for. There will be areas of practice and meaning which, almost by definition from its own limited character, or in its profound deformation, the dominant culture is unable in any real terms to recognize. This gives us a bearing on the observable difference between, for example, the practices of a capitalist state and a state like the contemporary Soviet Union in relation to writers. Since from the whole Marxist tradition literature was seen as an important activity, indeed a crucial activity, the Soviet state is very much sharper in investigating areas where different versions of practice, different meanings and values, are being attempted and expressed. In capitalist practice, if the thing is not making a profit, or if it is not being widely circulated, then it can for some time be overlooked, at least while it remains alternative. When it becomes oppositional in an explicit way, it does, of course, get approached or attacked.

I am saying then that in relation to the full range of human practice at any one time, the dominant mode is a conscious selection and organization. At least in its fully formed state it is conscious. But there are always sources of actual human practice which it neglects or excludes. And these can be different in quality from the developing and articulate interests of a rising class. They can include, for example, alternative perceptions of others, in immediate personal relationships, or new perceptions of material and media, in art and science, and within certain limits these new perceptions can be practised. The relations between the two kinds of source—the emerging class and either the dominatively excluded or the more generally new practices—are by no means necessarily contradictory. At times they can be very close, and on the relations between them much in political practice depends. But culturally and as a matter of theory the areas can be seen as distinct.

Now if we go back to the cultural question in its most usual form—what are the relations between art and society, or literature and society?—in the light of the preceding discussion, we have to say first that there are no relations between literature and society in that abstracted way. The literature is there from the beginning as a practice in the society. Indeed until it and all other practices are present, the society cannot be seen as fully formed. A society is not fully available for analysis until each of its practices is included. But if we make that emphasis we must make a corresponding emphasis: that we cannot separate literature and art from other kinds of social practice, in such a way as to make them subject to quite special and distinct laws. They may have quite specific features as practices, but they cannot be separated from the general social process. Indeed one way of emphasizing this is to say, to insist, that literature is not restricted to operating in any one of the sectors I have been seeking to describe in this model. It would be easy to say, it is a familiar rhetoric, that literature operates in the emergent cultural sector, that it represents the new feelings, the new meanings, the new values. We might persuade ourselves of this theoretically, by abstract argument, but when we read much literature, over the whole range, without the sleight-of-hand of calling Literature only that which we have already selected as embodying certain meanings and values at a certain scale of intensity, we are bound to recognize that the act of writing, the practices of discourse in writing and speech, the making of novels and poems and plays and theories, all this activity takes place in all areas of the culture.

Literature appears by no means only in the emergent sector, which is always, in fact, quite rare. A great deal of writing is of a residual kind, and this has been deeply true of much English literature in the last half-century. Some of its fundamental meanings and values have belonged to the cultural achievements of long-past stages of society. So widespread is this fact, and the habits of mind it supports, that in many minds 'literature' and 'the past' acquire a certain identity, and it is then said that there is now no literature: all that glory is over. Yet most writing, in any period, including our own, is a form of contribution to the effective dominant culture. Indeed many of the specific qualities of literature—its capacity to embody and enact and perform certain meanings and values, or to create in single particular ways what would be otherwise merely general truths —enable it to fulfil this effective function with great power. To literature, of course, we must add the visual arts and music, and in our own society the powerful arts of film and of broadcasting. But the general theoretical point should be clear. If we are looking for the relations between literature and society, we cannot either separate out this one practice from a formed body of other practices, nor when we have identified a particular practice can we give it a uniform, static and ahistorical relation to some abstract social formation. The arts of writing and the arts of creation and performance, over their whole range, are parts of the cultural process in all the different ways, the different sectors, that I have been seeking to describe. They contribute to the effective dominant culture and are a central articulation of it. They embody residual meanings and values, not all of which are incorporated, though many are. They express also and significantly some emergent practices and meanings, yet some of these may eventually be incorporated, as they reach people and begin to move them. Thus it was very evident in the sixties, in some of the emergent arts of performance, that the dominant culture reached out to transform, or seek to transform, them. In this process, of course, the dominant culture itself changes, not in its central formation, but in many of its articulated features. But then in a modern society it must always change in this way, if it is to remain dominant, if it is still to be felt as in real ways central in all our many activities and interests.

Critical Theory as Consumption

What then are the implications of this general analysis for the analysis of particular works of art? This is the question towards which most discussion of cultural theory seems to be directed: the discovery of a method, perhaps even a methodology, through which particular works of art can be understood and described. I would not myself agree that this is the central use of cultural theory, but let us for a moment consider it. What seems to me very striking is that nearly all forms of contemporary critical theory are theories of *consumption*. That is to say, they are concerned with understanding an object in such a way that it can profitably or correctly be consumed. The earliest stage of consumption theory was the theory of 'taste', where the link between the practice and the theory was direct in the metaphor. From taste there came the mᴗre elevated notion of 'sensibility', in which it was the consumption by sensibility of elevated or insightful works that was held to be the essential practice of reading, and critical activity was then a function of this sensibility. There were then more developed theories, in the 1920s with I.A. Richards, and later in New Criticism, in which the effects of consumption were studied directly. The language of the work of art as object then became more overt. 'What effect does this work ("the poem" as it was ordinarily described) have on me?' Or, 'what impact does it have on me?', as it was later to be put in a much wider area of communication studies. Naturally enough, the notion of the work of art as *object*, as *text*, as an isolated artefact, became central in all these later consumption theories. It was not only that the practices of *production* were then overlooked, though this fused with the notion that most important literature anyway was from the past. The real social conditions of production were in any case neglected because they were believed to be at best secondary. The true relationship was seen always as between the taste, the sensibility or the training of the reader and this isolated work, this object 'as in itself it really is', as most people came to put it. But the notion of the work of art as object had a further large theoretical effect. If you ask questions about the work of art seen as object, they may include questions about the components of its production. Now, as it happened, there was a use of the formula of base and superstructure which was precisely in line with this. The components of a work of art were the real activities of the base, and you could study the object to discover these components. Sometimes you even studied the components and then projected the object. But in any case the relationship that was looked for was one between an object and its components. But this was not only true of Marxist suppositions of a base and a superstructure. It was true also of various kinds of psychological theory, whether in the form of archetypes, or the images of the collective unconscious, or the myths and symbols which were seen as the *components* of particular works of art. Or again there was biography, or psychobiography and its like, where the components were in the man's life and the work of art was an object in which components of this kind were discovered. Even in some of the more rigorous forms of New Criticism and of structuralist criticism, this essential procedure of regarding the work as an object which has to be reduced to its components, even if later it may be reconstituted, came to persist.

Objects and Practices

Now I think the true crisis in cultural theory, in our own time, is between this view of the work of art as object and the alternative view of art as a practice. Of course it is at once argued that the work of art *is* an object: that various works have survived from the past, particular sculptures, particular paintings, particular buildings, and these are objects. This is of course true, but the same way of thinking is applied to works which have no such singular existence. There is no *Hamlet*, no *Brothers Karamazov*, no *Wuthering Heights*, in the sense that there is a particular great painting. There is no *Fifth Symphony*, there is no work in the whole area of music and dance and performance, which is an object in any way comparable to those works in the visual arts which have survived. And yet the habit of treating all such works as objects has persisted because this is a basic theoretical and practical presupposition. But in literature (especially in drama), in music and in a very wide area of the performing arts, what we permanently have are not objects but *notations*. These notations have then to be interpreted in an active way, according to the particular conventions. But indeed this is true over an even wider field. The relationship between the making of a work of art and its reception is always active, and subject to conventions, which in themselves are forms of (changing) social organization and relationship, and this is radically different from the production and consumption of an object. It is indeed an activity and a practice, and in its accessible forms, although it may in some arts have the character of a singular object, it is still only accessible through active perception and interpretation. This makes the case of notation, in arts like drama and literature and music, only a special case of a much wider truth. What this can show us here about the practice of analysis is that we have to break from the common procedure of isolating the object and then discovering its components. On the contrary we have to discover the nature of a practice and then its conditions.

Often these two procedures may in part resemble each other, but in many other cases they are of radically different kinds, and I would conclude with an observation on the way this distinction bears on the Marxist tradition of the relation between primary economic and social practices, and cultural practices. If we suppose that what is produced in cultural practice is a series of objects, we shall, as in most current forms of sociological-critical procedure, set about discovering their components. Within a Marxist emphasis these components will be from what we have been in the habit of calling the base. We then isolate certain features which we can so to say recognize *in component form*, or we ask what processes of transformation or mediation these components have gone through before they arrived in this accessible state.

But I am saying that we should look not for the components of a product but for the conditions of a practice. When we find ourselves looking at a particular work, or group of works, often realizing, as we do so, their essential community as well as their irreducible individuality, we should find ourselves attending first to the reality of their practice and the conditions of the practice as it was then executed. And from this I think we ask essentially different questions. Take for example the way in which an object—'a text'—is related to a genre, in orthodox criticism. We identify it by certain leading features, we then assign it to a larger cate-gory, the genre, and then we may find the components of the genre in a particular social history (although in some variants of criticism not even that is done, and the genre is supposed to be some permanent category of the mind).

It is not that way of proceeding that is now required. The recognition of the relation of a collective mode and an individual project—and these are the only categories that we can initially presume—is a recognition of related practices. That is to say, the irreducibly individual projects that particular works are, may come in experience and in analysis to show resemblances which allow us to group them into collective modes. These are by no means always genres. They may exist as resemblances within and across genres. They may be the practice of a group in a period, rather than the practice of a phase in a genre. But as we discover the nature of a particular practice, and the nature of the relation between an individual project and a collective mode, we find that we are analysing, as two forms of the same process, both its active composition and its conditions of composition, and in either direction this is a complex of extending active relationships. This means, of course, that we have no built-in procedure of the kind which is indicated by the fixed character of an object. We have the principles of the relations of practices, within a discoverably intentional organization, and we have the available hypotheses of dominant, residual and emergent. But what we are actively seeking is the true practice which has been alienated to an object, and the true conditions of practice—whether as literary conventions or as social relationships—which have been alienated to components or to mere background.

As a general proposition this is only an emphasis, but it seems to me to suggest at once the point of break and the point of departure, in practical and theoretical work, within an active and self-renewing Marxist cultural tradition.

Means of Communication as Means of Production

As a matter of general theory it is useful to recognize that means of communication are themselves means of production. It is true that means of communication, from the simplest physical forms of language to the most advanced forms of communications technology, are themselves always socially and materially produced, and of course reproduced. Yet they are not only forms but means of production, since communication and its material means are intrinsic to all distinctively human forms of labour and social organization, thus constituting indispensable elements both of the productive forces and of the social relations of production.

Moreover the means of communication, both as produced and as means of production, are directly subject to historical development. This is so, first, because the means of communication have a specific productive history, which is always more or less directly related to general historical phases of productive and technical capacity. It is so, second, because the historically changing means of communication have historically variable relations to the general complex of productive forces and to the general social relationships which are produced by them and which the general productive forces both produce and reproduce. These historical variations include both relative homologies between the means of communication and more general social productive forces and relationships, and, most marked in certain periods, contradictions of both general and particular kinds.

Three Ideological Blocks

This theoretical view of the means of communication, within a perspective of historical materialism, is, in our own time, overlaid or blocked by three characteristic ideological positions.

First, the means of communication, having been reduced from their status as means of social production, are seen only as 'media' : devices for the passing of 'information' and 'messages' between persons who either generally, or in terms of some specific act of production, are abstracted from the communication process as unproblematic 'senders' or 'receivers'. People are seen, that is to say, as abstract individuals, who are then either diagrammatically represented in terms of these abstract functions, or are at best broadly characterised (i) as bearers of a generalized ('human') sociality (communication as abstract 'socialization' or 'social process'); (ii) as bearers of a specified but still abstract sociality (communications between 'members' of a social group, usually national or cultural, without intrinsic reference to the differential social relations within any such group); or (iii), in an extreme form related to 'expressivist' theories of language, as unspecified 'individuals' (communication as transmission, but implying reception, by abstracted individuals, each with 'something of his own to say'). Much otherwise sophisticated work in information and communication theory rests on, and frequently conceals, this first, deeply bourgeois, ideological position.

Then, second, in a more plausible attempt to recognize *some* means of communication as means of production, there is the now commonplace distinction between 'natural' and 'technological' means of communication: the former characterized, and then usually neglected, as 'ordinary, everyday language', in 'face-to-face' situations; the latter grouped around developed mechanical and electronic communication devices and then generalized—with an especially noticeable ideological shift from technical means to abstracted social relationships—as 'mass communication'. This position has dominated a large area of modern bourgeois cultural science, but it has also, under the same title of 'mass communications', been uncritically imported into significant areas of socialist thinking, especially in its more applied forms.

It is theoretically inadmissible for two reasons. First, because the separation of 'mass communications' from 'ordinary, everyday language' practice conceals the fact that 'mass communication' processes include, in most cases necessarily, forms of 'ordinary, everyday language' use, to be sure in variably differential modes; and include also the simulation or conventional production of generally significant communication *situations.* Second, because the grouping of all or most mechanical and electronic means as 'mass communications' conceals (under the cover of a formula drawn from capitalist practice, in which an 'audience' or a 'public', itself always socially specific and differentiated, is seen as a 'mass market' of opinion and consumption) the radical variations between different kinds of mechanical and electronic means. In fact, in their differences, these necessarily carry both variable relations to 'ordinary, everyday language' in 'face-to-face situations' (the most obvious example is the radical difference of usage and communicative situation as between print and television) and the variable relations between the specific communicative relationships and other forms of social relationship (the variable extent and composition of audiences; variability of the social conditions of reception—the assembled cinema audience; the home-based television audience; group reading; isolated reading).

A variant of this second ideological position, associated especially with McLuhan, recognizes the specific differences between 'media' but then succumbs to a localized technological determinism, in which uses and relationships are technically determined by the properties of different media, irrespective of the whole complex of social productive forces and relationships within which they are developed and used. Thus the means of communication are recognized, but abstractly, as means of production, and are indeed, ideologically, projected as the only means of production, in which what will be produced is 're-tribalization', the supposed 'global village' of restored, 'unfallen' natural man. The superficial attraction of this position, beyond the essentially abstract materialism of its specification of media, rests on the characteristically rhetorical isolation of 'mass communications' from the complex historical development of the means of communication as intrinsic, related and determined parts of the whole historical social and material process.

There is then, third, an ideological position which has entered into some variants of Marxism, and which permits some accommodation with the bourgeois concept of 'mass communications'. This rests on an abstract and *a priori* separation of means of communication from means of production. It is related, first, to the specialized use of the term 'production' as if its only forms were either capitalist production—that is, the production of commodities, or more general 'market' production, in which all that is ever produced takes the form of isolable and disposable objects. Within Marxism it is further related to, and indeed dependent on, mechanical formulations of base and superstructure, in which the inherent role of means of communication in every form of production, including the production of objects, is ignored, and communication becomes a second-order or second-stage process, entered into only *after* the decisive productive and social-material relationships have been established.

This received position must be quite generally corrected, so that the variable, dynamic and contradictory forms of both 'base' and 'superstructure' can be seen historically, rather than subsumed, from a bourgeois habituation, as necessary universal forms and relations. But also in twentieth-century societies, it requires an especially sharp contemporary correction, since the means of communication as means of social production, and in relation to this the production of the means of communication themselves, have taken on a quite new significance, within the generally extended communicative character of modern societies and between modern societies. This can be seen, very strikingly, within the totality of modern 'economic' and 'industrial' production, where, in the transport, printing and electronic industries 'communicative production' has reached a qualitatively different place in its relation to—more strictly its proportion of—production in general. Moreover this outstanding development is still at a relatively early stage, and in electronics especially is certain to go very much further. Failure then to recognize this qualitative change not only postpones correction of the mechanical formulations of 'a base' and 'a superstructure', but prevents or displaces analysis of the significant relations of communicational means and processes to the crises and problems of advanced capitalist societies and—it would seem—to the different crises and problems of advanced industrial socialist societies.

Towards a History of 'Communicative Production'

A theoretical emphasis on the means of communication as means of production, within a complex of general social-productive forces, should allow and encourage new approaches to the history of the means of communication themselves. This history is, as yet, relatively little developed, although in some areas there is notable empirical work. Within the ideological positions outlined above, the most familiar kinds of history have been specialized technical studies of what are seen as new 'media'—from writing to alphabets through printing to motion pictures, radio and television. Much indispensable detail has been gathered in these specialist histories, but it is ordinarily relatively isolated from the history of the development of general productive forces and social orders and relationships. Another familiar kind of history is the social history of 'audiences' or 'publics': again containing indispensable detail but ordinarily undertaken within a perspective of 'consumption' which is unable to develop the always significant and sometimes decisive relations between these modes of consumption, which are commonly also forms of more general social organization, and the specific modes of production, which are at once technological and social.

The main result of a restated theoretical position should be sustained historical inquiry into the general history of the development of means of communication, including that especially active historical phase which includes current developments in our own societies. These remarkable developments have of course already directed attention to the crises and problems of modern communications systems. But in general, within the terms of one or other of the initial ideological positions, these tend to be treated statically or to be discussed as mere effects of other systems and other, as it were completed (or in general completely understood) historical developments. In few fields of contemporary social reality is there such a lack of solid historical understanding. The popularity of shallowly-rooted and ideological applications of other histories and other analytic methods and terms is a direct and damaging consequence of this lack. The necessary work, so immense in scope and variety, will be collaborative and relatively long-term. All that is possible now, in a theoretical intervention, is an indication of some of its possible lines.

Thus it is possible, in considering means of communication as means of production, to indicate, theoretically, those boundaries between different technical means which, as they are drawn, indicate basic differences in modes of communication itself. It should also then be possible to indicate the main questions about the relations of these modes to more general productive modes, to different kinds of social order, and (which in our own period is crucial) to the basic questions of skills, capitalization and controls.

It is useful, first, to distinguish between modes of communication which depend on immediate human physical resources and those other modes which depend on the transformation, by labour, of non-human material. The former, of course, can not be abstracted as 'natural'. Spoken languages and the rich area of physical communicative acts now commonly generalized as 'non-verbal communication' are themselves, inevitably, forms of social production: fundamental qualitative and dynamic developments of evolutionary human resources; developments moreover which are not only post-evolutionary but which were crucial processes in human evolution itself. All such forms are early in human history, but their centrality does not diminish during the remarkable subsequent stages in which, by conscious social labour, men developed means of communication which depended on the use or transformation of non-human material. In all modern and in all foreseeable societies, physical speech and physical non-verbal communication ('body language') remain as the central and decisive communicative means.

It is then possible to distinguish types of use or transformation of non-human material, for communicative purposes, in relation to this persistent direct centrality. This yields a different typology from that indicated by simple chronological succession. There are three main types of such use or transformation: (i) *amplificatory*; (ii) *durative* (storing); (iii) *alternative*. Some examples will make this preliminary classificaiton clearer. Thus, in relation to the continuing centrality of direct physical communicative means, the *amplificatory* ranges from such simple devices as the megaphone to the advanced technologies of directly transmitted radio and television. The *durative*, in relation to direct physical resources, is, in general, a comparatively late development; some kinds of non-verbal communication are made durable in painting and sculpture, but speech, apart from the important special case of repetitive (conventional) oral transmission, has been made durable only since the invention of sound recording. The type of the *alternative*, on the other hand, is comparatively early in human history: the conventional use or transformation of physical objects as signs; the rich and historically crucial development of writing, of graphics, and of means of their reproduction.

This typology, while still abstract, bears centrally on questions of social relationships and social order within the communicative process. Thus, at a first level of generality, both the amplificatory and the durative can be differentiated, socially, from the alternative. At least at each end of the amplificatory and most durative processes the skills involved—and thus the general potential for social access—are of a kind already developed in primary social communication: to speak, to hear, to gesture, to observe and to interpret. Many blocks supervene, even at a primary level, as in the different languages and gesture-systems of different societies, but within the communicative process itself there is no *a priori* social differentiation. Problems of social order and relationship in these processes centre in issues of control of and access to the developed means of amplification or duration. Characteristically these are of direct interest to a ruling class; all kinds of control and restriction of access have been repeatedly practised. But it is still a shorter route, for any excluded class, from such control and restriction to at least partial use of such means, than in the case of alternative means, in which not only access but a crucial primary skill—for example, writing or reading—has also to be mastered.

The problem of social order cannot be left as one of simple class differentiation. There is a reasonably direct and important relation between the relative powers of amplification and duration and the amounts of capital involved in their installation and use. It is much easier, obviously, to establish a capitalist or state-capitalist monopoly in radio-transmission than in megaphones. Such monopolies are still of crucial social and political importance. Yet within the amplificatory and durative means there are many historical contradictions. The very directness of access, at each end of the process, allows substantial flexibility. The short-wave radio receiver, and now especially the transistor radio, enable many of us to listen to voices beyond our own social system. The crucial phase of monopoly-capitalist development, including capitalist control of the advanced technologies of centralized amplification and recording, came also to include the intensive development of such machines as transistor radios and tape-recorders, which were intended for the ordinary channels of capitalist consumption, but as machines involving only primary communicative skills gave limited facilities also for alternative speaking, listening and recording, and for some direct autonomous production. This is still only a marginal area, by comparison with the huge centralized systems of amplification and recording, based on varying but always substantial degrees of control and selection in the interests of the central social order. Yet though marginal it is not insignificant, in contemporary political life.

Moreover there are many technical developments which, within the always contradictory social productive process, are extending this range: cheaper radio transmitters, for example. Within a socialist perspective these means of autonomous communication can be seen not only, as under capitalism or in the difficult early stages of socialism, as alternatives to the central dominant amplificatory and durative systems, but in a perspective of democratic communal use in which, for the first time in human history, there could be a full potential correspondence between the primary physical communicative resources and the labour-created forms of amplification and duration. Moreover this profound act of social liberation would itself be a qualitative development of the existing direct physical resources. It is in this perspective that we can reasonably and practically achieve Marx's sense of communism as 'the production of the very form of communication', in which, with the ending of the division of labour within the mode of production of communication itself, individuals would speak '*as* individuals', as integral human beings.

There are greater but not insuperable difficulties in those communicative processes which are technically *alternative* to the use of direct physical communicative resources. The most remarkable fact of electronic communications technology is that, coming very much later in human history than the technologies of writing and printing, it has nevertheless, in some of its main uses (with certain critical exceptions which we shall have to discuss), a much closer modal correspondence to direct physical communicative forms: speaking, listening, gesturing, observing. This means that there are in fact fewer obstacles, within this general mode, to abolition of the technical division of labour. The problems of the general social and economic—revolutionary—abolition of the division of labour are of course common to all modes, but there are here, as in other areas of production, significant technical differentiae which, even within a revolutionary society, will affect at least the timing of the practical ending of such divisions.

The first fact about the alternative communicative modes is that they require, for their very performance, skills beyond those which are developed in the most basic forms of social intercourse. Writing and reading are obvious examples, and the extent of illiteracy or imperfect literacy, even in advanced industrial societies, to say nothing of pre-industrial or industrializing societies, is evidently a major obstacle to abolition of the division of labour within this vital area of communication. Literacy programmes are thus basic within any socialist perspective. But their success, essential as it is, reaches only to the point already achieved within more direct physical communicative processes, in that there is then potential access at each end of the process. The problems encountered in the direct modes remain for solution: problems of effective access, of alternatives to class and state control and selection, and of the economics of general distribution. Theoretically these are of the same order as those encountered in democratization of the direct modes, but the costs of the transformation processes which are inherent in all alternative forms may significantly affect at least the timing of their solution.

Here also, however, technical developments are making some kinds of common access simpler. Mechanical and electronic forms of printing and reproduction are now available at relatively low capital costs. Beyond these there is a dynamic area of technical development which is socially and economically more ambiguous. From computer typesetting to the electronically direct composition of type—and beyond these, perhaps, though it is still some years away, direct electronic interchange, each way, between voice and print—there are now changes in the means of communicative production which at once affect class relations within the processes, and lead also to changes—indeed a rapid rise, at least in the first phase —in the necessary level of capitalization. Thus the relationship between writing and printing, developed in traditional technology, has been an outstanding instance of what is at once a technical and a social division of labour, in which writers do not print, but that is seen as only a technicality, and, crucially, printers do not write but are seen as merely instrumental in the transmission of the writing of others. The class relations within newspapers, for example—between editors and journalists who have things to say and who write them, and a range of craftsmen who then technically produce and reproduce the words of these others—are obvious and now acute. There is an ideological crisis within the capitalist press whenever, on important occasions, print craftsmen assert their presence as more than instrumentality, refusing to print what others have written, or, more rarely, offering themselves to write as well as print. This is denounced, within bourgeois ideology, as a threat to the 'freedom of the press', but the terms allow us to see how this bourgeois definition of freedom is founded, deeply, in a supposedly permanent division not only of labour but of human status (those who have something to say and those who do not).

Yet now, in the new technology, journalists, who 'write', may also, in a direct process, compose type. Traditional crafts are threatened, and there is a familiar kind of industrial dispute. Its terms are limited, but in any pre-revolutionary society the limits are an inevitable consequence of the basic social division of labour. Theoretically the solution is evident. Any gain in immediate access to print is a social gain comparable with the gains of direct transmission and reception of voices. But the capital costs are high, and the realities of access will be in direct relation to the forms of control over capital and the related general social order. Even where these forms have become democratic, there is still a range of questions about the real costs of universal-access communication, and obviously about the comparative costs of such access in different media. Much of the advanced technology, is being developed within firmly capitalist social relations, and investment, though variably, is directed within a perspective of capitalist reproduction, in immediate and in more general terms. At present it seems more probable that self-managing communication systems, with forms of universal access that have genuinely transcended the received cultural divisions of labour, will come earlier in voice systems than in print systems, and will continue to have important economic advantages.

'Direct' and 'Indirect' Communication

Thus far we have made only a first-level comparison between amplificatory and durative systems, on the one hand, and alternative systems, on the other. This comparison takes us a long way into the problem, but there is an important second-level comparison to which we must now turn.

The technical forms which are primarily amplificatory and durative include, as we have seen, within any class-divided society, certain social conditions which qualify their abstract definitions of general availability. Amplification can be, and indeed almost everywhere is, highly selective; only some voices are amplified. Duration is radically affected by this and by further selective processes. But what has then to be distinguished, theoretically, is a qualitative difference, within the means of communication as means of production, between the amplificatory (and to a lesser extent the durative) and those alternative systems which now include not only such modes as writing and print but modes which in some of their uses seem to be only amplificatory or durative.

Thus in radio and television there can, technically (leaving aside, for the moment, the powerful processes of social control and selection), be direct transmission and reception of already generalized communicative means: speech and gestures. But most radio and television—and this tendency is necessarily strengthened when a durative function is in question—involve further labour of a transforming or partly transforming kind. The processes of editing, in the broadest sense—from shortening and rearranging to the composition of new deliberate sequences—are qualitatively similar, at least in effect, to fully alternative systems. Yet this is very difficult to realize just because what is then transmitted has the appearance of direct transmission and reception of the most generalized communicative means. We hear a man speaking with his own voice, or he 'appears as himself' on the screen. Yet what is actually being communicated, after the normal processes of editing, is a mode in which the primary physical resources have been—usually in what are by definition hidden ways; the edited-out words cannot be heard—transformed by further intermediate labour, in which the primary communicative means have become material with which and on which another communicator works.

It is not only a matter of excision and selection. New positive relations of a signifying kind can be made by the processes of arrangement and juxtaposition, and this can be true even in those unusual cases in which the original primary units are left in their original state. In film, in which by definition there is no direct transmission of primary physical communicative resources—since all are intermediately recorded—there is a variation of this general position, and the central communicative act is customarily taken as precisely this composition, in which the primary communicative processes of others, whether or not under specific direction, are in effect raw material for communicative transformation by others.

It is in this sense that radio and television, in all forms other than the simplest direct transmission, and then video and film, have to be seen finally as alternative modes, rather than as simply amplificatory or durative. Even in direct transmission in television, so apparently technical a matter as the positioning of the camera is a crucial signifying element. In a confrontation between police and demonstrators it matters absolutely, for example, whether the camera is placed (as so regularly) behind the police, or, as in a different social perspective it can be, behind the demonstrators, or again, which can sometimes happen, in impartial relations to both. What is 'being seen' in what appears to be a natural form is, evidently, then in part or large part what is 'being made to be seen'. The traditional alternative systems, in which speech is rendered or recorded in print, or in which, by habituation, there is direct communicative composition for print, are then often easier to *recognize* as alternative systems, with all their initial social difficulties of acquiring the necessary skills, than these effectively alternative systems in which the appearance of direct communication has in effect been produced, by specific processes of technical labour.

Thus Marx's revolutionary perspective, within which modern universal communication can be subordinated to individuals only by surbodinating it to all of them, raises problems of a new kind in addition to those problems which are inherent in any such social transformation. We can foresee a stage of social development in which general appropriation of the means of communicative production can, by integrated movements of social revolution and the utilization of new technical capacities, be quite practically achieved. For example the creation of democratic, autonomous and self-managing systems of communal radio is already within our reach, to include not only 'broadcasting', in its traditional forms, but very flexible and complex multi-way interactive modes, which can take us beyond 'representative' and selective transmission into direct person-to-person and persons-to-persons communication. Similar though perhaps more expensive systems can be envisaged for teletext, where there is a broad area for the general appropriation of communicative and especially durative means of production. Yet at the same time, within other modern alternative systems, which include many of the most valuable communicative acts and processes, there are problems in the modalities of any such appropriation which are of a more intractable kind. It is true that modes of communal autonomy and self-management will go much of the way, within the intrinsically transforming processes, to alter the generally existing character of such production. But whereas in the simpler and more direct modes there are readily accessible forms of truly general (universal) appropriation—by direct access to a technology which utilizes only primary and already distributed communicative resources—it must for a long time be the case, in those processes which depend on transformations, that a relatively abstract appropriation is more practical, and therefore more likely, than that more substantial appropriation—general and universal—of the detailed means of production which such systems necessarily employ. Of critical importance, in this respect, and as the necessary ground for any effective transition, is sustained discussion and demonstration of the inherent transforming processes involved in, for example, television and film. The modes of 'naturalization' of these means of communicative production need to be repeatedly analyzed and emphasized, for they are indeed so powerful, and new generations are becoming so habituated to them that here as strongly as anywhere, in the modern socio-economic process, the real activities and relations of men are hidden behind a reified form, a reified mode, a 'modern medium'.

But critical demystification can take us only part of the way. Reification will have to be distinguished from the open, conscious composition of works, or the only results will be negative, as in some contemporary semiotic tendencies, which demystify the practice by calling all such practice into question, and then predictably fall back on ideas of universal (inherent and unsurpassable) alienation, within the terms of a pessimistic and universalist psychology. The critical demystification has indeed to continue, but always in association with practice: regular practice, as part of a normal education, in this transforming labour process itself: practice in the production of alternative 'images' of the 'same event'; practice in processes of basic editing and the making of sequences; practice, following this, in direct autonomous composition.

We shall already have entered a new social world when we have brought the means and systems of the most direct communication under our own direct and general control. We shall have transformed them from their normal contemporary functions as commodities or as elements of a power structure. We shall have recovered these central elements of our social production from the many kinds of expropriator. But socialism is not only about the theoretical and practical 'recovery' of those means of production, including the means of communicative production, which have been expropriated by capitalism. In the case of communications, especially, it is not only, though it may certainly include, the recovery of a 'primitive' directness and community. Even in the direct modes, it should be institution much more than recovery, for it will have to include the transforming elements of access and extension over an unprecedentedly wide social and inter-cultural range.

In this, but even more in the advanced indirect communicative modes, socialism is then not only the general 'recovery' of specifically alienated human capacities but is also, and much more decisively, the necessary institution of new and very complex communicative capacities and relationships. In this it is above all a production of new means (new forces and new relations) of production, in a central part of the social material process; and through these new means of production a more advanced and more complex realization of the decisive productive relationships between communication and community.

3

Ideas of Nature

One touch of nature may make the whole world kin, but usually, when we say nature, do we mean to include ourselves? I know some people would say that the other kind of nature—trees, hills, brooks, animals—has a kindly effect. But I've noticed that they then often contrast it with the world of humans and their relationships.

I begin from this ordinary problem of meaning and reference because I want this inquiry to be active, and because I intend an emphasis when I say that the idea of nature contains, though often unnoticed, an extraordinary amount of human history. Like some other fundamental ideas which express mankind's vision of itself and its place in the world, 'nature' has a nominal continuity, over many centuries, but can be seen, in analysis, to be both complicated and changing, as other ideas and experiences change. I've previously attempted to analyse some comparable ideas, critically and historically. Among them were culture, society, individual, class, art, tragedy. But I'd better say at the outset that, difficult as all those ideas are, the idea of nature makes them seem comparatively simple. It has been central, over a very long period, to many different kinds of thought. Moreover it has some quite radical difficulties at the very first stages of its expression: difficulties which seem to me to persist.

Some people, when they see a word, think the first thing to do is to define it. Dictionaries are produced, and, with a show of authority no less confident because it is usually so limited in place and time, what is called a proper meaning is attached. But while it may be possible to do this, more or less satisfactorily, with certain simple names of things and effects, it is not only impossible but irrelevant in the case of more complicated ideas. What matters in them is not the proper meaning but the history and complexity of meanings: the conscious changes, or consciously different uses: and just as often those changes and differences which, masked by a nominal continuity, come to express radically different and often at first unnoticed changes in experience and history. I'd then better say at once that any reasonably complete analysis of these changes in the idea of nature would be very far beyond the scope of a lecture, but I want to try to indicate some of the main points, the general outlines, of such an analysis, and to see what effects these may have on some of our contemporary arguments and concerns.

The central point of the analysis can be expressed at once in the singular formation of the term. As I understand it, we have here a case of a definition of quality which becomes, through real usage, based on certain assumptions, a description of the world. Some of the early linguistic history is difficult to interpret, but we still have, as in the very early uses, these two very different bearings. I can perhaps illustrate them from a well-known passage in Burke:

> In a state of *rude* nature there is no such thing as a people.... The
> idea of a people is the idea of a corporation. It is wholly artificial;
> and made, like all other legal fictions, by common agreement. What
> the particular nature of that agreement was, is collected from the
> form into which the particular society has been cast.

Perhaps *rude*, there, makes some slight difference, but what is most striking is the coexistence of that common idea, *a state of nature*, with the almost unnoticed because so habitual use of *nature* to indicate the inherent quality of the agreement. That sense of nature as the inherent and essential quality of any particular thing is, of course, much more than accidental. Indeed there is evidence that it is historically the earliest use. In Latin one would have said *natura rerum*, keeping nature to the essential quality and adding the definition of things. But then also in Latin *natura* came to be used on its own, to express the same general meaning: the essential constitution of the world. Many of the earliest speculations about nature seem to have been in this sense physical, but with the underlying assumption that in the course of the physical inquiries one was discovering the essential, inherent and indeed immutable laws of the world. The association and then the fusion of a name for the quality with a name for the things observed has a precise history. It is a central formation of idealist thought. What was being looked for in nature was an essential principle. The multiplicity of things, and of living processes, might then be mentally organized around a single essence or principle: a nature.

Now I would not want to deny, I would prefer to emphasize, that this singular abstraction was a major advance in consciousness. But I think we have got so used to it, in a nominal continuity over more than two millennia, that we may not always realize quite all that it commits us to. A singular name for the real multiplicity of things and living processes may be held, with an effort, to be neutral, but I am sure it is very often the case that it offers, from the beginning, a dominant kind of interpretation: idealist, metaphysical, or religious. And I think this is especially apparent if we look at its subsequent history. From many early cultures we have records of what we would now call nature spirits or nature gods: beings believed to embody or direct the wind or the sea or the forest or the moon. Under the weight of Christian interpretation we are accustomed to calling these gods or spirits pagan: diverse and variable manifestations before the revelation of the one true God. But just as in religion the moment of monotheism is a critical development, so, in human responses to the physical world, is the moment of a singular Nature.

Singular, Abstracted and Personified

When Nature herself, as people learnt to say, became a goddess, a divine Mother, we had something very different from the spirits of wind and sea and forest and moon. And it is all the more striking that this singular abstracted and often personified principle, based on responses to the physical world, had of course (if the expression may be allowed) a competitor, in the singular, abstracted and personified religious being: the monotheistic God. The history of that interaction is immense. In the orthodox western medieval world a general formula was arrived at, which preserved the singularity of both: God is the first absolute, but Nature is His minister and deputy. As in many other treaties, this relationship went on being controversial. There was a long argument, preceding the revival of systematic physical inquiry—what we would now call science—as to the propriety and then the mode of this inquiry into a minister, with the obvious question of whether the ultimate sovereignty was being infringed or shown insufficient respect. It is an old argument now, but it is interesting that when it was revived in the nineteenth century, in the arguments about evolution, even men who were prepared to dispense with the first singular principle—to dispense with the idea of God— usually retained and even emphasized that other and very comparable principle: the singular and abstracted, indeed still often and in some new ways personified, Nature.

Perhaps this does not puzzle others as much as it puzzles me. But I might mention at this stage one of its evident practical effects. In some serious argument, but even more in popular controversy and in various kinds of contemporary rhetoric, we continually come across propositions of the form 'Nature is...', or 'Nature shows...', or 'Nature teaches...'. And what is usually apparent about what is then said is that it is selective, according to the speaker's general purpose. 'Nature is...' —what? Red in tooth and claw; a ruthlessly competitive struggle for existence; an extraordinary interlocking system of mutual advantage; a paradigm of interdependence and cooperation.

And 'Nature is' any one of these things according to the processes we select: the food-chain, dramatized as the shark or the tiger; the jungle of plants competing for space and light and air; or the pollinator—the bee and the butterfly—or the symbiote and the parasite; even the scavenger, the population controller, the regulator of food supplies. In what is now seen so often as the physical crisis of our world many of us follow, with close attention, the latest reports from those who are observing and qualified to observe these particular processes and effects, these creatures and things and acts and consequences. And I am prepared to believe that one or other of the consequent generalizations may be more true than the rest, may be a better way of looking at the processes in which we also are involved and on which we can be said to depend. But I am bound to say I would feel in closer touch with the real situation if the observations, made with great skill and precision, were not so speedily gathered—I mean, of course, at the level of necessary generalization—into singular statements of essential, inherent and immutable characteristics; into principles of a singular nature. I have no competence to speak directly of any of these processes, but to put it as common experience: when I hear that nature is a ruthless competitive struggle I remember the butterfly, and when I hear that it is a system of ultimate mutual advantage I remember the cyclone. Intellectual armies may charge each other repeatedly with this or that selected example; but my own inclination is to ponder the effects of the idea they share: that of a singular and essential nature, with consistent and reconcilable laws. Indeed I find myself reflecting at this point on the full meaning of what I began by saying: that the idea of nature contains an extraordinary amount of human history. What is often being argued, it seems to me, in the idea of nature is the idea of man; and this not only generally, or in ultimate ways, but the idea of man in society, indeed the ideas of kinds of societies.

For the fact that nature was made singular and abstract, and was personified, has at least this convenience: that it allows us to look, with unusual clarity, at some quite fundamental interpretations of all our experience. Nature may indeed be a single thing or a force or a principle, but then what these are has a real history. I have already mentioned Nature the minister of God. To know Nature was to know God, although there was radical controversy about the means of knowing: whether by faith, by speculation, by right reason, or by physical inquiry and experiment. But Nature the minister or deputy was preceded and has been widely succeeded by Nature the absolute monarch. This is characteristic of certain phases of fatalism, in many cultures and periods. It is not that Nature is unknowable: as subjects we know our monarch. But his powers are so great, and their exercise at times so apparently capricious, that we make no pretensions to control. On the contrary we confine ourselves to various forms of petition or appeasement: the prayer against storm or for rain; the superstitious handling or abstention from handling of this or that object; the sacrifice for fertility or the planting of parsley on Good Friday. As so often, there is an indeterminate area between this absolute monarch and the more manageable notion of God's minister. An uncertainty of purpose is as evident in the personified Nature as in the personified God: is he provident or indifferent, settled or capricious? Everyone says that in the medieval world there was a conception of order which reached through every part of the universe, from the highest to the lowest: a divine order, of which the laws of nature were the practical expression. Certainly this was often believed and perhaps even more often taught. In Henry Medwall's play *Nature* or in Rastell's *The Four Elements*, Nature instructs man in his duties, under the eye of God; he can find his own nature and place from the instructions of nature. But in plague or famine, in what can be conveniently called not natural laws but natural catastrophes, the very different figure of the absolute and capricious monarch can be seen appearing, and the form of the struggle between a jealous God and a just God is very reminiscent of the struggle in men's minds between the real experiences of a provident and a destructive 'nature'. Many scholars believe that this conception of a natural order lasted into and dominated the Elizabethan and early Jacobean world, but what is striking in Shakespeare's *Lear*, for example, is the undertainty of the meaning of 'nature':

> Allow not nature more than nature needs,
> Man's life's as cheap as beast's...
> ...one daughter
> Who redeems nature from the general curse
> Which twain have brought her to.

> That nature, which contemns its origin,
> Cannot be border'd certain in itself...
> ...All shaking thunder...
> Crack nature's moulds, all germens spill at once,
> That make ungrateful man...

> ...Hear, nature hear; dear goddess, hear...

In just these few examples, we have a whole range of meanings: from nature as the primitive condition before human society; through the sense of an original innocence from which there has been a fall and a curse, requiring redemption; through the special sense of a quality of birth, as in the Latin root; through again the sense of the forms and moulds of nature which can yet, paradoxically, be destroyed by the natural force of thunder; to that simple and persistent form of the personified goddess, Nature herself. John Danby's analysis of the meanings of 'nature' in *Lear* shows an even wider range.[1]

What in the history of thought may be seen as a confusion or an overlapping is often the precise moment of the dramatic impulse, since it is because the meanings and the experiences are uncertain and complex that the dramatic mode is more powerful, includes more, than could any narrative or exposition: not the abstracted order, though its forms are still present, but at once the order, the known meanings, and that experience of order and meanings which is at the very edge of the intelligence and the senses, a complex interaction which is the new and dramatic form. All at once nature is innocent, is unprovided, is sure, is unsure, is fruitful, is destructive, is a pure force and is tainted and cursed. I can think of no better contrast to the mode of the singular meaning, which is the more accessible history of the idea.

Yet the simplifying ideas continued to emerge. God's deputy, or the absolute monarch (and real absolute monarchs were also, at least in the

---

[1]*Shakespeare's Doctrine of Nature*, London 1949.

image, the deputies of God) were succeeded by that Nature which, at least in the educated world, dominates seventeenth- to nineteenth-century European thought. It is a less grand, less imposing figure: in fact, a constitutional lawyer. Though lip-service is still often paid to the original giver of the laws (and in some cases, we need not doubt, it was more than lip-service), all practical attention is given to the details of the laws: to interpreting and classifying them, making predictions from precedents, discovering or reviving forgotten statutes, and then and most critically shaping new laws from new cases: the laws of nature in this quite new constitutional sense, not so much shaping and essential ideas but an accumulation and classification of cases.

The New Idea of Evolution

The power of this new emphasis hardly needs to be stressed. Its practicality and its detail had quite transforming results in the world. In its increasing secularism, indeed naturalism, it sometimes managed to escape the habit of singular personification, and nature, though often still singular, became an object, even at times a machine. In its earlier phases the sciences of this emphasis were predominantly physical: that complex of mathematics, physics, astronomy which was called natural philosophy. What was classically observed was a fixed state, or fixed laws of motion. The laws of nature were indeed constitutional, but unlike most real constitutions they had no effective history. In the life sciences the emphasis was on constitutive properties, and significantly, on classifications of orders. What changed this emphasis was of course the evidence and the idea of evolution: natural forms had not only a constitution but a history. From the late eighteenth century, and very markedly in the nineteenth century, the consequent personification of nature changed. From the underlying image of the constitutional lawyer, men moved to a different figure: the selective breeder; Nature the selective breeder. Indeed the habit of personification, which except in rather formal uses had been visibly weakening, was very strongly revived by this new concept of an actively shaping, indeed intervening, force. Natural selection could be interpreted either way, with natural as a simple unemphatic description of a process, or with the implication of nature, a specific force, which could do something as conscious as select. There are other reasons, as we shall see, for the vigour of the late eighteenth-century and nineteenth-century personifications, but this new emphasis, that nature itself had a history, and so might be seen as an historical, perhaps the historical force, was another major moment in the development of ideas.

It is already evident, if we look at only some of the great personifications or quasi-personifications, that the question of what is covered by nature, what it is held to include, is critical. There can be shifts of interest between the physical and the organic world, and indeed the distinction between these is one of the forms of the shaping inquiry. But the most critical question, in this matter of scope, was whether nature included man. It was, after all, a main factor in the evolution controversy: whether man could be properly seen in terms of strictly natural processes; whether he could be described, for example, in the same terms as animals. Though it now takes different forms, I think this question remains critical, and this is so for discoverable reasons in the history of the idea.

In the orthodox medieval concept of nature, man was, of course, included. The order of nature, which expressed God's creation, included, as a central element, the notion of hierarchy: man had a precise place in the order of creation, even though he was constituted from the universal elements which constituted nature as a whole. Moreover, this inclusion was not merely passive. The idea of a place in the order implied a destiny. The constitution of nature declared its purpose. By knowing the whole world, beginning with the four elements, man would come to know his own important place in it, and the definition of this importance was in discovering his relation to God.

Yet there is all the difference in the world between an idealist notion of a fixed nature, embodying permanent laws, and the same apparent notion with the idea of a future, a destiny, as the most fundamental law of them all. The latter, to put it mildly, is less likely to encourage physical enquiry as a priority; the purpose of the laws, and hence their nature, is already known: that is to say, assumed. And it is then not surprising that it is the bad angel who says, in Marlowe:

> Go forward, Faustus, in that famous art
> Wherein all Nature's treasure is contained.

What was worrying, obviously, was that in his dealings with nature man might see himself as

> Lord and Commander of these elements.

It was a real and prolonged difficulty:

> Nature that framed us of four elements
> Warring within our breasts for regiment
> Doth teach us all to have aspiring minds.

But though this might be so, aspiration was ambiguous: either to aspire to know the order of nature, or to know how to intervene in it, become its commander; or, putting it another way, whether to learn one's important place in the order of nature, or learn how to surpass it. It can seem an unreal argument. For many millennia men had been intervening, had been learning to control. From the beginning of farming and the domestication of animals this had been consciously done, quite apart from the many secondary consequences as men pursued what they thought of as their normal activities.

The Abstraction of Man

It is now well enough known that as a species we grew in confidence in our desire and in our capacity to intervene. But we cannot understand this process, indeed cannot even describe it, until we are clear as to what the idea of nature includes, and in particular whether it includes man. For, of course, to speak of man 'intervening' in natural processes is to suppose that he might find it possible not to do so, or to decide not to do so. Nature has to be thought of, that is to say, as separate from man, before any question of intervention or command, and the method and ethics of either, can arise. And then, of course, this is what we can see happening, in the development of the idea. It may at first seem paradoxical, but what we can now call the more secular and more rational ideas of nature depended on a new and very singular abstraction: the abstraction of Man. It is not so much a change from a metaphysical to a naturalist view, though that distinction has importance, as a change from one abstract notion to another, and one very similar in form.

Of course there had been a long argument about the relations between nature and social man. In early Greek thought this is the argument about nature and convention; in a sense an historical contrast between the state of nature and a formed human state with conventions and laws. A large part of all subsequent political and legal theory has been based on some sense of this relation. But then of course it is obvious that the state of nature, the condition of natural man, has been very differently inter-pre-ted. Seneca saw the state of nature as a golden age, in which men were happy, innocent and simple. This powerful myth often came to coincide with the myth of Eden: of man before the fall. But sometimes it did not: the fall from innocence could be seen as a fall into nature; the animal without grace, or the animal needing grace. Natural, that is to say, could mean wholly opposite conditions: the innocent man or the mere beast.

In political theory both images were used. Hobbes saw the state of men in nature as low, and the life of pre-social man as 'solitary, poor, nasty, brutish and short'. At the same time, right reason was itself a law of nature, in the rather different constitutive sense. Locke, opposing Hobbes, saw the state of nature as one of 'peace, goodwill, mutual assis-tance and cooperation'. A just society organized these natural qualities, whereas in Hobbes an effective society had overcome those natural disad-vantages. Rousseau saw natural man as instinctive, inarticulate, without property, and contrasted this with the competitive and selfish society of his own day. The point about property has a long history. It was a wide-spread medieval idea that common ownership was more natural than private property, which was a kind of fall from grace, and there have always been radicals, from the Diggers to Marx, who have relied on some form of this idea as a programme or as a critique. And indeed it is in this problem of property that many of the crucial questions about man and nature were put, often almost unconsciously. Locke produced a defence of private property based on the natural right of a man to that with which he has mixed his own labour, and many thousands of people believed and repeated this, in periods when it must have been obvious to everybody that those who most often and most fully mixed their labour with the earth were those who had no property, and when the very marks and stains of the mixing were in effect a definition of being propertyless. The argument can go either way, can be conservative or radical. But once we begin to speak of men mixing their labour with the earth, we are in a whole world of new relations between man and nature, and to separate natural history from social history becomes extremely problematic.

I think nature had to be seen as separate from man, for several purpo-ses. Perhaps the first form of the separation was the practical distinction between nature and God: that distinction which eventually made it possible to describe natural processes in their own terms; to examine them without any prior assumption of purpose or design, but simply as processes, or to use the historically earlier term, as machines. We could find out how nature 'worked'; what made it, as some still say, 'tick' (as if Paley's clock were still with us). We could see better how it worked by altering or isolating certain conditions, in experiment or in improvement. Some of this discovery was passively conceived: a separated mind observing separated matter; man looking at nature. But much more of it was active: not only observation but experiment; and of course not only science, the pure knowledge of nature, but applied science, the conscious intervention for human purposes. Agricultural improvement and the industrial revolution follow clearly from this emphasis, and many of the practical effects depended on seeing nature quite clearly and even coldly as a set of objects, on which men could operate. Of course we still have to remind ourselves of some of the consequences of that way of seeing things. Isolation of the object being treated led and still leads to unforeseen or uncared-for consequences. It led also, quite clearly, to major developments in human capacity, including the capacity to sustain and care for life in quite new ways.

But in the idea of nature itself there was then a very curious result. The physical scientists and the improvers, though in different ways, had no doubt that they were working on nature, and it would indeed be difficult to deny that this was so, taking any of the general meanings. Yet at just the first peak of this kind of activity another and now very popular meaning of nature emerged. Nature, in this new sense, was in another and different way all that was not man: all that was not touched by man, spoilt by man: nature as the lonely places, the wilderness.

The Natural and the Conventional

I want to describe this development in some detail, but because we are still so influenced by it I must first draw attention to the conventional character of this unspoilt nature; indeed the conventional terms in which it is separated out. There are some true wildernesses, some essentially untouched places. As a matter of fact (and of course almost by definition) few people going to 'nature' go to them. But here some of the earlier meanings of 'Nature' and 'natural' come in as a doubtful aid. This wild nature is essentially peaceful and quiet, you hear people say. Moreover it is innocent; it contrasts with man, except presumably with the man looking at it. It is unspoilt but also it is settled: a kind of primal settlement. And indeed there are places where in effect this is so.

But it is also very striking that the same thing is said about places which are in every sense man-made. I remember someone saying that it was unnatural, a kind of modern scientific madness, to cut down hedges; and as a matter of fact I agreed that they ought not to be cut down. But what was interesting was that the hedges were seen as natural, as parts of nature, though I should imagine everyone knows that they were planted and tended, and would indeed not be hedges if men had not made them so. A considerable part of what we call natural landscape has the same kind of history. It is the product of human design and human labour, and in admiring it as natural it matters very much whether we suppress that fact of labour or acknowledge it. Some forms of this popular modern idea of nature seem to me to depend on a suppression of the history of human labour, and the fact that they are often in conflict with what is seen as the exploitation or destruction of nature may in the end be less important than the no less certain fact that they often confuse us about what nature and the natural are and might be.

It is easy to contrast what can be called the improvers of nature and the lovers or admirers of nature. In the late eighteenth century, when this contrast began to be widely made, there was ample evidence of both kinds of response and activity. But though in the end they can be distinguished, and need to be distinguished, I think there are other and rather interesting relations between them.

We have first to remember that by the eighteenth century the idea of nature had become, in the main, a philosophical principle, a principle of order and right reason. Basil Willey's account of the main bearings of the idea, and of the effects and changes in Wordsworth, cannot, I think, be improved upon.[2] Yet it is not primarily ideas that have a history; it is societies. And then what often seem opposed ideas can in the end be seen as parts of a single social process. There is this familiar problem about the eighteenth century: that it is seen as a period of order, because order was talked about so often, and in close relation to the order of nature. Yet it is not only that at any real level it was a notably disorderly and corrupt period; it is also that it generated, from within this disorder, some of the most profound of all human changes. The use of nature, in the physical sense, was quite remarkably extended, and we have to remember— which we usually don't, because a successful image was imposed on us—

[2] *The Eighteenth Century Background*, London 1940.

that our first really ruthless capitalist class, taking up things and men in much the same spirit and imposing an at once profitable and pauperizing order on them, were those eighteenth-century agrarians who got themselves called an aristocracy, and who laid the real foundations, in spirit and practice (and of course themselves joining in), for the industrial capitalists who were to follow them.

A state of nature could be a reactionary idea, against change, or a reforming idea, against what was seen as decadence. But where the new ideas and images were being bred there was a quite different perspective. It is significant that the successful attack on the old idea of natural law should have been mounted just then. Not that it didn't need to be attacked; it was often in practice mystifying. But the utilitarians who attacked it were making a new and very much sharper tool, and in the end what had disappeared was any positive conception of a just society, and this was replaced by new and ratifying concepts of a mechanism and a market. That these, in turn, were deduced from the laws of nature is one of the ironies we are constantly meeting in the history of ideas. The new natural economic laws, the natural liberty of the entrepreneur to go ahead without interference, had in its projection of the market as the natural regulator a remnant—it is not necessarily a distortion—of the more abstract ideas of social harmony, within which self-interest and the common interest might ideally coincide. But what is gradually left behind, in the utilitarians, is any shadow of a principle by which a higher justice—to be appealed to against any particular activity or consequence —could be effectively imagined. And so we have this situation of the great interferers, some of the most effective interferers of all time, proclaiming the necessity of non-interference: a contradiction which as it worked itself through had chilling effects on later thinkers in the same tradition, through John Stuart Mill to the Fabians.

For and Against Improvement

And then it is at just this time, and first of all in the philosophy of the improvers, that nature is decisively seen as separate from men. Most earlier ideas of nature had included, in an integral way, ideas of human nature. But now nature, increasingly, was 'out there', and it was natural to reshape it to a dominant need, without having to consider very deeply what this reshaping might do to men. People talk of order in those cleared estates and those landscaped parks, but what was being moved about and rearranged was not only earth and water but men. Of course we must then say at once that this doesn't imply any previous state of social innocence. Men were more cruelly exploited and imposed on in the great ages of natural law and universal order; but not more thoroughly, for the thoroughness depended on new physical forces and means. Of course it soon happened that this process was denounced as unnatural: from Goldsmith to Blake, and from Cobbett to Ruskin and Dickens, this kind of attack on a new 'unnatural' civilization was powerfully deployed. The negative was clear enough, but the positive was always more doubtful. Concepts of natural order and harmony went on being repeated, against the increasingly evident disorder of society. Other appeals were attempted: to Christian brotherhood and to culture—that new idea of human growth, based on natural analogy. Yet set against the practical ideas of the improvers, these were always insufficient. The operation on nature was producing wealth, and objections to its other consequences could be dismissed as sentimental. Indeed the objections often were, often still are, sentimental. For it is a mark of the success of the new idea of nature—of nature as separated from man—that the real errors, the real consequences, could be described at first only in marginal terms. Nature in any other sense than that of the improvers indeed fled to the margins: to the remote, the inaccessible, the relatively barren areas. Nature was where industry was not, and then in that real but limited sense had very little to say about the operations on nature that were proceeding elsewhere.

Very little to say. But in another sense it had a great deal to say. New feelings for landscape: a new and more particular nature poetry; the green vision of Constable; the green language of Wordsworth and Clare. Thomson in *The Seasons*, like Cobbett on his rural rides, saw beauty in cultivated land. But as early as Thomson, and then with increasing power in Wordsworth and beyond him, there came the sense of nature as a refuge, a refuge from man; a place of healing, a solace, a retreat. Clare broke under the strain, for he had one significant disadvantage; he couldn't both live on the process and escape its products, as some of the others were doing and indeed as became a way of life—this is a very bitter irony—for some of the most successful exploiters. As the exploitation of nature continued, on a vast scale, and especially in the new extractive and industrial processes, the people who drew most profit from it went back, where they could find it (and they were very ingenious) to an unspoilt nature, to the purchased estates and the country retreats. And since that time there has always been this ambiguity in the defence of what is called nature, and in its associated ideas of conservation, in the weak sense, and the nature reserve. Some people in this defence are those who understand nature best, and who insist on making very full connections and relationships. But a significant number of others are in the plainest sense hypocrites. Established at powerful points in the very process which is creating the disorder, they change their clothes at week-ends, or when they can get down to the country; join appeals and campaigns to keep one last bit of England green and unspoilt; and then go back, spiritually refreshed, to invest in the smoke and the spoil.

They would not be able to go undetected so long if the idea they both use and abuse were not, in itself, so inadequate. When nature is separated out from the activities of men, it even ceases to be nature, in any full and effective sense. Men come to project on to nature their own unacknowledged activities and consequences. Or nature is split into unrelated parts: coal-bearing from heather-bearing; downwind from upwind. The real split, perhaps, is in men themselves: men seen, seeing themselves, as producers and consumers. The consumer wants only the intended product; all other products and by-products he must get away from, if he can. But get away—it really can't be overlooked—to treat leftover nature in much the same spirit: to consume it as scenery, landscape, image, fresh air. There is more similarity than we usually recognise between the industrial entrepreneur and the landscape gardener, each altering nature to a consumable form: and the client or beneficiary of the landscaper, who in turn has a view or a prospect to use, is often only at the lucky end of a common process, able to consume because others have produced, in a leisure that follows from quite precise work.

Men project, I said, their own unacknowledged activities and consequences. Into a green and quiet nature we project, I do not doubt, much of our own deepest feeling, our senses of growth and perspective and beauty. But is it then an accident that an opposite version of nature comes to force its way through? Nothing is more remarkable, in the second half of the nineteenth century, than the wholly opposite version of nature as cruel and savage. As Tennyson put it:

> A monster then, a dream,
> A discord. Dragons of the prime
> Which tear each other in the slime.

Those images of tearing and eating, of natural savagery, came to dominate much modern feeling. Disney, in some of his nature films, selects them with what seems an obsessive accuracy. Green nature goes on, in the fortunate places, but within it and all about it is this struggle and tearing, this ruthless competition for the right to live, this survival of the fittest. It is very interesting to see how Darwin's notion of natural selection passed into popular imagery—and by popular I mean the ordinary thoughts and feelings of educated men. 'Fittest', meaning those best adapted to a given and variable environment, became 'strongest', 'most ruthless'. The social jungle, the rat race, the territory-guarders, the naked apes: this, bitterly, was how an idea of man re-entered the idea of nature. A real experience of society was projected, by selective examples, on to a newly alienated nature. Under the veneer of civilization was this natural savagery: from Wells to Golding this could be believed, in increasingly commonplace ways. What had once been a ratification, a kind of natural condonation, of ruthless economic selfishness—the real ideology of early capitalism and of imperialism—became, towards our own day, not only this but a hopelessness, a despair, an end of significant social effort; because if that is what life is like, is naturally like, any idea of brotherhood is futile. Then build another refuge perhaps, clear another beach. Keep out not so much the shark and the tiger (though them when necessary) as other men, the grasping, the predatory, the selfish, the untidy, the herd. Let mid-Wales depopulate and then call it a wilderness area: a wilderness to go to from the jungle of the cities.

Ideas of nature, but these are the projected ideas of men. And I think nothing much can be done, nothing much can even be said, until we are able to see the causes of this alienation of nature, this separation of nature from human activity, which I have been trying to describe. But these causes cannot be seen, in a practical way, by returning to any earlier stage of the idea. In reaction against our existing situation, many writers have created an idea of a rural past: perhaps innocent, as in the first mythology of the Golden Age; but even more organic, with man not separated from nature. The impulse is understandable, but quite apart from its element of fantasy—its placing of such a period can be shown to be continually recessive—it is a serious underestimate of the complexity of the problem. A separation between man and nature is not simply the product of modern industry or urbanism; it is a characteristic of many earlier kinds of organized labour, including rural labour. Nor can we look with advantage to that other kind of reaction, which, correctly identifying one part of the problem in the idea of nature as a mechanism, would have us return to a traditional teleology, in which men's unity with nature is established through their common relation to a creator. That sense of an end and a purpose is in important ways even more alienated than the cold world of mechanism. Indeed the singular abstraction which it implies has much in common with that kind of abstract materialism. It directs our attention away from real and variable relations, and can be said to ratify the separation by making one of its forms permanent and its purpose fixed.

The point that has really to be made about the separation between man and nature which is characteristic of so many modern ideas is that—however hard this may be to express—the separation is a function of an increasing real interaction. It is easy to feel a limited unity on the basis of limited relationships, whether in animism, in monotheism, or in modern forms of pantheism. It is only when the real relations are extremely active, diverse, self-conscious, and in effect continuous—as our relations with the physical world can be seen to be in our own day— that the separation of human nature from nature becomes really problematic. I would illustrate this in two ways.

In our complex dealings with the physical world, we find it very difficult to recognize all the products of our own activities. We recognize some of the products, and call others by-products; but the slagheap is as real a product as the coal, just as the river stinking with sewage and detergent is as much our product as the reservoir. The enclosed and fertile land is our product, but so are the waste moors from which the poor cultivators were cleared, to leave what can be seen as an empty nature. Furthermore, we ourselves are in a sense products: the pollution of industrial society is to be found not only in the water and in the air but in the slums, the traffic jams, and not these only as physical objects but as ourselves in them and in relation to them. In this actual world there is then not much point in counterposing or restating the great abstractions of Man and Nature. We have mixed our labour with the earth, our forces with its forces too deeply to be able to draw back and separate either out. Except that if we mentally draw back, if we go on with the singular abstractions, we are spared the effort of looking, in any active way, at the whole complex of social and natural relationships which is at once our product and our activity.

The process, that is to say, has to be seen as a whole, but not in abstract or singular ways. We have to look at all our products and activities, good and bad, and to see the relationships between them which are our own real relationships. More clearly than anyone, Marx indicated this, though still in terms of quite singular forces. I think we have to develop that kind of indication. In industry, for example, we cannot afford to go on saying that a car is a product but a scrapyard a by-product, any more than we can take the paint-fumes and petrol-fumes, the jams, the mobility, the motorway, the torn city centre, the assembly line, the time-and-motion study, the unions, the strikes, as by-products rather than the real products they are. But then of course to express this we should need not only a more sophisticated but a more radically honest accounting than any we now have. It will be ironic if one of the last forms of the separation between abstracted Man and abstracted Nature is an intellectual separation between economics and ecology. It will be a sign that we are beginning to think in some necessary ways when we can conceive these becoming, as they ought to become, a single discipline.

But it is even harder than that. If we say only that we have mixed our labour with the earth, our forces with its forces, we are stopping short of the truth that we have done this unequally: that for the miner and the writer the mixing is different, though in both cases real; and that for the labourer and the man who manages his labour, the producer and the dealer in his products, the difference is wider again. Out of the ways in which we have interacted with the physical world we have made not only human nature and an altered natural order; we have also made societies. It is very significant that most of the terms we have used in this relationship—the conquest of nature, the domination of nature, the exploitation of nature—are derived from the real human practices: relations between men and men. Even the idea of the balance of nature has its social implications. If we talk only of singular Man and singular Nature we can compose a general history, but at the cost of excluding the real and altering social relations. Capitalism, of course, has relied on the terms of domination and exploitation; imperialism, in conquest, has similarly seen both men and physical products as raw material. But it is a measure of how far we have to go that socialists also still talk of the conquest of nature, which in any real terms will always include the conquest, the domination or the exploitation of some men by others. If we alienate the living processes of which we are a part, we end, though unequally, by alienating ourselves.

We need different ideas because we need different relationships.

> Nature and Nature's laws lay hid in night.
> God said, let Newton be, and all was light.[3]

> Now o'er the one half world
> Nature seems dead.[4]

Between the brisk confidence and the brooding reflection of those remembered lines we feel our own lives swing. We need and are perhaps beginning to find different ideas, different feelings, if we are to know nature as varied and variable nature, as the changing conditions of a human world.

---

[3] Alexander Pope, *Epitaph Intended for Sir Isaac Newton.*
[4] *Macbeth*, II, i.

Social Darwinism

Social Darwinism is the conventional term for a variant of social theory which emerged in the 1870s, mainly in Britain and the United States, and which I'm sorry to say has not entirely died out; indeed, under other names, is being widely revived. I want to describe its ideas in the context of an analysis of various applications of evolutionary theory to social theory, and of its use in creative literature. And so I shall be describing, first, the Social Darwinism which is conventionally known by that name, and which has been so well studied by Richard Hofstadter in *Social Darwinism in American Thought*; and then looking at some of the other variations.

In a sense, we can provide a very adequate analysis of Social Darwinism in terms of the errors of emphasis it makes in extending the theory of natural selection to social and political theory. We can say: this is a false extension or a false application of biology. But while that is true, I think it simplifies the matter a little too much, in that the biology itself has from the beginning a strong social component, as Robert Young has shown in detail.[1] Indeed, my own position is that theories of evolution and natural selection in biology had a social component before there was any question of reapplying them to social and political theory. We have to think of this dialectical movement between the two areas of study as a fact from the beginning. For example, in the case of Darwin himself, we have the impressive note on his reading of Malthus, whom he picked up to read for amusement: it's not the most likely motive for reading Malthus but there we are. He writes:

---

[1] Robert M. Young, 'The Human Limits of Nature' in *The Limits of Human Nature*, ed. J. Benthall, London 1973.

Being well-prepared to appreciate the struggle for existence which
everywhere goes on from long-continued observation of plants and
animals, it at once struck me that under these circumstances favourable
variations would tend to be preserved and unfavourable ones to be
destroyed; the result of this would be the formation of new species.

And Darwin's co-discoverer of natural selection, Wallace, says that
Malthus gave him the long-sought clue to the effective agent in the evolution of organic species. This has been disputed: many historians of
science have argued that the Malthus clue was a very minor element. But
to me it is significant that a theory about the relation between population
and resources—an explicit social theory which had great influence on
nineteenth-century social thought—was at any rate one of the organizing
elements in the emergence of the great generalization about natural selection.

But then one must make clear that Social Darwinism, the popular
application of the biological idea to social thought, comes not so much
from Darwin as from the whole tradition of evolutionary theory, which is
much older than Charles Darwin, which indeed goes back at least to his
grandfather, Erasmus, at the end of the eighteenth century, and which, in
the first half of the nineteenth century, is already a well-founded system
of thought. The explanation of the means of evolution might have to wait
on further discoveries, but the idea of evolution was there. It was in many
cases built into systems, and—above all for the purpose of understanding
Social Darwinism in the narrow sense—it was built into a system by
Herbert Spencer. Indeed, it was Spencer, as a social philosopher, who
first, in 1864, coined the phrase which was to have such a history in the
debate, 'the survival of the fittest'.

Spencer's view of progress, which, he said, was not an accident but a
necessity, a visible evolution in human history, carried some consequences which are the real origins of the narrow kind of Social Darwinism. He
believed, for example, that there was a principle of social selection
operative in human history, and that because this was so it was extremely
important that men didn't interfere with it, and in particular that governments didn't interfere with it. He opposed state aid to the poor on the
grounds that this would preserve the weaker and less successful members
of the race.

Whatever we may now think of the social ethics of this position, it was seen as a logically deducible consequence of the theory of progressive evolution by social selection. The weaker or less able members of society should not be artificially preserved, because the process of social selection which was creating the most vigorous and self-reliant types was something that ought not to be interfered with: its ultimate achievement would be human happiness of a general kind. So he was specifically against what he called artificial preservation of those least able to take care of themselves: a Spencerian theory which has, I suppose, survived to our own decade in the concept of the lame duck and beyond that quaint metaphor for a failing enterprise into the more virulent versions of a market economy and its consequent social order which are now again being put into practice. If you really believe this, if you really believe that there is a system of progressive social selection going on, it can seem wild infamy to interfere with it. And it is the confidence that evolution is leading to this development that forms the ethical or quasi-ethical component of what becomes Social Darwinism. Otherwise it seems the merest random cruelty and rationalization.

The idea of competition as a fundamental social principle is, of course, not new. It was most powerfully prefigured in English thought by Hobbes, who believed that life is the war of all against all, until some sovereign power intervenes and takes control of what would otherwise be a self-destroying horde. Until the intervention of the power to control men and to prevent them destroying one another, that is the natural condition of man. A critical constituent of the full Social Darwinist theory was the growing nineteenth-century belief that character was in a simple sense determined by environment: the doctrine of Robert Owen, for example, that you could wholly reform the moral character of the entire population in a short period of time by altering their environment. If you put the two things together you still don't have Social Darwinism in its full sense, but you have competition, inherent competition, as a natural state; and the idea of character being influenced by circumstances can very easily modulate into its being selected by favourable circumstances. Add to that the theory of historical progressive development and you have Social Darwinism in its developed form.

Darwin himself did not take a consistent position on any of these applications. In a letter he observed ironically that he had just received 'a squib', printed in a newspaper, showing that 'I have proved might is right and therefore that Napoleon is right and every cheating tradesman also right'—obviously a reaction to one of the first and crudest kinds of Social Darwinism. He was against anything which smacked to him of selfish and contentious policies. However he did, from his long early experience of the breeding of domestic creatures, the famous pigeons, take the view that a society was in some peril which didn't in a conscious way select and discard. He did say: 'We civilized men do our utmost to check the process of elimination. This must be highly injurious to the race of man.' In other words, if the weak or the unfavourable variations are, as Spencer would have put it, artificially preserved, the general condition of the race is likely to deteriorate. On the other hand, Darwin was much too humane a man to think in terms which were later to become possible—of the elimination of unfavourable variations, or of social policy in this conscious sense, to which he never fully applied himself.

Almost at once, however, the extensions began to be made: moving out from the social ideas of Spencer and gaining a lot of support from the general climate of harsh competitive individualism as a social ideology at that stage of industrial capitalism and general industrial development. And we can trace the process, in part in the work of particular thinkers, but as much in the ground-swell of a certain kind of public opinion. Look, for example, at Bagehot's *Physics and Politics*, published in 1876. Bagehot was a country banker, editor of the *Economist*, literary essayist, author of *The English Constitution*. In *Physics and Politics* he wrote a work which he subtitled 'Thoughts on the Application of the Principles of Natural Selection and Inheritance to Political Society'. It is one of the first conscious attempts to do just this. And in a sense it comes surprisingly from Bagehot, who was always a moderating man. His famous analysis of the English Constitution was in its way a superb piece of demystification, but of a rather special kind: demystification in order to remystify. He analysed the English Constitution in terms of its theatrical show—he wrote quite sharply about the Widow of Windsor – and he saw and approved the whole panoply of the British State as a means of creating deference in its subjects. He then argued with a quite new tone in Victorian social argument that this was necessary to any well-ordered state. In a way, the conclusions of *Physics and Politics*, after what seem some rather bolder speculations, are essentially similar. He takes from Spencer the idea of the progress of human society by certain well-ordered stages. Primitive or preliminary: the military stage in which human

relations are basically those of armed conflict. But then a stage of civilization which he thought he was living in, a stage of order in which conflict
is resolved by discussion. He did believe that in human societies there
was intrinsic competition: not so much of all against all, individual
against individual, but rather an intrinsic competition for the best shape
of the society. This or that notion of how the society might be had to
engage in competition with all other notions, and in a sense what emerged
as the constituting notion of any particular state was the superior notion.
This could be so, however, only in a period of ordered discussion, as
distinct from a period of military conflict in which a better idea might be
destroyed by a physically stronger enemy. Europe, having been the
central area of conflict between states founded on different notions,
different ideas of the social polity, different ideas of religion, was also the
centre of progress. The conflict and the progress were directly correlated.

This was soon overtaken by something which has a more sinister ring,
although many of the ideas of the next stage can already be found in
Spencer. Sumner in the 1880s offers what becomes, if you read in the
period, a very familiar definition: that civilization is the survival of the
fittest, that the survival of the unfittest is anti-civilization. Socialism is an
absurd notion because it proposes both the development of civilization
and the survival of the unfittest, which are manifestly contradictory, he
argues. Competition is a law of nature and to interfere with the results of
competition is radically to undermine civilization. So let no one pretend
to believe in civilization if on some other grounds he argues for intervention. Millionaires, Sumner said, are a product of natural selection. So we
can see that within twenty years of the formulation of the biological idea
of natural selection we have got a quite new phrase—not that earlier
phrases had been lacking to rationalize rich men—to describe the internal
logic and necessity of the social process.

Not surprisingly, Sumner was almost at once echoed by John D.
Rockefeller, who said that the growth of a large business is merely the
survival of the fittest and made a rather pretty analogy with a prize rose
bloom which has to be debudded of its subsidiary minor blooms before it
can come to its perfection. The processes of industrial monopoly which
were occurring at this time could be rationalized as the production either
of the most beautiful blooms or of the next stage in the social species.

Of course, this was an ideology: it was consciously in opposition to
liberal egalitarian tendencies, to measures of social welfare and reform,

and classically to ideas of socialism. Because it was an ideology, not all the implications of this rather stark and powerful theory were always welcome even to some of its exponents. It is very significant that along this line—through Spencer to Bagehot, Sumner and others—the main inheritance function which is assumed biologically is still that of Lamarck rather than Darwin: in other words, the physical inheritance of acquired characteristics rather than the kind of variation in adaptation to environment which Darwin relied on. Spencer continued to believe in Lamarck long after Darwin, and the concept of physical inheritance in this sense gave the ideologists of Social Darwinism a particularly fortunate opportunity to modify competition of an absolutely open kind when it came to the preservation of family property. After all, if you take their argument quite seriously, the war of all against all should never stop, because to interfere with it would prevent the emergence of the strongest types: so that inherited family property, which means that somebody who may not have strong individual talents which are going to evolve the higher kind of man starts with an advantage, is a kind of interference with competition. But if you have a Lamarckian notion of physical inheritance, then you can rationalize the family and family property as precisely the continuation of what you can now see to be the strongest and best species.

So, too, with the inheritance of capital: nobody could look at the nineteenth century and suppose that it was a society in which one day somebody fired a pistol and said: 'Go on, compete economically, and the strongest will come out at the top of the heap.' Quite evidently, huge fortunes were there at the start of the play, and the great majority of the players came to the table bearing nothing but their hands. If there is really to be competition in the full ruthless sense, then you must all come to the table with empty hands. But financial inheritance is defended with the ideology because the possession of capital provides a measure of continuity. It is really very painful to follow these convolutions of men who had committed themselves to a rhetorically powerful theory which rationalized competition as a principle of society, dismissing as sentimental all apparently ethical and moral objections to it, and then find them having to turn to defend things which were quite evidently qualifications of the competitive principle as such.

Nevertheless, the survival of the fittest, the struggle for existence—

nobody had to invent these as descriptions of nineteenth-century society, they were most people's everyday experience. Millions of men in this country went out each day knowing they had to be stronger or more cunning than their fellows if they were to survive or take anything home to their family. The idea is in a way as popular among the victims of that kind of competitive process as it is among its promoters, because it corresponds very directly to their daily experience of life. Whether or not anybody can conceive a better social order, the idea does seem to fit the experience of life as it is ordinarily lived. The popularity of phrases like 'the rat race' to describe our own society is a direct continuation of these earlier descriptions among the victims. And, of course, anyone who has succeeded, whether or not he has had advantages, has been very willing to invoke the principle of 'the survival of the fittest'.

There are two particular applications of this principle which ought to be noted before we go on to some of the other variants. First is the development of eugenics as a movement. It's a natural consequence of this theory that you should breed only from the most perfectly endowed types. The whole future of man was thought to depend upon this kind of selective physical inheritance. Although there are signs of it throughout the second half of the nineteenth century, it is in the nineties, and especially up to the period of the First World War, which did a little selection of its own, that eugenics gets put forward by a whole range of people otherwise sharing different views. Eugenics as a positive policy is one thing: it amounts to very little more than the argument that every encouragement to breed should be given to the most physically and intellectually favoured. The negative side of eugenics is a more serious matter. There is a direct link back to Malthus and to the thought that the unfit should be prevented from breeding.

Everything then depends on the concept of fitness. It is one thing to hear the eugenic argument about the breeding of children from the physically malformed or those carrying some hereditary disease: it is quite another to hear the eugenic argument against breeding from the disfavoured, the unsuccessful, the socially and economically weak. And yet it gets entangled with this, because very quickly it combines with theories of race, which again don't have a specific origin in the biological argument. Gobineau's argument about the inequality of races had appeared in 1853, well before this phase, but it is readily applicable to race because Darwin had at times used 'race' as a biological term for species—a continuing confusion—and so the idea of a particular human race—the Anglo-Saxon was a particular favourite—as the vigorous stock, the survivor in the competitive battle, inheriting a certain natural right to mastery, became a very powerful component of the ideology of imperialism. In the case for imperialism it was perfectly possible to argue, and many did, that the strongest, the best survivors, the Anglo-Saxon race, had a duty to humanity to continue to assert itself, not to limit its competition with weaker peoples out of some false ethical consideration for them or out of some legalistic notion of their rights. If the competitive struggle produces the strongest human types, then clearly the strongest race must in no way be limited.

You get an interesting variant of this in the North American theory that an even more vigorous hybrid of the Anglo-Saxon race happens to have established itself in the United States, and its turn will come. The general idea of the Aryans as a race with these attributes becomes intensely popular, and in a natural fit of self-defence somebody reinvents the Celts. For if you follow the logic of the crude argument of strength through competition, then you do arrive at imperialism, you do arrive at racist theories, although there may be different choices as to the most favoured race, according to where you happen to live. You also arrive at the rationalization of war. Von Moltke argued that war is the supreme example in human history of the Darwinian struggle for existence, because here, under the most intense conditions, men are set against one another, and the strongest survive, and it is right that it should be so, because only if the strongest survive can the future of humanity be assured.

Social Darwinism in this sense was not the only product of the application of these theories. It is very interesting to see that Marx in 1860, looking into *The Origin of Species*, wrote to Engels saying: 'Darwin's book is very important and serves me as a basis in natural science for the class struggle in history.' And immediately you turn it that way round you see that you can provide a basis for a theory of class struggle on the same analogy. Once again, human history is a struggle—but now between classes rather than races or individuals. On the other hand Engels was among the first to see the faults of the analogy. Arguing, if too simply, that

> the whole Darwinian theory of the struggle for existence is simply
> the transference from society to organic nature of Hobbes's theory of
> *bellum omnium contra omnes*, and of the bourgeois theory of
> competition, as well as the Malthusian theory of population

he went on, in the *The Dialectics of Nature*, to show that

> it is very easy to transfer these theories back again from natural
> history to the history of society, and altogether too naive to maintain
> that thereby these assertions have been proved as eternal natural laws
> of society.

The distinguishing feature of human society was production, and when

> the means of development are socially produced the categories taken
> from the animal kingdom are already totally inapplicable.

However, the concept of the struggle for existence must be retained. It
expresses the struggle of the producers against the capitalists who have
appropriated their means of production and reduced them to poverty.
Thus

> the conception of history as a series of class struggles is already
> much richer in content and deeper than merely reducing it to weakly
> distinguished phases of the struggle for existence.

This is complex. The analogy is criticized and rejected but then in a
way reinstated. Engels had earlier recognized that there was a different
kind of analogy from nature, its harmonious cooperative working, which
many thinkers had emphasized. But

> hardly was Darwin recognized before these same people saw
> everywhere nothing but struggle. Both views are justified within
> narrow limits, but both are equally one-sided and prejudiced.

This is right, but it can hardly be doubted that for his own version of
history Engels drew on the rhetorical strength—now differently applied
and directed—of the analogized 'struggle for existence'.

One of the results of Spencerian ideas of political development had
been the belief that although progress is going to happen by a natural
evolutionary mechanism, it can't be hurried. There's nothing you can do
about it. In the natural processes of social selection higher types eventually
emerge: this is the whole process, but you can't hurry it along. Therefore
evolution becomes a way of describing an attitude to social change. If
somebody says to you, 'Here is a wicked condition, a case of poverty or
corruption or exploitation,' you say: 'Yes, it is very bad, but there is
nothing we can do about it. The evolutionary process will eventually take
us beyond it and if we interfere now we shall merely prevent that happening.' Then this led to a popular contrast between evolution and

revolution, and the rhyme helped. You could not bring about change in society by intervention, let alone by violent intervention. 'We believe,' many thousands of people then started to say, 'in evolution, not revolution.' Yet given the bizarre nature of the analogies from biology, it is not surprising that when De Vries established the evolution of species from mutations, socialist writers who were engaged in the argument against the theorists of social evolution quickly seized on the mutation as the justification precisely for the sharp revolutionary break. 'There you are, you see,' they said: 'nature does not work by the inevitability of gradualism,' which had been the ordinary assumption and which was built into the ideology of the Fabians. 'It works by the sharp mutation which establishes a new . . . ' And then you say 'species' or 'order of society' according to which argument you're involved in. The argument between evolution and revolution, which ought to have been a social and political argument because it is really an argument about particular societies and about means of changing them, thus attracted very early a strong biological or pseudo-biological component.

Now let us look at some of the reactions from within the same tradition to some of these applications. Veblen, for example, in 1899, in *The Theory of the Leisure Class*, said, 'It is quite true that our social system selects certain men,' granting the point that Sumner had made, that millionaires are the product of 'natural selection': the point is, Veblen argued, does it select the right human traits? May not our social system be selecting altogether the wrong human qualities—for example, shrewd practice, chicanery or low cunning? Granted all your arguments about the mechanism of selection as inevitable, may not the social system be producing precisely the wrong emphases, and giving success and power to the wrong human types? This argument was very much developed around the turn of the century.

Benjamin Kidd in his *Social Evolution* said in 1894: 'We must above all take social action to preserve real competition.' At the moment the majority of men are shut out from effectively competing. They don't have the means to compete in society, they're not educated, they don't have money. He therefore uses a social democratic or liberal kind of argument about extending education, giving opportunity, but its purpose is to promote competition, to make the competitive struggle more active and more general. W.H. Mallock, on the other hand, taking a conservative view in his *Aristocracy and Evolution*, argued against democracy and the extension of education on the grounds—more in line with conventional Social Darwinism—that the one desirable product of the competitive process was the great man, the leader, and the one condition of a leader was that he should have enough power, that he should be instantly obeyed, that he should have the means of control to put his great visions into operation, because if the great man cannot put his visions into operation, dragged back by the mediocrity of the mass, human society will never solve its problems. This theory, with its biological component, became, in the twentieth century, first a theory of élites and then a theory of Fascism.

Meanwhile, however, there had been a response of a rather surprising kind. For Kropotkin, in *Mutual Aid* in 1902, said in effect: 'Yes, let us indeed learn from the order of nature. If we look at nature we find it full of examples of mutual aid. Look at the herds of deer, or of cattle. Look at the ants, look at the bees, look at all the social insects. We will find that everywhere there are examples of mutual aid.' Of course, this was co-operation within species. Most of the competitive theories had been based on struggle *between* species, and then covertly applied to competition within one species—man. Kropotkin reversed this: the order of nature, he argued, teaches us mutual aid, collectivism, a quite different sort of social order.

It was Thomas Huxley who made the decisive point, in his *Evolution and Ethics* in 1893. He said: 'The whole confusion has arisen from identifying fittest with best.' 'Fittest', after all, in the Darwinian sense, although not in the Spencerian sense, had meant those best adapted to their environment. If 'fittest' had meant strongest, most powerful, then presumably the dinosaurs would still be here and masters of the earth. 'Fittest' meaning 'adapted to the environment' didn't necessarily mean any of the things which it meant in the social analogy—the strongest, the fiercest, the most cunning, the most enduring. It meant that which in its situation was best adapted to survive. If this is so, Huxley argued, we realize that we can derive no ethical principle from a process of largely random survivals. If we look at the real process of the origins and survivals of species, we learn that fitness to environment cannot be based on any abstract principle and, therefore, that ethics cannot be founded on biological evidence.

Advanced societies, Huxley argued, develop ethical systems whose precise purpose is to modify natural law. Huxley assumes, which I take leave to doubt, that natural law, the order of nature, is a process of unrestrained struggle, and that ethics is then a qualifying mechanism to what, unrestrained, would be a cosmic law. Huxley is, surprisingly, as firm as many of the others that there is such a cosmic law, but he proposes social ethics, cultural development, as a way of modifying it. This position has been repeated by his grandson Julian, who argues that cultural evolution is now the main process, cultural evolution within man.

Meanwhile, this climate of ideas had been pervading imaginative literature in ways that went very deep, but in many different directions. You can pick it up, for example, in Strindberg, especially in the preface to *Miss Julie*, that remarkably powerful play about a single destructive relationship which he wrote in 1888. Strindberg in the preface describes the servant, Jean, as the rising type, the man who is sexually on the upgrade. Risen from a poor family, he is vigorous, adaptable and will survive in his struggle with Lady Julie, the weak aristocrat belonging to a fixed and therefore rather decadent strain. A powerfully-observed sexual relationship of a direct kind is thus interpreted in terms derived from the context of the Darwinist or pseudo-Darwinist argument.

I cannot reckon how many successors there have been to that proposition: the idea of a vigorous, rising working-class male, or a male from a submerged racial group, who enters into a relationship of sex and conflict with the representative of a comparatively weak, comparatively declining or fixed social stratum. A resolution which might be seen as destructive, as in the kind of imposed suicide of Julie which is Jean's culmination, can be ethically rationalized as the emergence of the most vigorous stock. The metaphors for such a process are everywhere apparent in subsequent imaginative literature.

There were more direct applications of the idea in, for example, Jack London, a socialist, a man deeply influenced by Spencer and Darwin, with experience of struggle under very primitive conditions and also with experience of the social jungle that, within the same order of analogy, was an increasingly popular way of describing the late-nineteenth-century city. London develops a characteristic imaginative structure in which struggle is a virtue. The survival of the most vigorous type is seen at once in terms of a kind of individual primitivism and also in terms of the rising class, the class which had hitherto been submerged. In some of his work—for example, *White Fang*—it is the emergence of the powerful individual who has competed under wilderness conditions; in *The Iron*

Heel it is the emergence of the class that has been long suppressed but is historically due to rise.

H.G. Wells's ideas on the subject derive most directly from Thomas Huxley's, but imaginatively he reaches well beyond them. Think, for example, of *The Time Machine*, which is the imaginative projection of a particular phase of evolution operating at several different levels. It is in one sense a projection of the division between the rich and the labouring poor in nineteenth-century industrial society. When the time traveller goes far into the future, he discovers two races of creatures sharing the earth. The race that he first finds is pretty, doll-like; it plays games with flowers, has charming manners, has a playful but weak kind of life in the sunshine, like children. Unnoticed at first, but eventually emerging from below the ground, there appears the other race, the Morlocks, who are dark and bestial.

You can see in all this the evolutionary projection of an idle playful rich and a working population submerged in the darkness and reduced to animal conditions. But the whole situation is imaginatively reversed because the Morlocks keep the Eloi as food: the pretty playmates on the surface of the earth are not the dominant race, for the Morlocks are waiting their time, in evolutionary terms, to come back to the surface again, and meanwhile they feed on the playful ones as cattle.

This idea of the struggle for existence, projected from deep social stratifications, resulting in a branching of the race of man into these two extremes, is one of Wells's most powerful ideas, unforgettably expressed, with the kind of horror with which so many of these ideas of the inevitable struggle for existence were imaginatively received. Wells uses everywhere in his imaginative fiction (and a whole tradition of Science Fiction and scientific romance has followed him) the idea of evolution into new physical types of man, the idea of differently evolving intelligent species on other planets and the idea of competition between them.

When alternative species meet they make war: this idea is deeply established in Science Fiction. *The War of the Worlds* and the whole vast tradition of intergalactic war that we've had ever since in books and films represent to some degree a reaction to twentieth-century experience of war. But the tradition began before the epoch of major wars, and represents also a reaction to the idea of the fundamental struggle for existence: if one species meets another, it will inevitably compete with it and try to destroy it. The extraordinary physical beings that we have been regaled with in Science Fiction are a product of this idea of evolution playing on situations of great tension, great fear.

Utopias have been quite differently projected. Instead of the static Utopias of pre-nineteenth-century writing, when men would find an ideal condition, an island or some point in the future, where their social problems would have been solved, Utopias now, as Wells observed, must be dynamic: they will not stand still. That is what we learn from Darwin, he said: there has to be progression through higher stages. Moreover, they are fraught with great threat: there is inherent danger and conflict in them. Wells's Utopias characteristically are arrived at only after a period of exceptionally destructive conflict.

Some other writers may be mentioned. Shaw, for example, takes a version of creative evolution which is, one might say, more naïve even than Spencer's. The evolution of the final ideal type in *Back to Methuselah* we might be happy to read as a caricature of Spencer. But it is clear from the preface that we are asked to take seriously the emergence of those He-Ancients and She-Ancients (and I think it isn't only the pronouns which remind us of goats) who have pressed on to human perfection, which is, guess what, the goal of redemption from the flesh: pure intelligence has emancipated itself from the body. This is the sort of thing that Wells imagined in his extraordinary race of Selenites on the Moon, with the enormous brain case and the tiny legs: but with Shaw it really was a kind of evolutionary idea that man should get rid of this flesh stuff.

In Ibsen and Hardy there is a very interesting preoccupation with heredity, directly influenced by Darwin and the evolutionary debate, but in each case the critical imaginative difference is this: survival is not unproblematically taken as a criterion of value. Ibsen and Hardy were perfectly prepared to accept that there is intense struggle and competition, that people do get defeated, often the most aspiring being the most deeply defeated. Nearly all Ibsen's heroes aspire, climb (spiritually in most cases) and are defeated in the very act of climbing, overwhelmed because they aspire.

In Hardy it is very often the aspiring or the exceptionally pure character, the Jude the Obscure or Tess, who is the most absolutely destroyed. You cannot read Ibsen or Hardy without realizing that survival is not the demonstration of value: struggle is a necessary process, but in a different sense from the rationalized struggle of the Social Darwinists. It is the constant self-urging towards the light, towards a different, higher kind of human life, which is repeatedly imagined in Hardy and in Ibsen. The attempt is defeated, but the manner of the defeat is such that what is confirmed is the impulse to the light, with a very sober, very sombre look at the possibility or probability that the darkness will win. It is not a teaching of darkness, nor is it any kind of rationalization of the results of crude struggle.

The final example I can give—and it is a surprising one in this context because he used to say he didn't believe in evolution and didn't believe in science much at all—is D.H. Lawrence. Like Strindberg, he uses the idea of the vital rising type and a rather decadent or fixed or imprisoned alternative social type: generally the vigorous rising man and the sexually imprisoned, socially imprisoned or socially declining woman.

He makes of the encounter a cosmic process: it is precisely the cosmic character of the Lawrence sexual relationships of this kind that gives them their place in this tradition. For these are not simple personal relationships: they have something to do with the future of the race, and the physically rising vigorous type is strongly emphasized. But beyond that, at the end of *Women in Love*, having reached a kind of deadlock in human relationships, having seen the failure of one cold, willed relationship between Gerald and Gudrun, having recognized that the relative warmth and friendliness of the relationship between Birkin and Ursula had its limits, that it was more decent but not necessarily complete, Lawrence suddenly in a very surprising version repeats the imaginative conclusion of so much of this tradition, that perhaps we shall have to evolve beyond being human. The merely human is the merely disappointing. He puts it in direct evolutionary terms: just as the horse, he writes, has taken the place of the mastodon, so the eternal creative mystery would dispose of man:

> Races came and went, species passed away, but ever new species arose, more lovely, or equally lovely, always surpassing wonder. The fountain-head was incorruptible and unsearchable. It had no limits. It could bring forth miracles, create utterly new races and new species in its own hour, new forms of consciousness, new forms of body, new units of being.

It is a positive transforming idea, that the creative mystery could evolve beyond man, if man in his present condition failed to attain an adequate consciousness. It is in that sense at the very opposite pole from the pessimistic rationalizations of struggle. But all these matters—issues of societies, of social, economic and political relationships, issues of human relationships between individuals—have been affected, both fundamentally and at the level of their persuasive content, by ideas of what is held to be a scientific process—which, as we have seen, can be applied in many different directions according to the main bearing of the argument or the work.

We then come back (or I at least come back, particularly remembering the social component in the biological theories themselves) to saying that man cannot derive lessons and laws from the processes of what he sees as a separated nature, lessons and laws supposed to be conditions of himself, conditions to which he must in some way conform. The nineteenth-century and early-twentieth-century examples have, at this distance, a certain faded air. Some of them, indeed, can be too easily introduced for mild astonishment or amusement. Yet in our own time, of course with a show of more up-to-date science, the crudest ideas of Social Darwinism, and the crudest analogical interpretations of human relationships in quasi-scientific terms, have been remarkably revived and given extraordinary publicity. Theories of unrestrained and in effect unrestrainable natural aggression have again been launched, with an extraordinary imaginative commitment to the jaws of the great predators. Advertising, typically, has used the tiger as an image for a brand of petrol, in effect animalizing—indeed making predatory—the car. The territoriality of some species has been rationalized as the natural basis of the nation-state and its means of armed defence. The actual complexities of territoriality in different animals and in different periods of human society are overridden by what are finally crude images of property and its defence. Again the highly differentiated internal relations between members of species have been selected and narrowed to crude images of necessary hierarchy—the 'pecking order'—which are used to ideologize and ratify contemporary class and status relationships.

In a familiar confusion and overlap between certain animal species and human prehistory, there has been a rhetorical projection of 'man the hunter', which typically overrides the varied evidence we have of the character of hunting societies, in their internal relations and in their often finely modulated attitudes to the animals they kill and eat. This is important because complex evidence is overriden by an image which is not really that of the hunter but of the aggressive hunter-killer, where not the food but the killing is taken as determining. And this in its turn is used to interpret violence in twentieth-century societies, as a 'more profound' alternative—the burden of the 'beast brain'—to political, economic and historical investigations. In the commercial culture of our own period—a culture which includes works passed off as scientific and theoretical—this new wave of Social Darwinism, now extended beyond its original matrix, is very pervasive and must be supposed to be influential.

It may then be necessary to do more than keep saying that most of the images are demonstrably false, in their characteristic selectivity and uncritical transference. That is a quiet point; quiet and perhaps insufficient, while these brutal images range. There is then another way of putting it, which this tradition seems to invite. If we must have an analogy, these theories and analogies are like one kind of scavenger: darting opportunists around the body of actual science. But then it is not the science that is dead. It is the social theory of that system which had promised order and progress and yet produced the twentieth century. Instead of facing that fact, in all its immense complexity, the rationalizers and the natural rhetoricians have now moved in to snap at and discourage us: not now to ratify an imperialist and capitalist order, but to universalize its breakdown and to persuade us that it has no alternatives, since all 'nature' is like that. In this respect they are worse than their predecessors and must be even more resolutely driven off.

Problems of Materialism

There are inevitable difficulties in any serious materialism. In its earliest phases it has a comparative simplicity of definition, since it rests on a rejection of presumptive hypotheses of non-material or metaphysical prime causes, and defines its own categories in terms of demonstrable physical investigations. Yet such definitions are subject to two inherent difficulties: first, that in the continuing process of investigation, the initial and all successive categories are inherently subject to radical revision, and in this are unlike the relatively protected categories of presumed or revealed truths; second, that in the very course of opposing systematic universal explanations of many of the common-ground processes, provisional and secular procedures and findings tend to be grouped into what appear but never can be systematic, universal and categorical explanations of the same general kind. Thus material investigation, grounded in the rejection of categorical hypotheses of an unverifiable kind, and basing its own confidence in a set of provisional working procedures and demonstrations, finds itself pulled nevertheless towards closed generalizing systems: finds itself material*ism* or *a* materialism. There is thus a tendency for any materialism, at any point in its history, to find itself stuck with its own recent generalizations, and in defence of these to mistake its own character: to suppose that it is a system like others, of a presumptive explanatory kind, or that it is reasonable to set up contrasts with other (categorical) systems, at the level not of procedures but of its own past 'findings' or 'laws'. What then happens is obvious. The results of new material investigations are interpreted as having outdated 'materialism'. Or, conversely, defence of 'the materialist world-view', specified in certain positions now frozen in time, involves contempt for or rejection of apparently incompatible evidence and procedures, and their categorical assignment to systems taken to be alternative and of the same kind: in the ordinary rhetoric, 'idealism'. Intellectual confusion is then severe enough, but it is made worse by the fact, on the one hand, that much of the new 'evidence' and 'procedures', especially in its interpreted and theoretically presumed forms, is indeed incompatible, not only (which is not important) with the frozen 'world-view' but with the significant criteria of the materialist enterprise; and by the fact, on the other hand, that within the world-view, however frozen, there is still hard, often very hard evidence of a kind that is indeed likely to be smothered in the difficult process of the search for genuine compatibilities and necessary reformulations.

These are among the most evident intellectual difficulties of the contemporary argument about materialism, but there is a further set of political and cultural considerations. Materialist modes of investigation have been historically connected, though never exclusively, with certain radical forms of social and political struggle. In Marxism, especially, this connection has been raised to the level of a conscious alliance. It is then not only that there can be confusion between certain frozen forms and certain kinds of political commitment and action: a confusion that reached bizarre extremes in identification of socialism with selected received generalizations—the brutal equation of certain (material) 'laws' with certain (political) loyalties. It is also that, in other political areas, affiliation to socialism appeared to involve affiliation to 'materialism', not as a body of evidence and procedures but as a verbal category: to be a socialist was to be, by definition, a materialist, even if the relevant actual positions held were of a kind to which material investigation would be (indeed sometimes by prior theoretical assertion) inappropriate or inapplicable. Again, more widely, necessary processes of investigation and re-investigation, over a range from political strategies to philosophical problems and cultural practices, were either dismissed, within the received verbal categories, as 'anti-materialist' or 'idealist', or were, by the proponents themselves, in reaction against the frozen forms and their political and cultural consequences, carefully distanced from materialism or the more convenient 'vulgar materialism'.

It is in this confused and complex situation, within the interactions and the failures to interact of politics, science and philosophy, that the question of 'materialism' has to be raised again, at the most general level. The significance of the recent work of Sebastiano Timpanaro is that he has not only raised the question; adequately read, he has provoked it.

Timpanaro's work is available in English in two volumes: *On Materialism* and *The Freudian Slip*.[1] He has also published studies of nineteenth-century Italian culture, including an important account of Leopardi. *On Materialism* is a collection of essays, of which the most substantial are 'Considerations on Materialism' and 'Structuralism and its Successors'. The other three essays are on 'Praxis and Materialism', the materialism of Engels, and Korsch and Lenin. *The Freudian Slip* is a more consecutive volume, beginning from a philological examination of Freud's interpretations of verbal errors and proceeding to a substantial examination of the relations between materialism and psychoanalysis. The mode of the writing is in the best sense polemical. There are substantial occasional statements of position, and other significant references and allusions. But the writing is strongest when it has another position and text to engage with; indeed, in the case of the professionally minute investigation of the relevant Freudian texts, so strong as to be overpowering. Yet in substance the writing is not criticism; it is a deeply engaged polemic, with substantial political implications and intentions, against major contemporary tendencies in Western Marxism, notably the work and the effects of the Frankfurt School and of Althusser, and, more broadly, what Timpanaro calls 'voluntarism' and 'Platonist scientism'. His central point of attack is on the question of materialism, from which all these tendencies are seen as divergent, and he is unusual in summoning to his aid, in what remains primarily a set of philosophical arguments, the work of natural scientists. For a generation, now, there has been an unusual uneasiness between Marxism and the natural sciences. Timpanaro regrets this, and argues to overcome it, not only because there are then gaps in knowledge and failures in its development, but because through the gaps, and from both sides, pour the enemies of materialism.

This is an attractive and provocative stance. Its many challenges deserve the most careful consideration. Dissenting immediately from one of his most basic formulations, on 'the links between the struggle for communism and the struggle against nature', I find, nevertheless, so close a convergence of interests and sympathies that it is not only an exceptional pleasure to read his books but important to try to engage with them. I propose to discuss, centrally, the very difficult relations between his

[1] *On Materialism*, NLB 1975; *The Freudian Slip*, NLB 1976.

understanding of materialism and his uses of the concept of 'nature'; and then, more briefly, his critique of psychoanalysis and his spirited and indispensable critique of structural linguistics and its extensions to structuralism.

Man and Nature

Timpanaro's most general definition of the fundamentals of materialism can be accepted, at first sight, as it stands: 'By materialism we understand above all acknowledgment of the priority of nature over "mind", or if you like, of the physical level over the biological level, and of the biological level over the socio-economic and cultural level; both in the sense of chronological priority (the very long time which supervened before life appeared on earth, and between the origin of life and the origin of man), and in the sense of the conditioning which nature *still* exercises on man and will continue to exercise at least for the foreseeable future.'[2] It is difficult to see how anyone could deny the intention of the first proposition, though it is better expressed in its specifying than in its general terms. The cautionary notation of 'mind' needs to be extended also to 'nature', but there can be no serious argument against the existence of a physical world before life and of other life-forms before man. And it is important that while these facts are never denied, within any relevant area of argument, they are quite often dismissed as banalities which have little practical bearing on the more interesting questions that lie ahead. One of the excuses for this impatience is that the general terms used to summarize the enormous and complex body of facts, on which the propositions necessarily rest, are shot through with inherently subsequent interpretations of a philosophical and cultural character. Thus it is not unproblematic to say that 'nature' has 'priority over' 'mind', but we can only approach these problems in good faith if we have, with full seriousness, taken the weight of the astronomical, geological and biological evidence before entering the more congenial ground of the humanist categories. And it is in this area, at first sight, that the effect of the declining contribution of the natural sciences to the general culture of Marxism has been most apparent. While the sense of proportion imposed by this fundamental materialism is either forgotten or dismissed as a

[2] *On Materialism*, p. 34.

preliminary banality, the way is indeed open for every kind of obscurantism and evasion.

Yet it is in the area of the second proposition that the most serious damage is actually done. And this is more difficult to see, because the language in which its undoubtedly correct intention is expressed is even more inherently problematic. 'The conditioning which nature *still* exercises on man': the problem here is the use of 'nature', coming through in the language as the humanist personification of all that is 'not man', to describe a very complex set of conditions which are indeed, in part, quite extrinsic or extrinsic with only marginal qualifications (the range is from the solar system through the physical composition of the planet to the atmosphere), but which are also, and crucially, *intrinsic* to human beings (evolved physical organs, the genetic inheritance). Thus a particular linguistic structure, the separation and contrast between 'nature' and 'man', largely developed in periods of the dominance of idealist and humanist thought, makes it very difficult for us to move from the complex and differential facts which are indeed our material and physical conditions to any statement of the general relationship between these 'conditions' and what, within the linguistic complex, we still isolate as 'conditioned'.

Timpanaro writes: 'We cannot ... deny or evade the element of passivity in experience: the external situation which we do not create but which imposes itself on us.'[3] This is another attempt to express 'the conditioning which nature *still* exercises on man'. But it leaves much unresolved. There is indeed an 'external situation' which is beyond human choice or control: the far and middle reaches of our material environment. It is right to emphasize this, while adding that there are near reaches, even at this level, which are already interactive with human industry and politics. And it is right to describe all these reaches as *conditions*. To see them either as simple 'raw material' for 'man's conquest of nature', as in the dominative progressivism shared by many tendencies in the nineteenth century but now—late in the twentieth century—more exclusive to a predatory late capitalism, or on the other hand as mere banal pre-conditions for the more interesting human social enterprise, is indeed damaging. They are necessary conditions and as such necessary elements of the relations of all life. But then what can properly be described as an 'external situation' modulates, in complex ways, into

[3] Ibid., p. 34.

what is already an 'interactive situation', and then, crucially, into an area of material conditions in which it is wholly unreasonable to speak of 'nature' as distinct from 'man' or to use the (political) language of 'impose on' and 'exercise', now terms of a (dualist) relationship which misrepresent the precise *constituted materiality* which the argument began by offering to emphasize.

Thus 'the element of passivity in experience' emerges as a key question. 'Passive' is already a curious description of our actual relations to the far and middle reaches of the physical universe, and would be misleading in its near reaches. For it is not at these levels a question of passivity or activity, as alternative human responses. There are dimensions quite beyond us, or there are basic forces—the obvious examples are gravity and light—which have entered so deeply into our constituted existence that they are conditions of everything we are and do, over the whole range from the most passive to the most active modes. What 'passive', in one of its senses—the relatively 'given', the relatively 'unwilled'—might usefully emphasize is, first, the character of many of our basic physical processes, which are indeed conditions of life; and second, though with more difficulty, something of the character of our participation in such matters as our genetic inheritance. In either case 'constitutive' would be better than 'passive', for what matters is what follows from the striking of this particular relational and emotional note. To re-emphasize, as a fundamental materialism, the inherent physical conditions—a specific universe, a specific planet, a specific evolution, specific physical lives—from which all labour and all consciousness must take their origins, is right and necessary. Failure not only to acknowledge these conditions, but to continue to take them into active account, has indeed, as Timpanaro indicates, led to shallow and limited kinds of Marxist and other political and social thought, and has left open a large and unavoidable area of experience and knowledge which has been repeatedly occupied by an indifferent positivism or, worse, by significantly popular kinds of irrationalism (astrology, earth-cults, new theologies of collective subjectivity, forms of organized psychic manipulation).

The direction of Timpanaro's response is, then, initially very welcome. But 'passive', we soon come to see, carries its own freight. When he is arguing, correctly, that many Marxists overlook, or acknowledge as mere banalities, our fundamental physical-material existence and processes, it is remarkable how often he specifies this existence and these processes in their negative and limiting capacity, and how rarely in any other sense. He is, of course, right to specify the effects of old age, of disease, of inherited physical disabilities; as he is right also to specify the predictable end of the solar system and the continuing conditioning presence of many more immediate natural forces. But this leads us to an argument which has already taken place, in response to existentialism and its interactions with Marxism. The existentialist emphasis of anguish, isolation and 'the absurd' was replied to with socialist emphases of comradeship, solidarity and 'the future', or with more general emphases of love, relatedness and 'community'. Each emphasis is a version of *response*, but is presented as an account of the true 'human condition'. One level of argument is then the exchange of alternative specifications. But the most serious level of argument must be the analysis of how the really basic conditions of life—the conditions of physical existence and survival—are perceived, selected and interpreted.

For the crucial question is the extent to which these fundamental physical conditions and processes affect or qualify the social and historical interpretations and projects which are the central specifications of Marxism. But then it is at once necessary to resolve this general question, resting on its general categories of 'nature' and 'man', into more precise and more differentiated questions. These seem to me to be three in number. First, what is the effect of scientific evidence of a physical kind, notably that of the solar system and of our planet and its atmosphere, on the proposition (ideology?) of the 'conquest of nature' which has often been associated with Marxism? Second, what factors, if any, in our evolutionary inheritance qualify the project (ideology?) of absolute human liberation? Third, what is the real relation between projects of human liberation cast in collective and epochal terms and the physical conditions which determine or affect actual individual human lives?

The 'Conquest of Nature'

On the first question it is undeniable, historically, that Marxism includes a triumphalist version of 'man's conquest of nature'. Nor is this merely a variant of the tradition; in one form or another it lies near the source. But it is then important to recognize that, in both its moderate and its extreme forms, the notion of the 'conquest of nature' belongs not simply to Marxism but to a whole period of bourgeois thought. Indeed, it became an almost inevitable generalization from the extraordinary achievements in material transformation of the industrial revolution and of advances in the physical sciences. And in one relatively unproblematic emphasis, it is a sustainable generalization, giving substance to the basic emphasis of historical materialism. Human beings have, by associated labour, moved in thousands of ways out of passive dependence on their environment, and out of mere adaptive marginality at its edges. The reshaping, remaking and innovative transformation of the pre-human material world is absolutely significant, historically. But of course this can only be described as the 'conquest of nature' if the initial terms of a separated 'man' and 'nature' are taken for granted. And it is to the extent that they have been taken for granted that real theoretical deformations have occurred.

For it is of course apparent, after all the achievements and projected achievements, that there are major natural forces, and these not only at the level of the physical universe and the solar system, which are still and in any reasonable projection beyond our control. Moreover, even within the more practical definition of the project, of sustaining full and free human life on our planet within foreseeable historical terms, that part of the 'conquest' which is represented by scientific knowledge now increasingly shows us the complexities and the often unwanted effects of that other part of the 'conquest' which is physical appropriation and transformation. The triumphalist version overrides all this real knowledge. Faced with the predictable end of the solar system, it responds with the by no means exclusively or even predominantly Marxist projection of emigration of the species to new stars, and by-passes the question of whether this remote project would not also be a change of species. Faced with the limits and complexities of appropriation and transformation, on our own planet, it extends the correct and reasonable response of improved knowledge and renewed effort into a brash mystique of 'overcoming all obstacles'. But it can now be clearly seen that this triumphalist version is, in an exceptionally close correspondence, the specific ideology of imperialism and capitalism, whose basic concepts—limitless and conquering expansion; reduction of the labour process to the appropriation and transformation of raw materials—it exactly repeats.

How then did Marxism, at any stage, come to be compromised by it? In part by the infection of its formative period. Engels, influentially, in *The Dialectics of Nature*, emphasized *mastering* nature as 'the final, essential distinction' between 'man and other animals'. Yet in the course of the same argument,[4] he made a necessary criticism of just this idea. Detailing the unforeseen effects of many such 'conquests', he wrote:

> Thus at every step we are reminded that we by no means rule over nature like a conqueror over a foreign people, like someone standing outside nature—but that we, with flesh, blood and brain, belong to nature, and exist in its midst, and that all our mastery of it consists in the fact that we have the advantage over all other creatures of being able to know and correctly apply its laws.

This is a profound (if still potentially ambiguous) correction of the ordinary notions of 'mastery' and 'conquest'. Moving in a materialist way from labour to science, Engels indeed saw the development of science, as both knowledge and control, leading to a situation in which men 'once more' (a separable but revealing and unsustainable reference)

> not only feel, but also know, themselves to be one with nature, and thus the more impossible will become the senseless and anti-natural idea of a contradiction between mind and matter, man and nature.

This is again a profound correction, but the ideas of 'control' and of 'mastery' nevertheless survive it, in some real ambiguities. By the point in the argument at which he has made these corrections, it is necessary, in fact, to abandon the notion of 'mastery', to see even 'controls' in a more secular and more qualified perspective, and to bring through, instead, the full materialist consciousness of associated labour and science within definite but knowable material conditions. Instead, partly here, but even more in a derived orthodox tradition, the enhanced notions of 'mastery' and 'conquest' went on being powerfully asserted. For a long time, then, there was a failure in Marxism to carry through its own fundamental restatement of the 'man'-'nature' relationship: its decisive emphasis on the intricate and constitutive processes of 'man-in-nature', with labour as the specifying instance of an always significant, always dynamic, and always—though differentially—limited set of material relationships. In this world of a properly materialist history there is no room for the separated abstract categories of 'nature' and 'man', but then what often happened was that they were made falsely equivalent, or that the historical process was seen as substituting one—'man'—for the other. This soon

---

[4] *The Dialectics of Nature*, Moscow 1954, pp. 241-243.

became a compromise with triumphalism. But it is then ironic to see the argument merely running in reverse. Timpanaro correctly and valuably re-emphasizes the weight of the natural forces that are beyond our actual or probable control, yet comes to sum them up as 'nature's oppression of man'.[5] Given that relationship, his argument then moves to consideration of the appropriate philosophical and ethical response to that kind of 'fact': a materialist pessimism, which adds rejection of the consolations of triumphalism to the established rejection of the consolations of religion.

But at one level, certainly, this is beside the point. Settled and universalizing emotional or philosophical responses to the complexities of the real material process are in fact themselves residual from pre-materialist religion and philosophy. Neither materialist triumphalism nor materialist pessimism is of any material help in the necessary processes of an extended secular knowledge and of definitions and redefinitions of our social processes in its light. To the extent that these are genuinely secular and materialist, they involve the whole range from new major opportunities of the kind triumphalism had generalized—say plant-breeding and land-reclamation—to new major difficulties—say the plutonium economy. In all relevant secular terms, what is needed at this level is not 'philosophy' at all, but associated science and labour, under conditions to be achieved only by socialist transformation of control of these means of production.

Biology and Liberation

The second question, on the limiting factors of our evolutionary inheritance, has been widely posed in contemporary bourgeois thought. There has been an extraordinary revival of some of the crudest forms of Social Darwinism, with emphasis on the inherent and controlling force of the aggressive instinct, the territorial imperative, the genetically determined 'hunter killer', the lower 'beast' brain, and so on. These crude evasions of historical and cultural variation, these even cruder rationalizations of the crises of the imperialist and capitalist social order, have to be patiently analysed and refuted, point by point. But the difficulty to which Timpanaro draws attention has also to be remembered. There is indeed some danger, in response to these intolerable confusions of biological and social facts, of another kind of triumphalism, in which the emphasis of

[5] *On Materialism*, p. 67.

human history and human culture simply ignores or treats as a preliminary banality the relatively stable biological conditions which are at least
elements of much human cultural activity. Timpanaro relates this problem, correctly, to some well-known difficulties of the formula of base and
superstructure, and in particular to certain kinds of art which clearly
relate to elements of our biological condition, often much more strongly
than to elements of our socio-historical experience. It is, of course, at once
added that these elements of the biological condition are mediated by
socio-historical experience and by its cultural forms; but Timpanaro is
right to argue that this mediation provides no basis for that still common
kind of reduction, in which the biological is a mere datum and all the
effective working social and historical. He usefully reminds us that
certain works of art expressing feelings of sexual love, of fear of death, of
grief and loss at the death of others, while undoubtedly varied by particular cultural forms, retain elements of common content which enable
them to communicate, actively and not only as documents, beyond and
across historical periods and cultures.

As a matter of fact he could have taken even stronger examples, since
these are cultural responses to and within biological conditions, and what
needs to be estimated, in each case, is the character of the mix. The
deepest cultural significance of a relatively unchanging biological human
condition is probably to be found in some of the basic material processes
of the making of art: in the significance of rhythms in music and dance
and language, or of shapes and colours in sculpture and painting. Because
art is always *made*, there can of course be no reduction of works of this
kind to biological conditions. But equally, where these fundamental
physical conditions and processes are in question, there can be no reduction either to simple social and historical circumstances. What matters
here—and it is a very significant amendment of orthodox Marxist thinking about art—is that art-work is itself, before everything, a material process; and that, although differentially, the material process of the
production of art includes certain biological processes, especially those
relating to body movements and to the voice, which are not a mere
substratum but are at times the most powerful elements of the work.

Yet to put the matter in this way is again to emphasize an open, secular
recognition and inquiry. It is not to reserve a 'human nature' as a 'long
wave' against the 'short waves' of history, as Timpana.o comes close to
implying. It is rather to acknowledge—and indeed to emphasize against

the simpler forms of sociological and superstructural reductionism—that intricate and varying set of productive processes, and of the human situations which they realize and communicate, in which the physical facts of the human condition are permanently and irreducibly important. Once again, it is not a matter of limits only. Moreover, though these real physical conditions qualify some projects of absolute liberation—such as the Shavian-progressivist 'liberation from this flesh-stuff'—it is significant that many contemporary projects of liberation, though at times too exclusively, and even as false alternatives to social liberation, have decisively reclaimed our physical existence and fulfilment as inseparable from any significant project of political and economic liberation.

Social Projects and the Individual

The second question here blends with the third, on the relation between our physical conditions and our social projects. Timpanaro argues eloquently for the acknowledgment of those physical realities which are there whether there is social change or not. We become ill, we become old, we die, and it is indeed a kind of petty bullying, at times a seemingly incurable shallowness, to respond to these conditions with an overriding reference to history or to a cause or to a future. That kind of reference belongs to the cultures of absolutism or to the closer contemporary cultures of bureaucracy. To die *for* a cause, and to be honoured for it, is one thing. To attempt to override the physical realities which persist in and through and beyond all historical causes is quite another. Indeed to restore this substance of human life to all effective social perspectives is a matter of great urgency. First, because no significant social perspective can exclude these substantial experiences, or treat them as marginal. It is only by infection from the social orders that we are fighting that any such exclusion or reduction is possible. But also, second, it is the perspective that then suffers, since the people who hold to it, and who struggle according to it, are all themselves within these conditions. What happens as this becomes clear, in millions of individual lives, is profoundly difficult to analyse. Many people have said, as they become old or ill, and as they now *know* that they will die, that the long historical project becomes meaningless or indifferent. Timpanaro is properly on his guard against this, for it is the mere converse of the error of overriding such realities in the name of a historical cause.

Yet the emotional freight which is carried by his particular definition of our basic physical conditions exerts, at just this point, an ambiguous influence. For consider another very relevant relation. It is another inescapable fact of 'our' physical condition that for a time 'we' are young and healthy and active. It is also a fact that this condition offers us abundant opportunities of physical fulfilment which, though of course related to the character of our specific social order, are hardly ever wholly determined by it. Thus in one equally relevant definition of our basic physical condition we have many, and at times more immediately accessible, opportunities of happiness in the exercise of our physical resources than in the project of social liberation. In the advanced capitalist countries, in our own day, a deduction of priorities from this version of the basic relations has been very widely made. It is not just when staring death or disability in the face that we can question or draw back from revolutionary effort. It is also when sexual love, the love of children, the pleasures of the physical world are immediately and very powerfully present. To attempt to deny the reality of the kinds of fulfilment that are possible in these ways, even under repressive social orders, to say nothing of social systems which have cleared significant space for them, comes in the end to appear a desperate dogmatism.

But then why is the question posed in such ways, leading to every kind of false solution? Timpanaro's purpose is almost equally to check both collective and subjectivist forms of triumphalism. Intellectually he is then on sure if not fully worked ground. But emotionally there is less real balance. The profound sadness of our epoch is fully expressed in his necessary reminders of our continuing physical limits. Yet the true sources of this depth of sadness are surely predominantly historical. For in the most basic physical terms our epoch can be characterized as (if the ethical term is appropriate) one of widening happiness: the limits of old age, of disease, of infant mortality, have been significantly pushed back, in an extending area of world society. More people are living longer, are healthier and better fed, than at any time in human history. The barriers to extending these conditions from the richer to the poorer countries are economic and political, and not of some basic physical character. Even the relation between population and resources is a political and economic issue. So why then a materialist pessimism? There is ground for a sense of tragedy in the long and bloody crisis of the ending of an imperialist and capitalist order. But at the most basic physical level there is only the contradiction intrinsic to any conscious life process, and this is not a settled but a dynamic contradiction, in which life is not only negated by death but affirmed by birth, and practical consciousness itself at once defines and redefines its proper limits. In any fully materialist perspective, it then seems impossible to rely on any singular political or ethical dimension, and especially on the received alternatives of triumphalism or pessimism. The properly objective process, to which these alternatives are directed, is itself contradictory and dynamic; while at any point, in the life of an individual or in the history of a movement, there is an intrinsic variability in the positions from which this nevertheless objective process is seen. A materialist ethics, like a materialist politics, has then to be grounded in these inherent relational conditions, only not as relativism, which is merely their registration, but as activity, which is the conscious effort towards their common realization as human history.

Psychoanalysis and Materialism

Interestingly, it is in his critique of psychoanalysis that Timpanaro most clearly moves from the presumptive selectivity of a materialist pessimism, basically derived from Leopardi, to more open materialist perspectives. Yet it is to be expected that this part of his work will encounter the most negative reactions, ranging from suspicion and hostility to indifference. The ideological roots and the vocabulary of psychoanalysis are now very deep in Western culture. The arrival of Timpanaro's kind of sceptic, deploying analytic skills very similar to those of the 'higher criticism' of religion, seems likely to repeat a moment of cultural history. For what Timpanaro first engages, from the whole psychoanalytic system, is Freud's analysis of verbal slips and errors—the persuasive 'psychopathology of everyday life'. Some central concepts of memory and forgetting, and then of repression and of ways of overcoming it, are thus tackled from an unusual direction.

Now to anyone trained in the interpretation of texts the Freudian analysis of specific errors ought always to have seemed problematic. I remember my own scepticism at first reading, and the instant diagnosis of this scepticism which the epigoni deployed. But Timpanaro is much better than a sceptic; he uses, with exceptional thoroughness and precision, the material evidence of a whole body of practice and analysis concerned with errors and failures of memory, and especially the manifest evidence of successive texts as studied in philology and textual criticism. It is then not only that he can show the arbitrary and tendentious character of certain Freudian interpretations but, much more usefully, that he contributes a body of relatively remote specialist knowledge to the central task of classifying varying types of verbal error and failure of memory: a classification which need not be taken as excluding certain psychoanalytic hypotheses for certain kinds of error. If this is set beside the now very extensive physiological investigations of the processes of memory and especially short-term memory, we reach a fully materialist position in which the evidence of cultural history, of situational analysis and of physiological investigation can be brought together and cross-checked.

Yet what has ordinarily happened, even inside 'psychology', with its variation into what are often non-communicating schools, but even more in the general culture,with its eclectic reliance on 'scientifically founded concepts' derived from evidence and procedures never rigorously examined, is the diffusion of a set of systems which even when they are materialist in character—and many of the most widely diffused are evidently and even proudly not—take on the appearance of general human explanations. Thus one can be asked, in the same mode as for an opinion of a film or a novel, whether one 'accepts the findings' of Freud or of Skinner or of Lacan, without any significant realization that all such 'findings' depend on criteria of evidence and on the (contested) theoretical presuppositions of both the evidence and the criteria. (These considerations would be relevant, of course, also to the 'opinion' of the film or the novel.) What Timpanaro has then done is to indicate, and especially to the 'literary' reader of psychology and psychoanalytic theory, certain indispensable considerations on the nature of verbal analysis as evidence. If at times it reads like taking a sledge-hammer to a nut, we do not have to read very far elsewhere to find how many nuts there are.

There are then two further considerations. First that in psychology and psychoanalytic theory, as in the related areas of anthropology and theoretical sociology, there are special problems for any materialist critique in their typical employment of concepts—which may or may not be 'theory'—which have a unique double character, in that they are internally held to be 'findings' from empirical evidence and yet at the same time are quite rapidly diffused in forms of discourse usually dependent on concepts founded in a more 'normal' linguistic mode, in the development of a language in social and historical experience. 'The unconscious' is the most evident example; 'id', 'ego', 'the mirror-phase' are others. Materialist analysis of 'normal' linguistic concepts, taken from general political and cultural discourse, is necessarily historical; its linguistic procedures are then directly scientific. But in this special class of concepts, with a very limited or specialized history, with general currency yet with this inherent reference to 'evidence' of a technical kind lying well beyond them, the methodological difficulties are acute. There is also the problem of that other class of concepts, including most notably 'memory', 'sex' and 'repression', which have both a substantive general history, preceding their specialized applications, and highly specialized and derived meanings within particular intellectual systems. Analysis of these varying classes of concepts is fundamentally necessary, as a new form of historical and cultural linguistics. It cannot be said that Timpanaro establishes new procedures; but so very little work of this kind is being done, anywhere, that some of his ways of approaching the problem—and notably on 'memory'—are extraordinarily interesting.

Second, and more generally, it is a fact about classical Marxism that it neglected, to its great cost, not only the basic human physical conditions which Timpanaro emphasizes in his reconsideration of materialism, but also the emotional conditions and situations which make up so large a part of all direct human relationship and practice. Problems of sexuality, including problematic sexuality, are among the most prominent omissions; and it is within this area that the attempts to supplement, deepen, go beyond historical materialism have inevitably occurred. This is sometimes even described as turning from 'materialism' to 'human considerations', with some but insufficient warrant in the more bizarre 'materialist' physio-chemical reductions of personal and relational experiences. But what is also increasingly claimed is that psychoanalysis, or certain variants of it, are themselves 'materialist'; the description appears sometimes serious, sometimes as a kind of loyalist affiliation.

Two things then need to be said. First, that it is wholly unreasonable to go on claiming as 'materialist' (and therefore as complementing or compatible with Marxism) systems of psychological explanation uncritically assimilated, at the level of 'findings', while ignoring or dismissing as mere 'positivism' or 'empiricism' the large body of experimental psychology concerned, for example, with problems of perception, memory, dreaming and language-development. There are undoubted theoretical problems arising from this work, but the grasp at fluently learned 'systems' is no way, and certainly no materialist way, of resolving them. Then, second, there is need for many more examples of the kind of rigorous theoretical and historical critique of psychological theory as mixed 'science' and 'ideology', which Timpanaro exemplifies in his analysis of the 'smothered materialism' of Freud and more briefly of Lacan and of other successors. It seems improbable that this can be done without confronting more directly, in historical-materialist terms, the much larger body of non-psychoanalytic psychological evidence and theory, and thereby (for this has been the cultural effect though hardly the scientific achievement of psychoanalytic revisionism) re-examining the received formulations of historical materialism itself, as at once historically limited and insufficiently materialist.

Language and Science

In his writings on nature and on psychoanalysis, Timpanaro is either deploying general arguments or using certain specialized skills to re-examine types of formulation, interpretation and analysis. In his essay on 'Structuralism and its Successors' he is, as a philologist, on more centrally familiar ground; and the brilliance of detail, both analytic and historical, is at once remarkable. There are those, at the level of general discourse, who tacitly assume that linguistics began with Saussure as psychology began with Freud. Timpanaro's masterly summary of the crisis in historical linguistics which preceded Saussure gives a depth to his subsequent critique, which in other respects and especially in certain passages is, though powerful, not entirely original. The critique is at its best when he is fully engaged professionally, as in the case of Saussure or of Hjelmslev, though the discussions of Lévi-Strauss, Althusser, Barthes and others may have more political effect. The polemic against structuralism, in the sense of its extensions beyond linguistics, as an 'objective idealism', is vigorous and convincing, and there is a shrewd observation that some of the most influential forms of post-structuralism have been reactions not against its idealism but against its objectivity. The fact remains, however, that a good deal of this section is in effect categorical argument against abusers of categories, and it is above all in an account of language that we look for more than this; look indeed for the outlines of a productive materialism.

It is in Timpanaro's discussion of Chomsky that some of these can be discerned. Recognizing the value of Chomsky's emphasis on the '*creative* side of linguistic activity', as against the mechanistic and merely reproductive positions of nineteenth-century biological linguistics and of orthodox behaviourism and structuralism, he at the same time correctly identifies a reversion, at the level of the most general principles, to what are clearly metaphysical forms of 'innatism'. Timpanaro's exceptionally wide knowledge of the history of linguistic studies is especially useful at this point. But it is in moving beyond the history of ideas to hypotheses adequate to contemporary scientific investigation that all the real problems begin. One significant theoretical distinction clears some ground: an important emphasis on the character of much scientific discovery, especially in studies of language, as the formulation of *tendencies* rather than the revelation of *laws*. This bears with close relevance on the tone and vocabulary of many structuralist and post-structuralist arguments and of structuralist Marxism; it might be added that it bears also on other more central kinds of Marxism, in which the (political) language of a providential universe, complete with its 'law-maker', has evidently infected even historical materialism.

But then, more specifically, in a challenge to Chomsky's rejection of 'evolutionism', Timpanaro reasserts the importance of neuro-physiological studies of language and of other communicative processes. This reminds us of the gap which has arisen everywhere, but with most damaging effect in Marxist work in the human sciences, between primarily philosophical and primarily natural-scientific traditions and formations. What can still be seen, within the external difficulties of Soviet linguistics, as a unity or at least a mode of contact in Vygotsky and his successors, has in the West become an almost incomprehensible split. The physical investigation of sense-data, of stimuli from the natural and social environment, of language and non-verbal communicative development, continues to produce an enormous body of work; but it has seemed possible, behind the defensive screens of the categories of 'positivism' and 'empiricism', to carry on the most fundamental arguments, involving quite universal definitions of the nature of 'man' and of 'reality', without much reference or with only carefully selective reference to it.

So striking a deformation of a whole intellectual enterprise must, for a Marxist, have deep roots in a social order and in its cultural formations; yet I am not sure that Timpanaro is right in looking only to a 'new sociopolitical situation' to 'release' us from it. His work, more than any other, draws attention to the split and the consequent deformation. It is markedly more useful than, for example, Snow's reasonable but limited description of the 'two cultures', since it is not only the relations between the literary-philosophical and the natural-scientific cultures that need to be questioned, but the complex relations of both to the socio-historical culture and process: relations, moreover, which cannot be reduced to the terms of a base-superstructure formula. The real lesson is a challenge to begin building intellectual formations of a new kind, and for many reasons the field of language and of non-verbal communication seems to be a good and practicable place to start.

The Materialist Project

Meanwhile, and for a start, how is Materialism? How is our brother Historical, and those quarrelling great-uncles, Dialectical and Mechanical? We do not mention Vulgar. In any materialist study of language, these sceptical questions have to be asked—as once, and with shock, about the significations of God. We have to inquire, demonstrably, into these linguistic formations and bearings: elements of a material practice within a continuing social process.

We may quickly come to know where we are with historical materialism. There is a demonstrable body of theory and practice, of method and evidence, within but also beyond the persuasive verbal formulation. Indeed it is tempting, so much is this so, to limit Marxism to this substantial work, in which our central political and economic struggles can be firmly though always openly grounded. Yet it soon becomes clear that we cannot impose such a limit, and not only because of the pride, the received pride, of the original limitless challenge. Too much social and cultural practice is necessarily directed beyond human history, to material that at once precedes it and persists. To neglect or withdraw from these directions would be a major cultural defeat. For the enemies are various and powerful: from the spiritualisms that are flourishing within a disintegrating social order, through the contemporary mythologizing, often sophisticated, of so many of our least understood conditions and practices, to the now vaulting ambition of epistemology to become the universal science. The reiteration of concepts and of universalizing systems is then almost beside the point.

For the special character of materialism, and that which alone gives it value, is its rigorous openness to physical evidence. The point is put interestingly in question in a remark of Chomsky's: 'We can, however, be fairly sure that there will be a physical explanation for the phenomena in question, if they can be explained at all, for an uninteresting terminological reason, namely that the concept of "physical explanation" will no doubt be extended to incorporate whatever is discovered in this domain, exactly as it was extended to accommodate gravitational and electromagnetic force, massless particles, and numerous other entities and processes that would have offended the common sense of earlier generations.'[6] This remark upsets and even outrages Timpanaro.[7] He takes it as implying that science has not extended its real understanding but has merely incorporated new phenomena by a series of verbal tricks. But it is not science that is in question; it is the concept of the 'physical', or, if you will, the 'material'. And the answer to Chomsky, who is indeed trying to discourage inquiry into his own basic version of the 'innate', is that what is in question is not an 'uninteresting terminological' process, but the necessary social process through which the materialist enterprise defines and redefines its procedures, its findings and its concepts, and in the course of this moves beyond one after another 'materialism'. There are only two real barriers to this continuing process: one, against which Timpanaro has sufficiently warned us, of mythologizing or recuperating to received presumptions all that which we do not yet understand or understand imperfectly; the other, closer to home, of seeming to know in advance, and as a test of our political fidelity, the changing materialist content of materialism.

[6] Noam Chomsky, *Language and Mind*, New York 1972, p. 97.
[7] *On Materialism*, pp. 202 ff.

4

Social Environment and Theatrical Environment

The Case of English Naturalism

There are three relevant senses of 'naturalism', and of the associated 'naturalist' and 'naturalistic'. The first, and most popular, indicates a method of 'accurate' or 'lifelike' reproduction. The second, and historically earliest, indicates a philosophical position allied to science, natural history and materialism. The third, and most significant in the history of drama, indicates a movement 'in which the method of accurate production and the specific philosophical position are intended to be organically fused.

The first sense began in English around 1850, mainly in relation to painting and especially landscape painting. Thus: 'the mannerism of the Italians, and the naturalism of the Flemish painters' (1852),[1]; 'the Gothic naturalism advancing gradually from the Byzantine severity' (1853);[2] 'the Naturalist-landscape school, a group of painters who threw overboard the traditions of Turner' (1893).[3] There was a common association of such a method with simplicity of attitude—'a naturalism without afterthought' (1850)[4]—and, through the association with 'nature' and 'natural', of subject.

The second sense was already more generally established. It began in the late sixteenth century in a form of conscious opposition, or at least distinction, between revealed (divine) and observed (human) knowledge, and was used in close association with accusations of atheism: 'atheists or men . . . who will admit of nothing but Morality, but Naturalismes, and

---

[1] *Naturalism*, 3,b in *A New English Dictionary on Historical Principles* (OED) (13 vols, Oxford, 1933).
[2] OED, *Naturalism*, 3,b.
[3] OED, *Naturalist*, 6,b.
[4] OED, *Naturalism*, 3,a.

humane reason' (1641);[5] 'those blasphemous truth-opposing Heretikes, and Atheisticall naturalists' (1612).[6] With growing confidence from the seventeenth through to the nineteenth centuries it acquired the more positive associations of a method and practice and body of knowledge, in natural history and the natural sciences. 'Naturalist' in this sense became neutral, but 'naturalism' was still a doctrine in which there was appeal to and reliance on natural laws, forces and explanations, as distinct from and eventually consciously opposed to 'supernaturalism', and also in which, in matters of morality, there was appeal to and reliance on human reason and a (secular) natural law.

The third sense, in specific application to a particular kind of novel or play, and thence to a literary movement, appeared in French in the late 1860s and is common in English from the 1880s. Its relations with the two earlier senses are complex. On the one hand its conscious linkage of literary method with scientific method and with the laws of natural history was sharp, distinct and at times aggressive. On the other hand, in very general tendencies in fiction and drama before this period, many steps in this linkage had been practically taken. The link between painting and science had been made by Constable:

> Painting is a science, and should be pursued as an inquiry into the laws of nature. Why, then, may not landscape painting be considered as a branch of natural philosophy, of which pictures are but the experiments?[7]

This was indeed the landscape-painting which had attracted the apparently simple technical term 'naturalist'. More generally, since the early eighteenth century, in plays and novels, there had been a practical reliance on a secular human dimension, in action, description and interpretation. Bourgeois literature, with increasing confidence, was in a distinguishing sense, by comparison with earlier literature, secular and social; an explicitly or implicitly metaphysical dimension was steadily and in the end without argument excluded. This is particularly evident in the drama, most clearly in bourgeois tragedy (from Lillo, *The London Merchant*, 1731), with its consciously secular, contemporary, social and

---

[5] OED, *Naturalism*, I.
[6] OED, *Naturalist*, I.
[7] John Constable, *Fourth Lecture at the Royal Institution* (1836), in *John Constable's Discourses*, ed. R.B. Beckett, Ipswich 1970, p. 69.

socially extended emphasis, but it had many seventeenth-century precedents in prose comedy and in isolated examples of what would later be
called 'domestic drama'. Within this powerful general movement
towards a predominantly secular and social literature, many elements of
'naturalism' became habitual, but the conscious description awaited one
further emphasis, in which the key term is 'environment'. It is one thing
to present character and action in exclusively secular and social terms. It
is or can be quite another to see and to show character and action as determined or profoundly influenced by environment, either natural or social.
The novelty of the naturalist emphasis was its demonstration of the
production of character or action by a powerful natural or social environment. This is radically distinct from exemplifications of 'permanent'
human characteristics in an accurately reproduced natural or social
'setting'. The intellectual basis for the new emphasis is then a sense of
historical production, both in the social sense that character is determined or profoundly influenced by its social environment, with the later
and more penetrating observation that this social environment is itself
historically produced, and in the wider sense of natural history, in the
evolution of human nature itself within a natural world of which it is an
interacting part. The theory of naturalism, in fiction and drama, is then a
conscious presentation of human character and action *within* a natural
and social environment. It is a specific culmination of a long tendency of
bourgeois theory and practice. It only ceases to be bourgeois (and then,
strictly, ceases to be naturalism) when, as in Marxist theory, action is seen
not only within an environment but as itself, within certain limits and
pressures, producing an environment.

Relations between the first and third senses of 'naturalism', in descriptions of works of art, are then inevitably complex. In popular and
semi-professional usage naturalism means no more than accurate or lifelike reproduction of a character, an action or a scene. In a stricter historical use naturalism is an artistic method in which a particular environment
is reproduced, of course as accurately and fully as possible, not because it
is an observed feature but because it is a causal or symptomatic feature.
Naturalism in the first sense is a general product of a bourgeois secular
tendency, with its preference for a practical and recognizable everyday
world. Naturalism in the third sense is the extension to art of the philosophical positions originally described as 'naturalism', in a conscious
reliance on observed natural history and on human reason. Dramatic

naturalism in the first sense can be plausibly related, but with complications that we shall notice, to developments in the means of production of physical theatrical effects. Dramatic naturalism in the third sense can never be so reduced, since it does not reproduce a physical feature or environment because it is technically available or interesting, but because such features and environments are integral parts of the dramatic action, indeed, in a true sense, are themselves actors and agencies.

It is a curiosity of dramatic history that naturalism, in the third sense, was relatively weak in England, by comparison with France, Scandinavia and Russia. Indeed, paradoxically, it was only after naturalism in the first sense had been modified that there were significant naturalist plays, in the third sense, in English. This is at first sight very surprising, since the intellectual movements which led to conscious naturalism were especially strong in England. The purest doctrines of the production of character by environment were those of William Godwin and of Robert Owen, from the late eighteenth and early nineteenth centuries. The most influential exponent of natural history as the production of human nature was, of course, Darwin. If anywhere, it might then seem, conscious naturalism were to be developed it would be in England, and indeed the case can be positively argued in the development of English painting and the English novel. In the drama, however, the case is quite otherwise, and the specific reasons for this need careful examination.

Physical Reproduction in the Theatre

Limited to the first sense of naturalism, the history of 'lifelike' reproduction on the English stage has often been traced. It is worth looking at the main elements of this history, both for their own sake and for the light they throw on the limitations of any merely technical definition of naturalism.

'The modern stage affects reality infinitely beyond the proper objects of dramatic representations', complained an observer in 1827.[8] This was no sudden development. The indoor theatres, from the Restoration, had developed more and more complicated and effective types of painted scenery, but in the turn from the eighteenth to the nineteenth century there was a further decisive change. This can be summarized as the

---

[8] J. Boaden, *Memoirs of Mrs Siddons*, 2 vols, London 1827, II, p. 355.

development of the 'set scene' from the system of scenic mobility which had dominated the eighteenth-century theatre. A crucial element in this was the steady reduction and eventual abolition of the apron-stage. This, together with the elaboration of backcloths and profiles as an alternative to moveable flats and wings, made the stage at once more integrated, more static and more enclosed. It was not until much later in the century, after prolonged controversy about the old kind of proscenium doors, that the fully enclosed picture-frame stage was established. The first was perhaps the Gaiety of 1869, but a description of the new Haymarket, in 1880, makes the point:

> A rich and elaborate gold border, about two feet broad, after the pattern of a picture frame, is continued all round the proscenium, and carried even below the actor's feet. There can be no doubt the sense of illusion is increased, and for the reason just given; the actors seem cut off from the domain of prose; there is no borderland or platform in front; and, stranger still, the whole has the air of a picture projected on a surface.[9]

The whole development thus achieved points forward, certainly, to major features of the naturalist drama; in particular its specific central feature of the stage as a room. It points forward also, interestingly, to film and television drama: 'a picture projected on a surface'. Yet the dramatic intentions within this development have an ambiguous relation to naturalism. Vestris and Mathews, at the Olympic between 1831 and 1838, were perhaps the first to develop the drawing-room stage, and a reviewer noted that the 'more perfect enclosure gives the appearance of a private chamber, infinitely better than the old contrivance of wings'.[10] Moreover, in a further innovation, these rooms were fully furnished, including floors and 'walls'. But the plays performed in them, usually adapted French short comedies, were hardly concerned with the 'life-like', and a sense of luxury rather than accuracy seems to have been the main staging motive. The wider development of technical means for more 'realistic' production is at an even greater distance from naturalism. Indeed, in all its early phases, technical innovation was primarily for spectacle. It is often asserted that naturalistic staging owed much to the introduction of gas-lighting, which was getting into theatres by 1820. Yet the main use of the new lighting was for new spectacular effects, such as

[9] P. Fitzgerald, *The World Behind the Scenes*, London 1881, pp. 20-1.
[10] Cit. G. Rowell, *The Victorian Theatre*, Oxford 1956, p. 18.

sunrise dispersing early mist. Indeed one of its most powerful applications, burning lime in a gas-jet to produce limelight, became almost synonymous with a new kind of spectacle, and was extensively used in the development of melodrama. Perhaps the most interesting, because intermediate, case is the development of technical staging for historical productions and in particular for the staging of Shakespeare. Elsewhere the new means of production made for increased spectacle; here, while spectacle remained as an intention, there was also an emphasis on 'correctness' of setting. This is evident as early as Planché's work for Kemble in the 1820s and is best known from Kean's 'antiquarian' productions in the 1850s. The interest in 'historical accuracy', and its intended priority over what Kean distinguished as 'theatrical effect',[11] has something genuinely in common with elements of naturalism. What is intended is a *reconstructed* environment, and, as in the case of the historical novel, with its formative effects on the novel of social realism, this is a transitional phase towards the presentation of a specific physical environment as symptomatic or causal. Nevertheless, the very sense of historical reconstruction, looking backward, characteristically, to more splendidly clothed and furnished times, worked in the opposite direction, against the contemporary environment outside the theatre, which was eventually to be the decisive influence in naturalism.

It was in the 1870s that the fully enclosed box-set began to be used to replace wings, flats and back-cloths, in close relation, of course, to the fully enclosed picture-frame stage. This provided a technical means for one of the central conventions of naturalism: the stage as an enclosed room. Yet even in this development, as in technical developments throughout the century, dramatic intentions remained variable. Spectacular illusion was as common as naturalistic illusion; or, to put it another way, even the motive for much naturalistic illusion was spectacular: the impressive reproduction of a 'real' environment, for its own sake rather than as an integral dramatic agency. This reminds us that in the theatre as in any other area of cultural technology, the doctrine of technological determinism—the creation of a form seen as determined by technical development; naturalism as the consequence of improvements in stage-carpentry—is false. And this in turn allows us to see the distinction, so decisive in the history of the drama, between naturalism as a technique among others, a particular staging effect among other varieties of

[11] J.W. Cole, *The Life and Theatrical Times of Charles Kean*, London 1835, II, p. 382.

spectacle, and naturalism as a dramatic form, in which the production or reproduction of a social environment, symptomatic or causal, is not just the setting for an action but is part of the action itself.

Changing Social Relations in Drama and Theatre

One dimension especially excluded by merely technical accounts of the development of naturalism is that of social relationships in the theatre. This is an especially significant exclusion in the case of English nineteenth-century theatre, where the changes in social relationships, in the course of the century, were radical.

We can distinguish three periods: that before 1830; from 1830 to 1860; and from 1860 to 1914. In the first period there was a completion of the long process, traceable from around 1700, in which the theatre moved back towards a more popular audience. This is not, in spite of some accounts, the entry of the 'mob' into the theatres. On the contrary it was the narrowing of the theatre audience which preceded this movement, from the 1620s to the 1690s and reaching a point of extreme class selectivity in the Restoration theatre, which was the novel phenomenon. In the course of the eighteenth century the audience broadened again, as well as increasing. In 1600 there had been some six successful theatres in London; in 1700, after the narrowing of the Restoration, there were only two. By 1750 there were again seven theatres in London, and a growing number of established theatres in the provinces. This process is usually summarized as the return of the middle class to the theatres. But social classes are not immortal, and the new eighteenth-century playgoers were in fact a new class: the greatly extended middle and lower-middle class of the developing cities: in a modern sense, a bourgeoisie. Until the end of the eighteenth century this was much more evident in London than elsewhere, for it was there that the explosive growth of a new kind of city had begun. By the beginning of the nineteenth century this urban bourgeoisie and petit-bourgeoisie had in effect taken over the London theatres, and a similarly 'popular' audience had become the mainstay of the multiplying provincial theatres. Many of the internal changes in theatre structure—the pit driving back the apron stage, the conversion of upper galleries to boxes—were directly related to this at once growing and changing audience. The Old Price riots (demonstrations about admission charges) at Covent Garden in 1809 are only the most striking among many manifestations of these class tensions and changes. 'Polite society', as it called itself, was in effect first invaded, then driven from the ' pit to boxes, then driven out altogether. This made the tension between the monopoly patent theatres, established under Restoration conditions to restrict serious drama to minority audiences, and the so-called 'minor theatres', pushing up everywhere, using every device and exploiting every ambiguity of definition, very much more severe. In the period before 1830, 'minor theatres' such as the Lyceum, the Haymarket and the Adelphi were only nominally distinguishable from the old patent theatres, Covent Garden and Drury Lane, while south of the Thames, especially at Astley's and Surreyside, the 'transpontine theatre', more open, more popular and more spectacular in style, was serving new audiences.

The inevitable happened. A repeal of the monopoly legislation passed the House of Commons in that classic year of middle-class triumph, 1832, but was thrown out by the House of Lords. In 1843 the law was finally changed. Covent Garden, in 1847, became an opera house, with a more fashionable audience. Drury Lane became the centre of spectacles. The majority development of the English theatre went on in the middle-class theatres, which grew from seven in 1800 to nineteen in 1850. Astley's became the Royal, Surreyside the Olympic. In outlying districts new large theatres were opened, and from the 1840s the music-halls began their extraordinary development, both taking over variety from the minor theatres which had now moved up to drama and providing newly organised entertainment for the vastly growing population of the city. London had grown from just over a million to over two and a half millions in the first half of the century. The industrial cities now followed the same patterns. In this period, between 1830 and 1860, the theatre, like the press and publishing, became open, varied and in its own forms vigorous. It could have gone in any of a number of ways.

What actually happened in the third period, after 1860, is again characteristic of general developments in the culture. There was an even faster rate of growth, but new dividing lines appeared between the 'respectable' and the 'popular', and at the respectable end there was an integration of middle-class and fashionable audiences and tastes. This integration, decisive in so many areas, had marked effects in the theatre. The 'popular' audience was now, in the new terms of an urban industrial society, largely working-class and lower middle-class, but on the whole they were not in these theatres, except on special occasions; they were in the music halls and yet newer places of performance, within a widening labour movement. In the central London theatres what was happening was the process usually described as making theatre 'respectable' again: a process which included putting carpets and seats into the old pit; serving more discreet refreshments; altering times to fit with other social engagements. In the Restoration theatre there had been early afternoon performances, for the Court and its circle. Through the eighteenth century the time was steadily moved towards the evening, when people could attend after business and work. Early nineteenth-century performances usually began at six and went on four or five hours: an entire night out at the theatre. From the 1860s the time was moved to eight o'clock, and the performance ended at about eleven: largely to allow for dinner and supper engagements on either side. Matinées came in, for a new kind of leisured audience. What we now think of as West End theatre was established.

This social change must be remembered within the impressive statistics of growth. The whole point of the newly respectable integration was that it offered to be self-recruiting; it was socially inclusive, at a given level of price, taste and behaviour, rather than categorically exclusive, as in an older kind of society. London grew from the two and a half millions of mid-century to six and a half millions by 1900. Internal transport, in railways, omnibuses, and eventually the underground both increased possible audiences and permitted the physical concentration of theatres. From the 1860s an extraordinary wave of building, rebuilding and refurnishing began. In 1850 there had been nineteen theatres; in 1900 there were sixty-one, as well as some forty music-halls. What we think of as the modern theatre and its audience—though it is not modern, since it pre-dates cinema, radio and television which were to cut it back again— had been more centrally and more solidly established than at any other time, before or since.

Melodrama

It is in relation to these connected social factors—changes in audiences and physical changes in the theatres—that we can begin to consider the development of dramatic forms. The first important problem, in a way just because it seems to be at the opposite pole from naturalism, is the case of melodrama which, at least in the first half of the nineteenth century, can be reasonably claimed to be the only significant formal innovation. Yet melodrama is an especially difficult 'form' to define.

Some elements of its development are clear. The original 'melodrama—mime to music in France, dialogue intermissions with music in opera in Germany—was not widely imitated in England, and where it was, usually passed under other names, connected with other precedents. By the time that it was recognized as a form in England its connection with music was little more than incidental or indeed tactical (one of the effects of the restriction of 'legitimate' drama to the patent theatres was to encourage the minor theatres to describe plays as anything but plays; if the inclusion of a song or a mime would do the trick with the Licensing Office—the Lord Chamberlain—then managers and authors would try it). What really came through, under this title, was a new kind of sensational drama, with close connections with the popularity of the Gothic novel. Monk Lewis's *The Castle Spectre* (1797) is an early English example, among a flood of similar imports from Germany (especially Kotzebue) and France. If we correlate this development with the changes of audience already noted, we can see connections between the replacement of sentimental comedy by melodrama and the replacement of a relatively restricted and 'polite' audience by a more open and more vigorous 'popular' audience. Yet within this, and also overriding it, are more complex elements. In France the melodrama, in the sense of sensational drama, had become overtly political during the Revolution, especially in the 'Bastille' plays (Pixérécourt). These sensational plays of prison, tyranny and liberation became popular in adaptation in England, but their political element was excluded, in the period of turbulence before 1830, when censorship of a conscious political kind was extensive. The English 'prison' melodrama then became more purely sensational. A certain radicalism, nevertheless, was inseparable from all English popular culture between about 1820 and 1850; a close correlate was the new kind of Sunday paper, combining sensation, scandal and radical politics. Much of the subsequent development of English social drama, with obvious effects on the case of English naturalism, was affected by this linkage and by its many contradictions and ambiguities. On the one hand, within the restrictions imposed by the status of the minor theatres, there was a constant pressure on authors to avoid more traditional dramatic forms, and the internal habits of these theatres, trained to action and to spectacle rather than to sustained dialogue, increased this. While it is still a question of the simple sensational drama there are no difficult analytic problems. Indeed in one sense this was the heir of Renaissance drama, in most of its external elements, but with the supernatural losing its metaphysical dimension, and the exploring moral and social energy declined to stereotypes: a process most evident in the reduction of dramatic language to rhetoric and stereotype, carriers of the shell of the action, the living body dead inside it. Yet from the 1820s onwards there was a discernible attempt to put new content into this sensational form. This is the attempt at once recognized and exaggerated by the description 'radical melodrama'.

The significant case is that of Douglas Jerrold. He had made his name in 1829 with *Black-Ey'd Susan*: melodrama in the simple transitional sense: a plot of innocence in danger, of miraculous rescue, tied, characteristically, to a ballad (Gay's), and with some marginal consciousness of the poor man (the sailor) as exposed and victimized. It is significant that then, in 1832, Jerrold wrote two plays, *The Rent Day* and *The Factory Girl*, which were quite open attempts to dramatize a new social consciousness. *The Rent Day*, which has survived, is again transitional. Based on a picture by David Wilkie, which the opening tableau directly reproduces, it is a 'domestic-drama' in which a farm-tenant suffers from an absentee landlord and a cheating steward: in this sense radical but assimilated to an older consciousness and an older kind of play. The absentee landlord, initially taken as the representative figure gambling away his rents, has returned in disguise to see what is happening; he exposes the dishonest steward. Thus the actual social tension, which was especially acute in the period when the play was written, is at once displaced—the agent substituting for the landlord as villain—and sensationalized, in that through the magic of disguised and providential authority a happy ending to what had in fact no ending is contrived. *The Factory Girl*, which we know only by report, has many features in common, but what happened to it is, in its way, a significant moment in nineteenth-century culture. This account is taken from the contemporary *Figaro in London*:

> Writers like Mr Jerrold deserve our gratitude as well as our admiration, for their aim is not merely to amuse, but to plead, through the medium of the stage, the cause of the poor and oppressed classes of society. Such is the author's object in *The Factory Girl*, in which he

has drawn with lamentable truth the picture of a weaver's lot, which
is to be the slave of the inhuman system of overworking in English
factories, and too often a victim of the petty tyranny of those who are
placed in authority over him ... The story has interest and incident
which would with the general good writing throughout the piece,
and the quaint satirical humour of Harley's part, have carried off
The Factory Girl triumphantly had it not been in some degree
marred by the dénouement, in which letters were pulled out of
bosoms, a labourer finds a brother in a rich merchant, and an
extensive relationship is discovered among the principal characters.
This comfortable arrangement for a happy ending naturally excited a
smile which gave to the ill-natured a plea for sending forth their
venomous breath in loud blackguard shouts of 'off'... [12]

This can be read in more than one way: as confirming the tendency, as in
The Rent Day, to solve the insoluble by the devices of the sensational
drama; as evidencing an audience which was becoming critical of this; or,
with the specification of the 'ill-natured', as an example of the cross-
pressures of the period. The play was taken off after two nights and never
printed. There may be many reasons, but the contrived ending is not
likely to be one of them, since it was, indeed, standard practice. Jerrold
himself was sure that it was the new theme of the victimized industrial
worker which made the play unpopular.

It is now some six years since the writer of this paper essayed a
drama, the purpose of which was an appeal to public sympathy in
the cause of the Factory Children: the drama was very summarily
condemned ... The subject of the piece 'was low, distressing'. The
truth is, it was not then *la mode* to affect an interest for the 'coarse
and vulgar' details of human life, and the author suffered because he
was two or three years before the fashion.[13]

He refers to the subsequent success, in such subjects, of a 'lady writer',
presumably Frances Trollope. The terms in which *The Factory Girl* was
attacked may remind us of the arguments that raged around naturalism in
the 1880s. Yet the history, again, is complex. There was nothing in the
new naturalist or realist drama of the 1880s which, in terms of the vulgarity of low life or of the violence of events, was new to the English
nineteenth-century theatre, and especially to the melodrama. There had
been a long run of crime plays, from the stories of Maria Marten and

[12] Cit. W. Jerrold, *Douglas Jerrold, Dramatist and Wit*, 2 vols, London 1914, I, p. 211.
[13] Ibid., I, p. 214.

Vidocq (both dramatized by Jerrold in the 1820s) through *The Factory Assassin* (Rayner, 1837), with a falsely accused mute, to the 'detective' plays beginning with Taylor's *The Ticket-of-Leave Man*—the appearance of the archetypical Hawkshaw—in 1863. Mayhew's *London Labour and the London Poor* was dramatized, with the sub-title *Want and Vice*, at the Whitechapel Pavilion in 1860. Plays of city poverty and orphanage, including many adaptations of Dickens, were commonplace. In *Lost in London* (1867) a miner's wife was abducted by a wealthy Londoner, and there were scenes of contrast between Bleakmore Mine and a London champagne party. In Charles Reade's *It's Never Too Late To Mend* (1865) an actress dressed as a boy 'died' on a meticulously staged treadmill (incidentally provoking a critic to get up in the theatre and shout 'Brutal realism'—one of the earliest examples of what was to become a standard phrase[14]). Sexual or at least marital scandals were common after the success of *East Lynne* (1861) and *Lady Audley's Secret* (1862), the latter including a scene of the wife hitting her husband with an iron bar and pushing him down a well, though he reappears in the final scene.

Moreover, to look at it another way, there was a certain radicalism in many of the most popular melodrama plots: wicked landlords seduced the daughters of tenants, foreclosed mortgages, turned mothers and children into the snow; wicked officers and other wealthy young men did their best to emulate them. It is possible, from these examples, to speak of the radical melodrama, with close connections to other elements of the new urban popular culture. What has then to be observed is a paradox: that elements of the social and moral consciousness which was to inform serious naturalism went mainly, in England, into the melodrama, which at the same time preserved, as the foundation of its conventions, providential notions of the righting of wrongs, the exposure of villainy, and the triumph or else the apotheosis of innocence. At the same time, as we shall see, the more naturalistic presentation of scenes, characters and actions moved in general away from themes based in a radical consciousness. The result was a muddle. Melodrama touched every nerve of nineteenth-century society, but usually only to play on the nerves and to resolve crisis in an external and providential dramatic world. Its methods became a byword for sensational exaggeration, against which the more blurred and muted tones of English domestic naturalism made their way with the

[14] Cit. M. Willson Disher, *Melodrama*, London 1954, p. 70.

false reputation of a more essential truth. But this is not simply an internal history of the forms. The changes already noted in the social character of the theatre, after 1860, including especially the split between a 'respectable' drama and 'popular' entertainment, prevented, on either hand, the emergence of any sustainable adequate form. Melodrama, which in its own way had got nearest to the crises of that dislocated, turbulent and cruel society, became, in the end, no more than sensational presentation and then, inevitably, a mode to be patronized or mocked.

Domestic Naturalism

It is orthodox to date the appearance of English naturalism from Robertson's *Caste* (1867), or perhaps the earlier *Society* (1865). But it is again a matter of definition. These plays are indeed a world away from melodrama. A preliminary definition might be comedy of manners with a consciously social topic. But then this does not begin with Robertson. Bulwer Lytton's *Money* (1840) is an obvious earlier example. Its plot involves the familiar scheming for an inheritance, and the readjustments of all the finer feelings after it is known where all the money has gone. In fact to come to *Money* after *The Plain Dealer* or *The Way of the World* is to feel a certain continuity, though its language and incident are firmly contemporary. Or take Jerrold's *Retired from Business* (1851), in which a greengrocer retires to the country and is persuaded by his wife, as a matter of prestige, to change his name from Pennyweight to Fitzpennyweight. The anxious snobbery of this (suburban) country society is mocked in the character of Creepmouse, who at any mention of the actual world can exclaim:

> Pumpkinfield is threatened with revolution. Retail marriage menaced at our firesides, and property barricaded with its own hearthstones.[15]

To go from Bulwer Lytton or Jerrold to Robertson's *Society* is hardly to feel the breeze of innovation. The plot is a standard account of the *nouveaux riches* trying to buy their way into fashionable society, and making the conventional coarse errors. In minor ways it is a nineteenth-century world: one of the Chodds' schemes, to acquire influence, is to start a newspaper, or rather two newspapers: the *Morning* and the *Evening*

---

[15] *The Writings of Douglas Jerrold*, Collected Edition, 7 vols, London 1853, VII, p. 286.

Earthquake. In the end, after scheming and counter-scheming, Chodd Junior rejects 'blue blood' and would 'rather have it the natural colour'.[16] But this does not prevent the play ending with the triumph of the impoverished barrister as Sir Sidney Daryl, Member of Parliament:

Countrymen, & c, wave hats—band plays, &c.[17]

Caste extends the social reference. An aristocratic officer courts the daughter of an unemployed and drunken workman; she is an actress. This outrages his mother, the Marquise. The girl, left with his child, becomes poor when he is reported killed in India and her father has spent the money left for her. But D'Alroy resurrects, the Marquise is reconciled, and the old workman, the only embarrassment, is pensioned off to drink himself to death in Jersey. Of course remarks are made about the silliness of 'caste' feeling when compared with the claims of true love, but to go from *Caste* or *Society* to the pushing world of mid-Victorian England, with its ready conversion of business fortunes into peerages, its movement of actresses into the old aristocracy, to say nothing of the general triumph of the new social integration of 'respectability', is to perceive a theatrical convention as impervious as anything in melodrama. It can then be said that the difference is the 'naturalness' of the dialogue, and it is true that the writing of *Society* and *Caste*, and for that matter of *Money* and *Retired from Business*, can be sharply contrasted with the exclamatory and incident-serving dialogue of, say, *Lady Audley's Secret*. In fact what is principally evident is a developed colloquialism at all but the critical points. Yet this again is not a novelty: *The Ticket-of-Leave Man*, slightly earlier, has more sustained colloquial speech, with less edge of caricature, within its 'melodramatic' plot. (Indeed it is an irony that the only words widely remembered from the play are the detective's, on emerging from disguise: 'Hawkshaw, the detective', which became a comic catch-phrase. The speech of most of the play is the most sustained 'naturalism', in the popular sense, in the English nineteenth-century theatre.)

What then is new in Robertson? It is naturalism in the most technical sense: that of the 'lifelike' stage. There were, as we have seen, precedents for this, in Vestris and Mathews and in the 'archaeological' productions.

---

[16] T.W. Robertson, *Society*, Act III, in *Great English Plays*, ed. H.F. Rubinstein, London 1928, p. 1060.
[17] Ibid., p. 1061.

But Robertson fixed the form, in the new theatres and the new staging of the 1860s. The changes in the social character of the theatre helped him: single-play evenings, at the new later hours; longer runs. The technical means had only to be brought together, in an integrated production of an 'enclosed' play. It is in this exact sense that it is true to say that Robertson invented stage-management, and indeed invented the modern figure of the producer or director, impressing an overall atmosphere and effect. Styles of acting were modified to fit into this general effect, and the plays, in a real sense, are scripts for these productions, in a way that has since become familiar. Robertson's detailed stage-directions are the most obvious evidence of this kind of integrated production, and the motive is undoubtedly, as in all technical definitions of naturalism, the 'appearance (illusion) of reality': 'the ivy to be real ivy, and the grass to be grass matting—not painted'.[18] In local ways these effects of environment are intended to be symptomatic: 'holding out kettle at arm's length. Hawtree looks at it through eyeglass', in a familiar contrast of social habits.[19] But the informing consciousness is always illustrative, and naturalism of this kind is properly described in terms of 'setting' or 'background'.

The distinction that then matters can be explored by comparing this kind of reproduction of a known and recognizable environment with the superficially similar production of a symptomatic or causal environment in high naturalism: for example, the room and the garret beyond it in Ibsen's *The Wild Duck*; the trapped interior of Strindberg's *The Father*; or the social presence and social history of the orchard in Chekhov's *The Cherry Orchard*. It is not only, though it is also, a matter of dramatic reach and scale. It is a question of a way of perceiving physical and social environment, not as setting or background through which, by other conventions, of providence, goodwill, freedom from prejudice, the characters may find their own ways. In high naturalism the lives of the characters have soaked into their environment. Its detailed presentation, production, is thus an additional dramatic dimension, often a common dimension within which they are to an important extent defined. Moreover, the environment has soaked into the lives. The relations between men and things are at a deep level interactive, because what is there physically, as a space or a means for living, is a whole shaped and shaping

[18] T.S. Robertson, *Birth*, Act III, Sc.i, cit. Rowell, *Victorian Theatre*, p. 79.
[19] T.W. Robertson, *Caste*, Act I, in *Nineteenth Century Plays*, ed. G. Rowell, 2nd edition, Oxford 1972, p. 354.

social history. It is characteristic that the actions of high naturalism are often struggles against this environment, of attempted extrication from it, and more often than not these fail. The pre-naturalist conventions of providential escape or of resolution through recognition fall away in the face of this sombre assessment of the weight of the world: not a world which is a background, nor an illustrative setting; but one which has entwined itself in the deepest layers of the personality. It is this practice which makes sense of Strindberg's argument:

> Naturalism is not a dramatic method like that of Becque, a simple photography which includes everything, even the speck of dust on the lens of the camera. That is realism; a method lately exalted to art, a tiny art which cannot see the wood for the trees. That is the false naturalism, which believes that art consists simply of sketching a piece of nature in a natural manner: but it is not the true naturalism, which seeks out those points in life where the great conflicts occur, which rejoices in seeing what cannot be seen every day.[20]

There is room for confusion, here, between 'naturalism' and 'realism', especially since later distinctions, of a comparable kind, have usually reversed the terms. But the central point is evident, and the reference to 'conflict' clarifies it. This view of a shaping physical environment and a shaping social environment is the intellectual legacy of the new natural history and the new sociology of the nineteenth century. Whatever the variations of subsequent attitude, among individual dramatists, this absolute sense of real limits and pressures—in physical inheritance, in types of family and social relationship, in social institutions and beliefs— is common and preoccupying. To produce these limits and pressures, in actually staged environments, was the common aim of the varied and brilliant period of dramatic experiment which this sombre consciousness provoked. Even where, eventually, the struggles and conflicts became internal, as in early expressionism, they were still between the physical limits and pressures of a shaped and shaping natural and social world, and the determined sense of a self, a possible self, which could try to get beyond them, though it usually failed.

It is hardly necessary to say that, set beside high naturalism, what became known as naturalism in the English theatre, after Robertson, is of another and much smaller dimension. But to follow the argument

---

[20] A. Strindberg, *On Modern Drama and Modern Theatre* (1889) in *Samlade Skrifter*, 55 vols, Stockholm 1912-19, XVII, pp. 288-9.

through we must look at what happened after Robertson, in the confident theatres of late Victorian and then Edwardian society.

Naturalism and the Problem Play

The key to an interpretation of the development of English drama between Robertson and the end of the century is the social character of the West End theatre, newly established in this form in the same period. Its audience, as we have seen, was not 'aristocratic' or even 'fashionable'; it was an integrated middle-class audience, in what was now at once a metropolitan and an imperial capital. But then, as in other areas of the culture of the period, and especially in those closely dependent on institutions (from parliament and education to the theatre) the dominant tones were those of an assumed and admired class: 'Society'. This is a radically different situation from theatres with a direct court or aristocratic linkage, notably the Restoration theatre, in which actions, audience and writers were, however narrowly, socially integrated. In the late Victorian theatre, to put it crudely, a largely middle-class audience was spellbound by an image of 'fashionable Society' and the theatres were among the principal agencies for its display. Dramatists such as Henry Arthur Jones, originally a commercial traveller with a nonconformist upbringing, or Pinero, a legal apprentice and then an actor, were not of this displayed class but, like other theatre people, serving it and, as agents of the image, making their way into it. It is striking evidence of the prepotence of the display form that Jones and Pinero did not, as might have been supposed, succeed in writing bourgeois drama but what it was agreed to call 'Society drama'. It was not that they did not briefly try. Jones's *Saints and Sinners* (1884) grafted the problems of nonconformist dullness and respectability on to the old melodrama plot of the innocent girl seduced by a villainous officer and, though rescued, dying of a lost reputation. Pinero, in a late play, *The Thunderbolt* (1908) moved away from London society to a provincial (brewing) middle-class family; the play was found to be drab. In what was now overwhelmingly a bourgeois commercial society, the displacement represented by 'Society drama' would be almost incredible, were it not for the special character of the institutional cultural integration. It is instructive to go from Jones's *Saints and Sinners* to Stanley Houghton's *Hindle Wakes* (1912), not only because Houghton has moved into a bourgeois manufacturing world,

but because Fanny Hawthorn, formal successor to the long line of compromised innocents (she has gone to Blackpool with the son of a rich
manufacturer) refuses her conventional fate: he is not man enough for her
to marry, she has had a good time and now she will make her own way. It
is a generation later, of course, but the more significant difference is that
the play developed and was produced outside the special atmosphere of
the London theatre, in Miss Horniman's Repertory at Manchester. In its
refreshing note of self-confidence it illuminates, by contrast, the extraordinary cultural subordination of the earlier bourgeois dramatists.

There is nothing difficult in the diagnosis of 'Society drama' as a form.
It is the intrigue play moved up-stage, with strong scenes for display.
What is more interesting is the interaction of this form with what became
known as the 'problem play', for this is a crucial question in the matter of
naturalism. Jones and Pinero, in their drawing-room plays, to some
extent muted and blurred—or to put it another way, simplified and
naturalized—the detail of the intrigue play. At the same time they
developed characteristic intrigues to the status of 'problems': notably the
old plot of the lady with a 'past'. The problem, here, was one of moral
judgment, and there was an obvious loosening from the rigidities of, say,
Lady Audley's Secret. The best-known example is Pinero's *The Second
Mrs Tanqueray*, in which the problem is directly discussed. Tanqueray's
first wife, a virtuous woman who also, it is suggested, 'kept a thermo-
meter in her stays and always registered ten degrees below zero'[21] has
insisted, before she dies, on a convent education for her daughter.
Tanqueray's second marriage is to a woman, Paula, whose 'past' is
known to him: a succession of premarital affairs. The problem of 'respectability' is then posed at two levels: the conventional prejudices of his
circle against the second Mrs Tanqueray, including their fears about her
influence on the daughter, but then also the explosive situation in which
the daughter falls in love with one of her stepmother's former men. Paula
tells the truth and kills herself. The daughter wishes she had 'only been
merciful'.[22]

It is a strongly emotional play, but it is the interaction of 'intrigue' and
'problem' that is significant, and that is significantly unresolved by the
form. The sensational coincidence of the daughter falling in love with

---

[21] A.W. Pinero, *The Second Mrs Tanqueray*, Act I, in *Late Victorian Plays*, 1890-1914, ed.
G. Rowell, 2nd edition, Oxford 1972, p. 13.
[22] Ibid., p. 79.

one of the stepmother's young men remains within the orbit of the intrigue drama, though one can easily see that, taken straight, it could lead directly to issues of relationship, including sexual rivalry and jealousy, which the major naturalist drama was exploring. It is not so taken, though the hint is there, and some of the ground has been laid for it, in the last scene of confrontation. On the other hand the generalized 'problem' is of a quite different kind. All the right questions are asked: do not men have 'pasts'; is not prejudice often hypocritical; even, are there not connections between respectability and frigidity? The points go to and fro, but of course that whole discussion is blown to pieces by the actual event, when the abstract question enters an intractable area of primary relationships. What happens is then a compromise, with neither the relationship nor the problem carried through.

Indeed the general character of the 'questioning' in the problem plays of Society drama is in the end strictly suggestive. The basic reason is that the conventions, alike of the structure of feeling and of the form, are restricted to the uneasy terms of the social integration. No sense of any life or any idea beyond the terms of this displayed society can be dramatically established; not even any strictly bourgeois viewpoint, since this is overlaid and compromised by the preoccupation with 'Society' (there is markedly less frankness about money, for example, than even earlier in the century). English naturalism, in this first phase, could then, inevitably, be little more than a technical matter.

Some breaks came. As in most other European situations, a new kind of drama needed a new kind of theatre audience. Virtually all the important new work in European drama of this period was done in breakaway independent theatres, based on a minority (fractional) audience which separated itself at once from its own class and from the 'theatrical' integration. In England this minority was already large, in other fields, but in the theatre it was slow to organize: The Dramatic Students (1886), the Independent Theatre Society (1891), the Stage Society (1899). But it was through these organizations that different work came into the theatres: Shaw's *Widower's Houses* at the Independent Theatre in 1892; the *Plays Pleasant and Unpleasant*; and ultimately the Vedrenne-Barker régime at the Court Theatre between 1904 and 1907. By the last ten years before the war a different kind of English drama had an independent base, though the West End continued to be dominated by Society drama (Sutro, Hankin, early Maugham) and, even more, by musical comedy.

Was this then, even if late, the period of English naturalism, in the most serious sense? In a way, yes. The plays of Galsworthy (*Strife*, 1909 and *Justice*, 1910) have a new breadth of reference and concern, and are specifically naturalist both in the technical sense and in the sense of a conscious correlation between character and environment. Barker's plays (*The Voysey Inheritance*, 1905, and *Waste*, 1907) are highly developed naturalism, in the technical sense, though their themes belong more to the anti-romantic, exposure-of-respectability, strain than to any positive naturalism. It is a significant but limited achievement, and the main reason for this is that Shaw, who most consciously adopted the naturalist philosophical standpoint, and indeed whose expositions of it are more conscious and explicit than those of any of the major naturalist dramatists, chose, for tactical reasons connected with the predominant styles of the orthodox theatre, to work mainly with old forms and then to alter them internally. In some plays, *Widowers' Houses*, *Mrs Warren's Profession* and the later *Heartbreak House*, the material is transformed; the last under the direct influence of a genuinely original naturalist form in Chekhov. But the main thrust of Shaw's drama is a sustained and brilliant polemic, in the plays and in the significantly ancillary prefaces, which as theatrical form stays generally within the terms of the established Society drama and the associated romantic intrigues, historical reconstructions and even the earlier melodrama and farce. It is the most effective body of drama of the period, but it never attempted, in any sustained way, the specifically naturalist conjunction of philosophy and form, and it was supported in this by the reaction against naturalism which was already evident in the avant-garde theatre elsewhere. For of course high naturalism, as a form, itself broke down, under the tensions of its own central theme: the interaction of character and environment. To go more deeply into the experience of a self trapped by an environment the new subjective expressionism of Strindberg was already necessary. Also, to see environment actively—not as a passive determining force, but as a dynamic history and society—needed the new and more mobile conventions of social expressionism. Shaw has connections with the second of these tendencies, though significantly none with the first, and this must be seen as a reason for his actual development. But another reason is the prepotence of the theatrical forms then current within the special case of the English (London West End) theatre.

To trace the subsequent development of English naturalist drama is beyond the scope of this essay. We can only briefly note the extraordinary revival of naturalist drama in the theatre of the mid- and late-1950s, and its extensive and dominant transfer into television drama. We can add that the persistence of a limited technical sense of naturalism has allowed many people, including especially directors and writers, to claim that they have abandoned, 'gone beyond', naturalism, when it is clear, on the one hand, that the great majority of plays now produced, in all media, are technically naturalist, and, on the other hand, that many 'non-naturalist' plays are evidently based on a naturalist philosophy: not only the assumptions about character and environment but the 'scientific' sense of natural history and especially physical inheritance. What remains to be emphasized is the special character of the social basis of theatre in England since the changes of the 1860s. It is significant that in centres other than London a different kind of drama has been evident. I have already given an example of the work at Manchester. Even more significant is the case of the Irish drama, which in spite of the very different pre-occupations and influence of Yeats, produced in Synge's *Riders to the Sea* an especially pure naturalist tragedy, in his *Playboy of the Western World* a significantly localized naturalist comedy, and in O'Casey's early plays, for all their difficulties, work which belongs in the mainstream of European naturalist drama. A final example is of a negative kind: D.H. Lawrence, in his early writing years, worked consistently and sometimes successfully in a kind of naturalist drama, with a quite different social base and with a language significantly revitalized by contrast with the terms of the middle-class problem plays. *The Widowing of Mrs Holroyd*, in spite of limitations which he overcame when writing the same experience in the more flexible form of narrative, would also take its place in a European mainstream, and more work might have followed, but for the fact that, in the special conditions of the English theatre, he could not get his plays produced and so came to rely, as generations of English writers had done before him, on the more open medium of print.

The special conditions for the limitation and lateness of English naturalism are then reasonably clear. Some of these conditions indeed still exist in parts of the English theatre, though television has bypassed them. What remains for reflection is the very difficult question of the relations between naturalist method and what can still be distinguished, though the labels are often changed, as naturalist world-views and structures of feeling. The specific fusion of method and structure which we know historically as high naturalist drama has always to be seen in these terms, but it also, quite as much as the fashionable London theatre, had its specific historical conditions. The question about other forms of such a fusion, both actual and potential, remains central in the history of twentieth-century drama, and it is made very much harder to ask, let alone to answer, if, in loose ways, we go on describing naturalism as if it were only a set of techniques. English naturalism, in its very limitations, provides, in its real history, ample evidence against that. It also provides evidence for what is still the central inquiry: into the formation of forms and, which is another way of saying the same thing, into the relations between forms and social formations, crucial everywhere in art but in the drama always especially central and evident.

The Bloomsbury Fraction

There are serious problems of method in the analysis of cultural groups. When we are analysing large social groups we have some obvious and useful methods at our disposal. The large numbers allow significant statistical analysis. There are usually organized institutions and relatively codified beliefs. There are still many problems in analysis, but we can at least begin with these reasonably hard facts.

In the case of a cultural group, the number of people involved is usually much too small for statistical analysis. There may or may not be organized institutions, through which the group works or develops, but even the most organized institutions are different in scale and kind from those of large groups. The principles which unite the group may or may not be codified. Where they are codified, one kind of analysis is immediately relevant. But there are many important cultural groups which have in common a body of practice or a distinguishable ethos, rather than the principles or stated aims of a manifesto. What the group itself has not formulated may indeed be reduced to a set of formulations, but some effects of reduction—simplification, even impoverishment—are then highly probable.

The social and cultural significance of all such groups, from the most to the least organized, can hardly be doubted. No history of modern culture could be written without attention to them. Yet both history and sociology are uneasy with them. We find histories of particular groups, but little comparative or analytic history. In the sociology of culture, we find the effect of general sociology in a tendency to concentrate on groups of a more familiar kind, with relatively organized institutions: churches for the sociology of religion, an educational system for the sociology of education. In other areas of culture—writing, painting, music, theatre, and for that matter philosophy and social thought—there is usually either specialization or neglect. The group, the movement, the circle, the tendency seem too marginal or too small or too ephemeral, to require historical and social analysis. Yet their importance, as a general social and cultural fact, especially in the last two centuries, is great: in what they achieved, and in what their modes of achievement can tell us about the larger societies to which they stand in such uncertain relations.

These are general considerations but they happen to be particularly important in the case of the Bloomsbury Group, if only because, influentially, they went out of their way, by assertion or innuendo, to deflect or deny them. For example, Leonard Woolf:

> What came to be called Bloomsbury by the outside world never
> existed in the form given to it by the outside world. For
> 'Bloomsbury' was and is currently used as a term—usually of
> abuse—applied to a largely imaginary group of persons with largely
> imaginary objects and characteristics... We were and always
> remained primarily and fundamentally a group of friends.'[1]

Of course when Leonard Woolf complained of misrepresentation, he had important things to say. But the theoretical interest of his observation is that, first, in discussing this 'largely imaginary group' he takes for granted the existence and the concept of 'the outside world', and, second, he counterposes 'a group of friends' to a group in some more general sense. But it is a central fact about many though not all such groups that they begin and develop as 'a group of friends'. What we have then to ask is whether any shared ideas or activities were elements of their friendship, contributing directly to their formation and distinction as a group, and, further, whether there was anything about the ways in which they became friends which indicate wider social and cultural factors. It is significant, for example, to continue the quotation:

> We were and always remained primarily and fundamentally a group
> of friends. Our roots and the roots of our friendship were in the
> University of Cambridge.[2]

For it is especially significant of Bloomsbury that 'the University of Cambridge' can be taken, in this way, as if it were a simple location, rather than the highly specific social and cultural institution which it was

---

[1] *Beginning Again*, London 1964, pp. 21, 23.
[2] Ibid., p. 23.

and is. Moreover the social and cultural roots of that particular form of perception—the 'group' and the 'outside world'—have in their turn to be traced to a precise social position and formation.

For this is the real point of social and cultural analysis, of any developed kind: to attend not only to the manifest ideas and activities, but also to the positions and ideas which are implicit or even taken for granted. This is especially necessary in the England of the last hundred years, in which the significance of groups like Bloomsbury or, to take another relevant example, F.R. Leavis and *Scrutiny*, has been widely acknowledged but within an especially weak general perspective. For the concepts to which such groups are referred belong, essentially, to the definitions and perspectives of the groups themselves, so that any analysis which follows tends to be internal and circular.

This is so, for example, in the concept of the 'intellectual aristocracy', which Lord Annan has popularized and documented, and in the concept of 'minority culture', which Clive Bell, of Bloomsbury, and F.R. Leavis, of *Scrutiny*, in their different ways relied on. The point is not to question the intelligence or the cultivation of such self-defining groups. It is rather to relate them, in their specific forms, to those wider conditions which the concepts of an 'aristocracy' or a 'minority' both imply and obscure. This means asking questions about the social formation of such groups, within a deliberate context of a much wider history, involving very general relationships of social class and education. It means asking, further, about the effects of the relative position of any particular formation on their substantive and self-defining activities: effects which may often be presented merely as evidence of the distinction but which, viewed in a different perspective, may be seen as defining in less realized ways.

Thus Annan's presentation of an intellectual aristocracy, defined by a number of intellectually distinguished families, has to be qualified by two different considerations: first, the effect, including the generational effect, of the social position of those families on their members' *opportunities* for intellectual distinction; and, second, the facts of those families as whole numbers of persons, who need not—except on the founding assumption—be described as it were from the most eminent outwards (a method which allows virtually indefinite inclusion by relationship, where inclusion by independent distinction might present more problems) but who, if distinguished families are the *starting point*, can all, by the apparently independent criterion of intellectual achievement, be included and praised. I believe it to be true that indeed, by independent criteria, in the case of many of Annan's subjects, some remarkable clusters of distinction are evident. But these may then be open to quite different kinds of analysis and conclusion from the ideological, and ideologically derived, notion of an 'intellectual aristocracy'.

The same considerations apply to the Bloomsbury Group, especially as we now see it at some historical distance. It can be presented, reasonably, as an extraordinary grouping of talents. Yet in Bloomsbury, quite clearly, there is also now eminence by association. It is interesting to go through Leonard Woolf's list of Old Bloomsbury and its later accessions.[3] It is difficult to be certain in these matters, but it is worth asking how many people on the list would be now independently and separately remembered, in any generally significant cultural sense, apart from their membership of the group. I mean that in one kind of presentation we can lead with Virginia Woolf, E.M. Forster and J.M. Keynes, and then go on through the widening circle to others. But suppose we take the list as it comes: Vanessa Bell, Virginia Woolf, Leonard Woolf, Adrian Stephen, Karin Stephen, Lytton Strachey, Clive Bell, Maynard Keynes, Duncan Grant, Morgan Forster, Saxon Sydney Turner, Roger Fry, Desmond MacCarthy, Molly MacCarthy, Julian Bell, Quentin Bell, Angelica Bell, David (Bunny) Garnett. It is a list of well-known and some other names. It is indeed exactly what we would expect from Leonard Woolf's accurate description of a group of friends and relations who included some people whose work would be widely respected if the group itself were not remembered, others of whom this is quite clearly not the case, and others again in whom it is difficult to distinguish between independent reputation and the effect of group association and group memoirs.

Yet the point is emphatically not to diminish anybody. That would, indeed, be a gross surrender to some of the very modes of human judgment which Bloomsbury and similar groups effectively popularized. The real point is to see the significance of the cultural group over and above the simple empirical presentation and self-definition as 'a group of friends'. It is to ask what the group was, socially and culturally, as a question distinct from (though still related to) the achievements of individuals and their own immediately perceived relationships. It is

3 Ibid., p. 22.

indeed just because so many significant modern cultural groups are formed and developed in this way that we have to ask, even against the rising eyebrows of Bloomsbury, certain (heavy) theoretical questions.

For it is clear that no analysis which neglects the elements of friendship and relationship, through which they recognized and came to define themselves, would begin to be adequate. At the same time any restriction to these terms would be a clear evasion of the general significance of the group. We have therefore to think about modes of analysis which avoid collapsing one kind of definition into another, either the generalized group or the empirical assembly. For it is just because of its specific internal formation and its evident general significance—the two qualities taken together—that Bloomsbury is so interesting. It is also an especially important case theoretically, since it is impossible to develop a modern cultural sociology unless we can find ways of discussing such formations which both acknowledge the terms in which they saw themselves and would wish to be presented, and at the same time enable us to analyze these terms and their general social and cultural significance. And because this is so, though I shall mainly discuss Bloomsbury, I shall say something also about Godwin and his circle and the Pre-Raphaelite Brotherhood. This is partly for comparison, including historical comparison, but it also a way of beginning to find terms for the more general discussion.

The Formation of Bloomsbury

Let us then notice first that certain of the declared founding principles of Bloomsbury were of a kind which corresponded directly to their precise mode of formation and to the activities for which most of them are remembered. One account after another emphasizes the centrality of the shared values of personal affection and aesthetic enjoyment. For any conscious formulation of these values, we are regularly referred to the great influence of G.E. Moore on the original friends at Cambridge. These shared values were modulated in specific ways. There was a sustained emphasis on candour: people were to say to each other exactly what they thought and felt. There was also great emphasis on clarity: the candid avowal, or any other kind of statement, must expect to be met by the question: 'what precisely do you mean by that?'. These shared values and habits are then immediately relevant to the internal formation of the group and to some of its external effects. The values and habits which brought them so closely together soon gave them a (self-regarding) sense of being different from others, and these others, in turn, could identify them as a clique. But then, in this as in other important respects, they were also one of the advanced formations of their class:

> When I went to Ceylon [*sc.*1904]—indeed even when I returned [*sc.*1911]— I still called Lytton Strachey Strachey and Maynard Keynes Keynes, and to them I was still Woolf. When I stayed for a week with the Stracheys in the country in 1904, or dined in Gordon Square with the Stephens, it would have been inconceivable that I should have called Lytton's or Toby's sisters by their Christian names. The social significance of using Christian instead of surnames and of kissing instead of shaking hands is curious. Their effect is greater, I think, than those who have never lived in a more formal society imagine. They produce a sense—often unconscious —of intimacy and freedom and so break down barriers to thought and feeling. It was this feeling of greater intimacy and freedom, of the sweeping away of formalities and barriers, which I found so new and so exhilarating in 1911. To have discussed some subjects or to have called a (sexual) spade a spade in the presence of Miss Strachey or Miss Stephen would seven years before have been unimaginable; here for the first time I found a much more intimate (and wider) circle in which complete freedom of thought and speech was now extended to Vanessa and Virginia, Pippa and Marjorie.[4]

This sense of liberation was a stage in the development of the original Cambridge friends. It was a local realization of their earlier bearings:

> We were convinced that everyone over twenty-five, with perhaps one or two remarkable exceptions, was 'hopeless', having lost the elan of youth, the capacity to feel, and the ability to distinguish truth from falsehood...We found ourselves living in the springtime of a conscious revolt against the social, political, religious, moral, intellectual and artistic institutions, beliefs and standards of our fathers and grandfathers...We were out to construct something new; we were in the van of the builders of a new society which should be free, rational, civilized, pursuing truth and beauty.[5]

It must of course be clear that this was a very much wider movement than Bloomsbury. In this very account, with a characteristic mixture of honesty and unawareness, Leonard Woolf noted that 'we felt ourselves

---

[4] Ibid., pp. 34-5.
[5] Idem, *Sowing*, London 1960, pp. 160-1.

to be the second generation in this exciting movement', though the attitude to almost everyone over twenty-five seems to have survived this. In fact most of the attitudes and opinions were derived, as here from Ibsen

> saying 'Bosh!' to that vast system of cant and hypocrisy which made lies a vested interest, the vested interest of the 'establishment', of the monarchy, aristocracy, upper classes, suburban bourgeoisie, the Church, the Army, the stock exchange.[6]

What Bloomsbury really represented, in the development of this wider movement, was a new *style*.

It was an effective style for the new critical frankness. But there were elements in its formation which brought other tones, and not only the cliquishness of the self-conscious advanced group. The frankness could modulate into tones of quite extraordinary rudeness about, and to, the 'hopeless'. There is also something very curious about the attachment to personal affections. This is difficult to estimate, at a distance and from outside, but 'affection', rather than any stronger word, does, as one reads, come to seem exact. A cool frankness as a dominant intellectual tone seems to have had its effect on certain levels of emotional life. This was, of course, already evident in Shaw, and in the related but wider Fabian formation. There is an unforgettable moment in a conversation between Virginia Woolf and Beatrice Webb in 1918:

> Beatrice had asked Virginia what she intended to do now that she was married. Virginia said that she wanted to go on writing novels. Beatrice seemed to approve and warned Virginia against allowing her work to be interfered with by emotional relations. 'Marriage, we always say', she said, 'is the waste paper basket of the emotions'. To which, just as they came to the level crossing, Virginia replied: 'But wouldn't an old servant do as well?'.[7]

The fact that in her own record of this conversation Virginia Woolf has 'waste pipe' for 'waste paper basket' only deepens its ironic fascination. There is a sense in which the rationality and the candour give 'affection' a limiting though still important definition. On the other hand, what is quite evident in the group is a significant tolerance in sexual and emotional matters. This valuable tolerance and the exact weight of 'affection' seem really to be linked.

[6] Ibid., p. 164.
[7] *Beginning Again*, p. 117.

A final factor which must be added to this initial definition of the structure of feeling of the group can be precisely represented by the phrase 'social conscience'. They were not its originators, and in any case it is a more evident factor after 1918 than before 1914. It relates, certainly, to the comprehensive irreverence for established ideas and institutions, in the earliest phase. But it becomes something more. Nothing more easily contradicts the received image of Bloomsbury as withdrawn and languid aesthetes than the remarkable record of political and organizational involvement, between the wars, by Leonard Woolf, by Keynes, but also by others, including Virginia Woolf, who had a branch of the Women's Cooperative Guild meeting regularly in her home. The public record of Keynes is well enough known. That of Leonard Woolf, in his prolonged work for the League of Nations, for the Cooperative movement, and for the Labour Party, especially on anti-imperialist questions, is especially honourable.

It might then come as a surprise, to Bloomsbury and to those formed in its image, to set a mark on 'social conscience'. The phrase itself, from just this period, has become widely naturalized, and it is then very difficult to question it. One way of doing so is to note its widespread association with that other significant phrase, 'concern for the underdog'. For what has most carefully to be defined is the specific association of what are really quite unchanged class feelings—a persistent sense of a quite clear line between an upper and a lower class—with very strong and effective feelings of sympathy with the lower class as victims. Thus political action is directed towards systematic reform at a ruling-class level; contempt for the stupidity of the dominant sectors of the ruling class survives, quite unchanged, from the earliest phase. The contradiction inherent in this— the search for systematic reform at the level of a ruling class which is known to be, in majority, short-sighted and stupid—is of course not ignored. It is a matter of social conscience to go on explaining and proposing, at official levels, and at the same time to help in organizing and educating the victims. The point is not that this social conscience is unreal; it is very real indeed. But it is the precise formulation of a particular social position, in which a fraction of an upper class, breaking from its dominant majority, relates to a lower class *as a matter of conscience*: not in solidarity, nor in affiliation, but as an extension of what are still felt as personal or small-group obligations, at once against the cruelty and stupidity of the system and towards its otherwise relatively helpless victims.

The complex of political attitudes, and eventually of political and social reforms of a certain kind, that flowed from this 'social conscience' has been especially important in England. It has indeed become consensual, from the right wing of the Labour Party through the Liberal Party to a few liberal Conservatives. Bloomsbury, including Keynes, was in this as in other matters well ahead of its times. In its organs, from the *New Statesman* through to the *Political Quarterly*, it was, in its period, second in importance in this consensus only to the closely related Fabian Society. In its hostility to imperialism, where the conscientious identification with victims was more negotiable than in England itself, its contribution was very significant. In its early and sustained hostility to militarism it represented an element of the consensus which was later, and especially in the Cold War, phased out. But what now matters most, in defining the group, is the nature of the connection between these important political bearings and the small, rational, candid group. The true link term is 'conscience'. It is a sense of individual obligation, ratified among civilized friends, which both governs immediate relationships and can be extended, without altering its own local base, to the widest 'social concerns'. It can then be distinguished, as the group itself always insisted, from the unfeeling, complacent and stupid state of mind of the dominant sector of the class. It has also to be distinguished—and this the group and its successors did not see—from the 'social *consciousness*' of a self-organizing subordinate class. These very different political bearings were not so much rejected as never taken seriously. Close contact with them, which the 'social conscience' required, produced a quite un-self-conscious and in its own way quite pure patronage. For if this were not given, these new forces could not be expected to be any more rational and civilized than their present masters.

In these initial definitions of the meanings and values which made this group more than just a group of friends—meanings and values, of course, which at every point, because of what they were, sustained their self-perception as *only* a group of friends, a few civilized individuals—we have come to the edge of the central definition of the social significance of the Bloomsbury Group. They were a true *fraction* of the existing English upper class. They were at once against its dominant ideas and values and still willingly, in all immediate ways, part of it. It is a very complex and delicate position, but the significance of such fractions has been very generally underestimated. It is not only a question of this problematic relationship within any particular section of time. It is also a question of the function of such relationships and such groups in the development and adaptation, through time, of the class as a whole.

Godwin and His Circle

It is here that we can look briefly, by way of comparison, at two important earlier English groups. William Godwin and his circle, in the 1780s and 1790s, came out of a quite differently based dissent. Their religious dissent, at the moment of their formation, already carried the specific social implications: of a relatively disadvantaged religious sector, but also the effects of a social and economic position which was very sharply different from that of the ruling and upper class of the day. That is to say, Godwin and his friends were relatively poor working professionals, an emerging small-bourgeois intelligentsia, with no other means of social or political influence. In their basic attempt to establish rationality, tolerance and liberty they were opposing, and knew they were opposing, a whole class and system beyond them. Within their own group they could argue for and try to practise the rational values of civilized equality, including, it should be remembered, for in this with Mary Wollstonecraft they were especially advanced, sexual equality. In their early phase they were wholly persuaded of the powers of rational explanation and persuasion. Vice was simply error, and error could be repaired by patient inquiry. Virtue could be assured by reasonable institutions. The stupidities and dogmas which now barred the way must be met by steady and careful enlightenment.

What then happened is still very striking. They encountered a ruling class, quite beyond them, which was not only arrogant and cruel but, at just that time, was under a new kind of threat from the effects of the French Revolution. The rational and civilizing proposals were met by the crudest kind of repression: prosecution, imprisonment and transportation. Godwin's novel, *Things as They Are*, is a remarkable evocation of this crisis, in which truth became a literal risk to life, and reasonable explanation was quite ruthlessly hunted down. It is a remarkable moment in English culture, still insufficiently honoured for the bravery of its initial attempt, and this mainly because the repression broke it so thoroughly and drove it underground for a generation. Failed groups are not easily respected, yet this one should be, in the nobility of its aspirations alongside the inherent character of its illusions. What we can so easily call failure was in fact defeat, and it was defeat by a vicious repression.

More generally, and decisively, this group was not a fraction, a break from an upper class. It was an emergent sector of a still relatively subordinate class, the smaller independent commercial bourgeoisie. Questioning everything, but within the assumption of a continuing rational discourse, they were hit by people who hardly even bothered to answer their arguments but who as threat and danger mounted simply bullied or locked them up. And then what we learn theoretically is that we cannot describe any of these cultural groups simply in internal terms: of what values they stood for, what meanings they tried to live. Taken only at this level, Godwin and his circle have some striking resemblances to Bloomsbury, although they were always stronger. But the level that matters, finally, is not that of the abstracted ideas, but of the real relations of the group to the social system as a whole.

The Pre-Raphaelite Brotherhood

The social system as a whole, but of course social systems change: in their general character and in their internal relations. By the time of the Pre-Raphaelite Brotherhood, in the middle of the nineteenth century, an industrial and commercial bourgeoisie was becoming dominant, and some parts of that earlier discourse had found a limited social base. For these and other reasons, the character of this new group was quite different. What they primarily opposed was the conventional philistinism of their day. In their earliest phase they were irreverent, impatient, contemptuous of shams; they were trying to find new and less formal ways of living among themselves. For a moment, which did not last, they were part of the democratic turbulence of 1848. But the central mode of their brief unity as a group was a declaration for truth in art, and a corresponding rejection of the received conventions. Their positive aim was truth to nature, 'rejecting nothing, selecting nothing and scorning nothing'. They defined a return to the old (pre-Raphaelite) as a means to the new. As an immediate group, they practised an easy and irreverent informality, an exceptional and now 'bohemian' tolerance, and some elements of a private group language (in slang such as 'stunner' and 'crib') which deliberately marked them off. They could be described as being, in their chosen area of art, in revolt against the commercial bourgeoisie, yet in majority they came from this same class. Holman Hunt's father was a warehouse manager, William Morris's a bill broker. Moreover, to a surprising extent as they developed, they found their patrons in this same class. Of course in the end they went their separate ways: towards the new and flattering integration represented by Millais, or to the break towards revolutionary socialism—though with the same immediate commercial links—of Morris. But in their effective moment, for all their difficulties, they were not only a break from their class—the irreverent and rebellious young—but a means towards the necessary next stage of development of that class itself. Indeed this happens again and again with bourgeois fractions: that a group detaches itself, as in this case of 'truth to nature', in terms which really belong to a phase of that class itself, but a phase now overlaid by the blockages of later development. It is then a revolt against the class but for the class, and it is no surprise that its emphases of style, suitably mediated, became the popular bourgeois art of the next historical period.

The Bloomsbury Fraction

There is always advantage in historical distance, and Godwin and his circle, or the Pre-Raphaelites, are in this sense more easily placed than Bloomsbury, which in certain of its tones and styles has still significant contemporary influence and even presence. Yet the purpose of this brief reference to these earlier groups is to emphasize, past some of the more obvious points in common, not only the ideal differences but the decisive social differences. And these in their turn can be understood only by following the development of the general society. For what happened in the second half of the nineteenth century was a comprehensive development and reform of the professional and cultural life of bourgeois England. The old universities were reformed and made more serious. The administrative services were both developed and reformed, by the new needs of imperial and state administration, and by the competitive examinations which interlocked with the reformed universities. The changing character of the society and the economy built, in fact, a new and very important professional and highly educated sector of the English upper class: very different in its bearings and values from either the old aristocracy or from the directly commercial bourgeoisie. And then—indeed as we look it is no surprise—it was from this sector, and especially from its second and third generations, that novel definitions and new groups emerged; and specifically, in its full sense, Bloomsbury.

The direct connections of the Bloomsbury Group with this new sector are well known. There is a significant frequency of connection with the upper levels of colonial (usually Indian) administration, as in the Stephen family, in Lytton Strachey's father, in Leonard Woolf's early career. There are continuities before and after in this respect: the Mills in the nineteenth century; Orwell in the twentieth. But the period of the emergence of Bloomsbury was the high point of this sector, as it was also the high point of the social order which it served. The sector is distinguishable but is still very closely connected with a wider area of the class. As Leonard Woolf says of the social world of the Stephens:

> That society consisted of the upper levels of the professional middle class and county families, interpenetrated to a certain extent by the aristocracy [Or more generally] The Stephens and the Stracheys, the Ritchies, Thackerays and Duckworths had an intricate tangle of ancient roots and tendrils stretching far and wide through the upper middle classes, the county families, and the aristocracy.[8]

One of the interests of Woolf's account is that he was himself entering this crucial sector from a rather different class background:

> I was an outsider to this class, because, although I and my father before me belonged to the professional middle class, we had only recently struggled up into it from the stratum of Jewish shopkeepers.[9]

He was thus able to observe the specific habits of the class from which Bloomsbury was to emerge:

> Socially they assumed things unconsciously which I could never assume either unconsciously or consciously. They lived in a peculiar atmosphere of influence, manners, respectability, and it was so natural to them that they were unaware of it as mammals are unaware of the air and fish of the water in which they live.[10]

But that was the class as a whole. What was decisive in the emergence of its professional sector was the social and intellectual atmosphere of the reformed ancient universities. It was here, after liberalization, after a significant recovery of seriousness, and after internal reorganization to

[8] Ibid., p. 74.
[9] Ibid., p. 74.
[10] Ibid., p. 75.

assure coached and competitive merit, that the specific qualities of the professional sector emerged within the general assumptions of the class. This allowed some new recruits, like Woolf himself. It promoted many significant and in a sense autonomous continuities, within the old universities. This is why it can still be seen, from a deliberately selective angle, as an 'intellectual aristocracy'.

> The male members of the British aristocracy of intellect went automatically to the best public schools, to Oxford and Cambridge, and then into all the most powerful and respectable professions. They intermarried to a considerable extent, and family influence and the high level of their individual intelligence carried a surprising number of them to the top of their professions. You found them as civil servants sitting in the seat of permanent under-secretaries of government departments; they became generals, admirals, editors, judges, or they retired with a KCSI or KCMG after distinguished careers in the Indian or Colonial Civil Services. Others again got fellowships at Oxford or Cambridge and ended as head of an Oxford or Cambridge college or headmaster of one of the great public schools.[11]

The confusion of this account is as remarkable as the local accuracy of its information. There is the very characteristic admission and yet blurring of the two factors in success: 'family influence', 'high level of...individual intelligence'. There is a related blurring of the 'aristocracy of intellect', supported by one range of examples (Fellows and Headmasters; Permanent Under-Secretaries and Editors) and rather different ruling-class figures (Generals, Admirals). Within each range, in fact, the proportionate effect of class provenance, including family influence, and examined or demonstrated individual intelligence would need to be very precisely estimated. For what is really being described is a sectoral composition, and the diversities within this composition need much more precise description than the self-presenting and self-recommending formula—with its deliberate and yet revealing metaphor—of an 'intellectual aristocracy'.

A further relevant point, in this significant sectoral composition, is raised by Woolf's accurate reference to 'male members'. One of the factors that was to affect the specific character of the Bloomsbury Group, as a formation distinguishable from this whole sector, was the delay in higher education for women of this class. Even in its early stages, a few women from these families were directly involved; one of the Strachey

[11] *Sowing*, p. 186.

sisters, Pernel, became Principal of Newnham. Yet a persistent sexual asymmetry was an important element in the composition of the Bloomsbury Group. As Woolf again puts it:

> Our roots and the roots of our friendship were in the University of Cambridge. Of the 13 persons mentioned above [as members of Old Bloomsbury] three are women and ten men; of the ten men nine had been at Cambridge.[12]

The effects of this asymmetry were ironically and at times indignantly noted by Virginia Woolf, in *A Room of One's Own* and *Three Guineas*.

What we have then to emphasize, in the sociological formation of Bloomsbury, is, first, the provenance of the group in the professional and highly educated sector of the English upper class, itself with wide and sustained connections with this class as a whole; second, the element of contradiction between some of these highly educated people and the ideas and institutions of their class as a whole (the 'intellectual aristocracy', in the narrower sense, or at least some or a few of them, were bringing their intelligence and education to bear on the 'vast system of cant and hypocrisy' sustained by many of the institutions—'monarchy, aristocracy, upper classes, suburban bourgeoisie, the Church, the Army, the stock exchange'—which were elsewhere included as the fields of success of this same 'aristocracy of intellect'); third, the specific contradiction between the presence of highly intelligent and intellectual women, within these families, and their relative exclusion from the dominant and formative male institutions; and, fourth and more generally, the internal needs and tensions of this class as a whole, and especially of its professional and highly educated sector, in a period which, for all its apparent stability, was one of social, political, cultural and intellectual crisis.

The Bloomsbury Group, we can then say, separated out as a distinct fraction on the basis of the second and third factors: the social and intellectual critique, and the ambiguity of the position of women. Taken together, these are the modes at once of its formation and of its achievements. But the first factor, of their general provenance, must be taken as defining the particular qualities of this fraction: their significant and sustained combination of dissenting influence and influential connection. And the fourth factor indicates something of their general historical

---

[12] *Beginning Again*, p. 23.

significance: that in certain fields, notably those of sexual equalization and tolerance, of attitudes to the arts and especially the visual arts, and of some private and semi-public informalities, the Bloomsbury Group was a forerunner in a more general mutation within the professional and highly educated sector, and to some extent in the English ruling class more generally. A fraction, as was noted, often performs this service for its class. There was thus a certain liberalization, at the level of personal relationships, aesthetic enjoyment and intellectual openness. There was some modernization, at the level of semi-public manners, of mobility and contact with other cultures, and of more extended and more adequate intellectual systems. Such liberalization and modernization were of course quite general tendencies, in changing social circumstances and especially after the shocks of the 1914-18 war and, later, the loss of Empire. It is not that the Bloomsbury Group *caused* either change; it is only (but it is something) that they were prominent and relatively coherent among its early representatives and agents. At the same time, the liberalization and modernization were more strictly adaptations than basic changes in the class, which in its function of directing the central ruling-class institutions has, for all the changes of manners and after some evident recruitment of others into its modes, not only persisted, but more successfully persisted *because* these adaptations have been made and continue to be made.

The Contribution of Bloomsbury

What has then finally to be discussed is the character of Bloomsbury's cultural, intellectual and artistic contributions within this context of their specific sociological formation and their historical significance. Yet any such discussion faces severe theoretical and methodological difficulties. There can be no question of reducing a number of highly specific individual contributions to some crude general content. Cultural groups of this kind—fractions by association rather than fractions or oppositional groups by manifesto or programme—can in any case never be treated in this way. Yet neither can the contributions be seen in mere random association. It is in this careful mood that we have to read Leonard Woolf's interesting summary:

> There have often been groups of people, writers and artists, who were not only friends, but were consciously united by a common

doctrine and object, or purpose artistic or social. The utilitarians, the Lake poets, the French impressionists, the English Pre-Raphaelites were groups of this kind. Our group was quite different. Its basis was friendship, which in some cases deepened into love and marriage. The colour of our minds and thought had been given to us by the climate of Cambridge and Moore's philosophy, much as the climate of England gives one colour to the face of an Englishman while the climate of India gives a quite different colour to the face of a Tamil. But we had no common theory, system or principles which we wanted to convert the world to; we were not proselytizers, missionaries, crusaders or even propagandists. It is true that Maynard produced the system or theory of Keynesian economics which has had a great effect upon the theory and practice of economics, finance and politics; and that Roger, Vanessa, Duncan and Clive played important parts, as painters or critics, in what came to be known as the Post-Impressionist Movement. But Maynard's crusade for Keynesian economics against the orthodoxy of the Banks and academic economists, and Roger's crusade for post-impressionism and 'significant form' against the orthodoxy of academic 'representational' painters and aestheticians were just as purely individual as Virginia's writing of *The Waves*—they had nothing to do with any group. For there was no more a communal connection between Roger's 'Critical and Speculative Essays on Art', Maynard's *The General Theory of Employment, Interest and Money*, and Virginia's *Orlando* than there was between Bentham's *Theory of Legislation*, Hazlitt's *Principal Picture Galleries in England*, and Byron's *Don Juan*.[13]

At the simplest empirical level this can be taken to be true, though the final comparison is merely rhetorical: Bentham, Hazlitt and Byron were never significantly associated, and their names beg the question. Nor is the characteristic rejection of 'common theory, system or principles' quite as convincing as it looks; Bloomsbury's attitudes to 'system', at least, were among their most evident common, and principled, characteristics.

Indeed there is something in the way in which Bloomsbury denied its existence as a formal group, while continuing to insist on its group qualities, which is the clue to the essential definition. The point was not to have any common—that is to say, general—theory or system, not only because this was not necessary—worse, it would probably be some imposed dogma—but primarily, and as a matter of principle, because

[13] Ibid., p. 26.

such theories and systems obstructed the true organizing value of the group, which was the unobstructed free expression of the civilized individual. The force which that adjective, 'civilized', carries or is meant to carry can hardly be overestimated.

> In the decade before the 1914 war there was a political and social movement in the world, and particularly in Europe and Britain, which seemed at the time wonderfully hopeful and exciting. It seemed as though human beings might really be on the brink of becoming civilized.[14]

In this sense, at its widest range, Bloomsbury was carrying the classical values of bourgeois enlightenment. It was against cant, superstition, hypocrisy, pretension and public show. It was also against ignorance, poverty, sexual and racial discrimination, militarism and imperialism. But it was against all these things in a specific moment of the development of liberal thought. What it appealed to, against all these evils, was not any alternative idea of a whole society. Instead it appealed to the supreme value of the civilized *individual*, whose pluralization, as more and more civilized individuals, was itself the only acceptable social direction.

The profoundly representative character of this perspective and commitment can now be more clearly seen. It is today the central definition of bourgeois ideology (bourgeois practice, of course, is something else again). It commands the public ideals of a very wide range of orthodox political opinion, from modern conservatives through liberals to the most representative social democrats. It is a philosophy of the sovereignty of the civilized individual, not only against all the dark forces of the past, but against all those other and actual social forces which, in conflicts of interest, in alternative claims, in other definitions of society and relationships, can be quickly seen as enemies and can as quickly be assigned to the far side of that border which is marked by its own definition of 'civilized'. The early confidence of the position, in the period before 1914, has in its long encounter with all these other and actual social forces gone in Leonard Woolf's title—'downhill all the way'. For all its continuing general orthodoxy, it appears now much more often as a beleagured than as an expanding position. The repetition of its tenets then in turn becomes more and more ideological.

Bloomsbury's moment in this history is significant. In its practice—as in the sensibility of the novels of Virginia Woolf and of E.M. Forster—

[14] Ibid., p. 36.

it could offer much more convincing evidence of the substance of the civilized individual than the orthodox rallying phrase. In its theory and practice, from Keynesian economics to its work for the League of Nations, it made powerful interventions towards the creation of economic, political and social conditions within which, freed from war and depression and prejudice, individuals could be free to be and to become civilized. Thus in its personal instances and in its public interventions Bloomsbury was as serious, as dedicated and as inventive as this position has ever, in the twentieth century, been. Indeed the paradox of many retrospective judgements of Bloomsbury is that the group lived and worked this position with a now embarrassing wholeheartedness: embarrassing, that is to say, to those many for whom 'civilized individualism' is a summary phrase for a process of conspicuous and privileged consumption. It is not that we can sever the positions of Bloomsbury from these later developments: there are some real continuities, as in the cult of conspicuous-appreciative-consumption; and certain traps were sprung, as in Keynesian economics and in monetary and military alliances. But we have still to see the difference between the fruit and its rotting, or between the hopefully planted seed and its fashionably distorted tree.

But then, as we see both the connections and the differences, we have to go on to analyze the obscurities and the faults of the original position around which Bloomsbury defined itself. This can be done either seriously or lightheartedly. Let us for a moment choose the latter, in one of Bloomsbury's own modes. It can be said, it was often said, that the group had no *general* position. But why did it need one? If you cared to look, there were Virginia and Morgan for literature, Roger and Clive and Vanessa and Duncan for art, Leonard for politics, Maynard for economics. Didn't these about cover the proper interests of all civilized people? With one exception perhaps, but in the twenties, significantly, this was remedied. A number of associates and relations of the group— Adrian and Karin Stephen, James Strachey—moved into the new practice of psychoanalysis, and Leonard and Virginia Woolf's Hogarth Press—their own direct and remarkable creation—effectively introduced Freudian thinking into English. Thus to the impressive list of Virginia and Morgan for literature, Roger and Clive and Vanessa and Duncan for art, Leonard for politics and Maynard for economics they could, so to say, add Sigmund for sex.

It is tempting to turn any mode back on itself, but the underlying point is serious. The work and thought of the Bloomsbury Group, and that other work and thought which it effectively associated with itself and presented—including, it should be said, the early 'communist' poetry of the thirties—are remarkable, at first sight, for their eclecticism, for their evident *dis*connections. In this sense it is understandable that anyone should turn and ask, rhetorically, what connections there could ever be between Clive Bell on art and Keynes on employment, or Virginia Woolf on fiction and Leonard Woolf on the League of Nations, or Lytton Strachey on history and the Freudians on psychoanalysis. It is true that we cannot put all this work together and make it into a general theory. But of course that is the point. The different positions which the Bloomsbury Group assembled, and which they effectively disseminated as the contents of the mind of a modern, educated, civilized individual, are all in effect *alternatives* to a general theory. We do not need to ask, while this impression holds, whether Freud's generalizations on aggression are compatible with single-minded work for the League of Nations, or whether his generalizations on art are compatible with Bell's 'significant form' and 'aesthetic ecstasy', or whether Keynes's ideas of public intervention in the market are compatible with the deep assumption of society as a group of friends and relations. We do not need to ask because the effective integration has already taken place, at the level of the 'civilized individual', the singular definition of all the best people, secure in their autonomy but turning their free attention this way and that, as occasion requires. And the governing object of all the public interventions is to secure this kind of autonomy, by finding ways of diminishing pressures and conflicts, and of avoiding disasters. The social conscience, in the end, is to protect the private consciousness.

Where this can be assured without that kind of protection—in the privileged forms of certain kinds of art, refusing the 'sacrifice . . . to representation' as 'something stolen from art',[15] or of certain kinds of fiction, as in Virginia Woolf mockingly rejecting social description—

> Begin by saying that her father kept a shop in Harrogate. Ascertain the rent. Ascertain the wages of shop assistants in 1878. Discover what her mother died of. Describe cancer. Describe calico. Describe . . . [16]

[15] Clive Bell, *Art*, London 1914, p. 44.
[16] *Mr Bennett and Mrs Brown*, London 1924, p. 18.

—or in the available significant forms of personal relationships and aesthetic enjoyments—there is still no conflict (in spite of the troublesome 'details') with social *conscience*. Rather this higher sensibility is the kind of life which is its aim and model, after the rational removal of ('unnecessary') conflicts and contradictions and modes of deprivation. For the sake of personal life and of art, as Clive Bell argued,

> Society can do something...because it can increase liberty...Even politicians can do something. They can repeal censorious laws and abolish restrictions on freedom of thought and speech and conduct. They can protect minorities. They can defend originality from the hatred of the mediocre mob.[17]

It is not always that specific blend of sweet and sour. It is indeed never free from class connotations, as again most explicitly in Bell:

> The liberation will not be complete until those who have already learned to despise the opinion of the lower-middle classes learn also to neglect the standards and the disapproval of people who are forced by their emotional limitations to regard art as an elegant amenity...Comfort is the enemy; luxury is merely the bugbear of the bourgeoisie.[18]

At its best it was brave, in its own best terms:

> The least that the State can do is to protect people who have something to say that may cause a riot. What will not cause a riot is probably not worth saying.[19]

Yet after so much saying, there were no riots. Because for all its eccentricities, including its valuable eccentricities, Bloomsbury was articulating a position which, if only in carefully diluted instances, was to become a 'civilized' norm. In the very power of their demonstration of a private sensibility that must be protected and extended by forms of public concern, they fashioned the effective forms of the contemporary ideological dissociation between 'public' and 'private' life. Awareness of their own formation as individuals within society, of that specific social formation which made them explicitly a group and implicitly a fraction of a class, was not only beyond their reach; it was directly ruled out, since the free and civilized individual was already their founding datum. Psycho-

[17] *Art*, p. 274-5.
[18] Ibid., pp. 273-4.
[19] Ibid., p. 275.

analysis could be integrated with this, while it remained an ahistorical study of specific individual formations. Public policies could be integrated with it, while they were directed to reforming and amending a social order which had at once produced these free and civilized individuals but which through stupidity or anachronism now threatened their existence and their indefinite and generalized reproduction. The final nature of Bloomsbury as a group is that it was indeed, and differentially, a group of and for the notion of free individuals. Any general position, as distinct from this special assumption, would then have disrupted it, yet a whole series of specialized positions was at the same time necessary, for the free individuals to be civilized. And the irony is that both the special assumption, and the range of specialized positions, have become naturalized—though now more evidently incoherent—in all later phases of English culture. It is in this exact sense that this group of free individuals must be seen, finally, as a (civilizing) fraction of their class.

Advertising: the Magic System

1. History

It is customary to begin even the shortest account of the history of advertising by recalling the three thousand year old papyrus from Thebes, offering a reward for a runaway slave, and to go on to such recollections as the crier in the streets of Athens, the paintings of gladiators, with sentences urging attendance at their combats, in ruined Pompeii, and the flybills on the pillars of the Forum in Rome. This pleasant little ritual can be quickly performed, and as quickly forgotten: it is, of course, altogether too modest. If by advertising we mean what was meant by Shakespeare and the translators of the Authorized Version—the processes of taking or giving notice of something—it is as old as human society, and some pleasant recollections from the Stone Age could be quite easily devised.

The real business of the historian of advertising is more difficult: to trace the development from processes of specific attention and information to an institutionalized system of commercial information and persuasion; to relate this to changes in society and in the economy: and to trace changes in method in the context of changing organizations and intentions.

The spreading of information, by the crier or by handwritten and printed broadsheets, is known from all periods of English society. The first signs of anything more organized come in the seventeenth century, with the development of newsbooks, mercuries and newspapers. Already certain places, such as St Paul's in London, were recognized as centres for the posting of specific bills, and the extension of such posting to the new printed publications was a natural development. The material of such advertisements ranged from offers and wants in personal service, notices of the publication of books, and details of runaway servants, apprentices, horses and dogs, to announcements of new commodities available at particular shops, enthusiastic announcements of remedies and specifics, and notices of the public showing of monsters, prodigies and freaks. While the majority were the simple, basically factual and specific notices we now call 'classified', there were also direct recommendations, as here, from 1658:

> That Excellent, and by all Physicians, approved China drink, called by the Chineans Tcha, by other nations *Tay* alias *Tee*, is sold at the Sultaness Head Cophee-House in Sweeting's Rents, by the Royal Exchange, London.

Mention of the physicians begins that process of extension from the conventional recommendations of books as 'excellent' or 'admirable' and the conventional adjectives which soon become part of the noun, in a given context (as in my native village, every dance is a Grand Dance). The most extravagant early extensions were in the field of medicines, and it was noted in 1652, of the writers of copy in news-books:

> There is never a mountebank who, either by professing of chymistry or any other art drains money from the people of the nation but these arch-cheats have a share in the booty—because the fellow cannot lye sufficiently himself he gets one of these to do't for him.

Looking up, in the 1950s, from the British Dental Association's complaints of misleading television advertising of toothpastes, we can recognize the advertisement, in 1660, of a 'most Excellent and Approved DENTIFRICE', which not only makes the teeth 'white as Ivory', but

> being constantly used, the Parties using it are never troubled with the Tooth-ache. It fastens the Teeth, sweetens the Breath, and preserves the Gums and Mouth from Cankers and Imposthumes.

Moreover

> the right are onely to be had at Thomas Rookes, Stationer, at the Holy Lamb at the east end of St Paul's Church, near the School, in sealed papers at 12d the paper.

In the year of the Plague, London was full of

> SOVEREIGN Cordials against the Corruption of the Air.

These did not exactly succeed, but a long and profitable trade, and certain means of promoting it, were now firmly established.

With the major growth of newspapers, from the 1690s, the volume of advertisements notably increased. The great majority of them were still of the specific 'classified' kind, and were grouped in regular sections of the paper or magazine. Ordinary household goods were rarely advertised; people knew where to get these. But, apart from the wants and the runaways, new things, from the latest book or play to new kinds of luxury or 'cosmatick' made their way through these columns. By and large, it was still only in the pseudo-medical and toilet advertisements that persuasion methods were evident. The announcements were conventionally printed, and there was hardly any illustration. Devices of emphasis—the hand, the asterisk, the NB—can be found, and sailing announcements had small woodcuts of a ship, runaway notices similar cuts of a man looking back over his shoulder. But, in the early eighteenth century, these conventional figures became too numerous, and most newspapers banned them. The manufacturer of a 'Spring Truss' who illustrated his device, had few early imitators.

A more general tendency was noted by Johnson in 1758:

> Advertisements are now so numerous that they are very negligently perused, and it is therefore become necessary to gain attention by magnificence of promises and by eloquence sometimes sublime and sometimes pathetick. Promise, large promise, is the soul of an advertisement. I remember a washball that had a quality truly wonderful—it gave *an exquisite edge to the razor*! The trade of advertising is now so near to perfection that it is not easy to propose any improvement.

This is one of the earliest of 'gone about as far as they can go' conclusions on advertisers, but Johnson, after all, was sane. Within the situation he knew, of newspapers directed to a small public largely centred on the coffee-houses, the natural range was from private notices (of service wanted and offered, of things lost, found, offered and needed) through shopkeepers' information (of actual goods in their establishments) to puffs for occasional and marginal products. In this last kind, and within the techniques open to them, the puffmen had indeed used, intensively, all the traditional forms of persuasion, and of cheating and lying. The mountebank and the huckster had got into print, and, while the majority of advertisements remained straightforward, the influence of this particular group was on its way to giving 'advertising' a more specialized meaning.

2. Development

There is no doubt that the Industrial Revolution, and the associated revolution in communications, fundamentally changed the nature of advertising. But the change was not simple, and must be understood in specific relation to particular developments. It is not true, for example, that with the coming of factory production large-scale advertising became economically necessary. By the 1850s, a century after Johnson's comment, and with Britain already an industrial nation, the advertising pages of the newspapers, whether *The Times* or the *News of the World*, were still basically similar to those in eighteenth-century journals, except that there were more of them, that they were more closely printed, and that there were certain exclusions (lists of whores, for example, were no longer advertised in the *Morning Post*).

The general increase was mainly due to the general growth in trade, but was aided by the reduction and then abolition of a long-standing Advertisement Tax. First imposed in 1712, at one shilling an announcement, this had been a means, with the Stamp Duty, of hampering the growth of newspapers, which successive Governments had good reason to fear. By the time of the worst repression, after the Napoleonic Wars, Stamp Duty was at 4d a sheet, and Advertisement Tax at 3s 6d. In 1833, Stamp Duty was reduced to 1d, and Advertisement Tax to 1s 6d. A comparison of figures for 1830 and 1838 shows the effect of this reduction: the number of advertisements in papers on the British mainland in the former year was 877,972; by the later date is stood at 1,491,991. Then in 1853 the Advertisement Tax was abolished, and in 1855 the Stamp Duty. The rise in the circulation of newspapers, and in the number of advertisements, was then rapid.

Yet still in the 1850s advertising was mainly of a classified kind, in specified parts of the publication. It was still widely felt, in many kinds of trade, that (as a local newspaper summarized the argument in 1859)

> it is not *respectable*. Advertising is resorted to for the purposes of introducing inferior articles into the market.

Rejecting this argument, the newspaper (*The Eastbourne Gazette and Fashionable Intelligencer*) continued:

> Competition is the soul of business, and what fairer or more legitimate means of competition can be adopted than the availing oneself of a

channel to recommend goods to public notice which is open to all?
Advertising is an open, fair, legitimate and respectable means of
competition; bearing upon its face the impress of free-trade, and of as
much advantage to the consumer as the producer.

The interesting thing is not so much the nature of this argument, but
that, in 1859, it still had to be put in quite this way. Of course the article
concluded by drawing attention to the paper's own advertising rates, but
even then, to get the feel of the whole situation, we have to look at the
actual advertisements flanking the article. Not only are they all from local
tradesmen, but their tone is still eighteenth-century, as for example:

> To all who pay cash and can appreciate
> GOOD AND FINE TEAS
> CHARLES LEA
> Begs most respectfully to solicit a trial of his present stock which has
> been selected with the greatest care, and paid for before being
> cleared from the Bonded warehouses in London...

In all papers, this was still the usual tone, but, as in the eighteenth
century, one class of product attracted different methods. Probably the
first nationally advertised product was Warren's Shoe Blacking, closely
followed by Rowland's Macassar Oil (which produced the counter-
offensive of the antimacassar), Spencer's Chinese Liquid Hair Dye, and
Morison's Universal Pill. In this familiar field, as in the eighteenth
century, the new advertising was effectively shaped, while for selling
cheap books the practice of including puffs in announcements was widely
extended. Warren's Shoe Blacking had a drawing of a cat spitting at its
own reflection, and hack verses were widely used:

> The goose that on our Ock's green shore
> Thrives to the size of Albatross
> Is twice the goose it was before
> When washed with Neighbour Goodman's sauce.

Commercial purple was another writing style, especially for pills:

> The spring and fall of the leaf has been always remarked as the
> periods when disease, if it be lurking in the system, is sure to show
> itself. (Parr's Life Pills, 1843).

The manner runs back to that of the eighteenth-century hucksters and
mountebanks, but what is new is its scale. The crowned heads of Europe
were being signed up for testimonials (the Tsar of all the Russias took and

recommended Revalenta Arabica, while the Balm of Syriacum, a 'sovereign remedy for both bodily and mental decay', was advertised as used in Queen Victoria's household). Holloway, of course a 'Professor', spent £5,000 a year, in the 1840s, spreading his Universal Ointment, and in 1855 exceeded £30,000.

Moreover, with the newspaper public still limited, the puffmen were going on the streets. Fly-posting, on every available space, was now a large and organized trade, though made hazardous by rival gangs (paste for your own, blacking for the others). It was necessary in 1837 to pass a London act prohibiting posting without the owner's consent (it proved extremely difficult to enforce). In 1862 came the United Kingdom Billposters Association, with an organized system of special hoardings, which had become steadily more necessary as the flood of paste swelled. Handbills ('throwaways') were distributed in the streets of Victorian London with extraordinary intensity of coverage; in some areas a walk down one street would collect as many as two hundred different leaflets. Advertising vans and vehicles of all sorts, such as the seven-foot lath-and-plaster Hat in the Strand, on which Carlyle commented, crowded the streets until 1853, when they were forbidden. Hundreds of casual labourers were sent out with placards and sandwich boards, and again in 1853 had to be officially removed from pavement to gutter. Thus the streets of Victorian London bore increasingly upon their face 'the impress of free trade', yet still, with such methods largely reserved to the sellers of pills, adornments and sensational literature, the basic relation between advertising and production had only partly changed. Carlyle said of the hatter, whose 'whole industry is turned to *persuade* us that he has made' better hats, that 'the quack has become God'. But as yet, on the whole, it was only the quack.

The period between the 1850s and the end of the century saw a further expansion in advertising, but still mainly along the lines already established. After the 1855 abolition of Stamp Duty, the circulation of newspapers rapidly increased, and many new ones were successfully founded. But the attitude of the Press to advertising, throughout the second half of the century, remained cautious. In particular, editors were extremely resistant to any break-up in the column layout of their pages, and hence to any increase in size of display type. Advertisers tried in many ways to get round this, but with little success.

As for products mainly advertised, the way was still led by the makers of pills, soaps and similar articles. Beecham's and Pears are important by reason of their introduction of the catch-phrase on a really large scale; 'Worth a Guinea a Box' and 'Good morning! Have you used Pears' Soap?' passed into everyday language. Behind this familiar vanguard came two heavily advertised classes: the patent food, which belongs technically to this period, and which by the end of the century had made Bovril, Hovis, Nestlé, Cadbury, Fry and Kellogg into 'household names'; and new inventions of a more serious kind, such as the sewing-machine, the camera, the bicycle and the typewriter. If we add the new department-stores, towards the end of the century, we have the effective range of general advertising in the period, and need only note that in method the patent foods followed the patent medicines, while the new appliances varied between genuine information and the now familiar technique of slogan and association.

The pressure on newspapers to adapt to techniques drawn from the poster began to be successful from the 1880s. The change came first in the illustrated magazines, with a crop of purity nudes and similar figures; the Borax nude, for example, dispelling Disease and Decay; girls delighted by cigarettes or soap or shampoos. The poster industry, with its organized hoardings, was able from 1867 to use large lithographs, and Pears introduced the 'Bubbles' poster in 1887. A mail-order catalogue used the first colour advertisement, of a rug. Slowly, a familiar world was forming, and in the first years of the new century came the coloured electric sign. The newspapers, with Northcliffe's *Daily Mail* in the lead, dropped their columns rule, and allowed large type and illustrations. It was noted in 1897 that '*The Times* itself' was permitting 'advertisements in type which three years ago would have been considered fit only for the street hoardings', while the front page of the *Daily Mail* already held rows of drawings of rather bashful women in combinations. Courtesy, Service and Integrity, as part of the same process, acquired the dignity of large-type abstractions. The draper, the grocer and their suppliers had followed the quack.

To many people, yet again, it seemed that the advertisers had 'gone about as far as they can go'. For many people, also, it was much too far. A society for Checking the Abuses of Public Advertising (SCAPA) had been formed in 1898, and of course had been described by the United Bill Posters Association as 'super-sensitive faddists'. SCAPA had local successes, in removing or checking some outdoor signs, and the 1890s saw other legislation: prohibiting uniform for sandwich-men (casual labourers, dressed as the Royal Marine Light Infantry or some other regiment, had been advertising soaps and pills); regulating skyline and balloon advertisements; restricting flashing electric signs, which had been blamed for street accidents. It is a familiar situation, this running fight between traditional standards (whether the familiar layout of newspapers or respect for building and landscape) and the vigorous inventiveness of advertisers (whether turning hoardings into the 'art-galleries of the people', or putting an eight-ton patent food sign halfway up the cliffs of Dover). Indeed ordinary public argument about advertising has stuck at this point, first clarified in the 1890s with 'taste' and 'the needs of commerce' as adversaries. In fact, however, even as this battle was raging, the whole situation was being transformed, by deep changes in the economy.

3. Transformation

The strange fact is, looking back, that the great bulk of products of the early stages of the factory system had been sold without extensive advertising, which had grown up mainly in relation to fringe products and novelties. Such advertising as there was, of basic articles, was mainly by shopkeepers, drawing attention to the quality and competitive pricing of the goods they stocked. In this comparatively simple phase of competition, large-scale advertising and the brand-naming of goods were necessary only at the margin, or in genuinely new things. The real signs of change began to appear in the 1880s and 1890s, though they can only be correctly interpreted when seen in the light of the fully developed 'new' advertising of the period between the wars.

The formation of modern advertising has to be traced, essentially, to certain characteristics of the new 'monopoly' (corporate) capitalism, first clearly evident in this same period of the end and turn of the nineteenth century. The Great Depression which in general dominated the period from 1875 to the middle 1890s (though broken by occasional recoveries and local strengths) marked the turning point between two modes of industrial organization and two basically different approaches to distribution. After the Depression, and its big falls in prices, there was a more general and growing fear of productive capacity, a marked tendency to reorganize industrial ownership into larger units and combines, and a growing desire, by different methods, to organize and where possible control the market. Among the means of achieving the latter purposes, advertising on a new scale, and applied to an increasing range of products, took an important place.

Modern advertising, that is to say, belongs to the system of market-control which, at its full development, includes the growth of tariffs and privileged areas, cartel-quotas, trade campaigns, price-fixing by manufacturers, and that form of economic imperialism which assured certain markets overseas by political control of their territories. There was a concerted expansion of export advertising, and at home the biggest advertising campaign yet seen accompanied the merger of several tobacco firms into the Imperial Tobacco Company, to resist American competition. In 1901, a 'fabulous sum' was offered for the entire eight pages of *The Star*, by a British tobacco advertiser, and when this was refused four pages were taken, a 'world's record', to print 'the most costly, colossal and convincing advertisement ever used in an evening newspaper the wide world o'er'. Since the American firms retaliated, with larger advertisements of their own, the campaign was both heavy and prolonged. This can be taken as the first major example of a new advertising situation.

That this period of fundamental change in the economy is the key to the emergence of full-scale modern advertising is shown also by radical changes within the organization of advertising itself. From the eighteenth century, certain shops had been recognized as collecting agencies for advertisements, on behalf of newspapers. In the nineteenth century, this system (which still holds today for some classified advertisements) was extended to the buying of space by individual agents, who then sold it to advertisers. With the growth in the volume of advertising, this kind of space-selling, and then a more developed system of space-brokerage, led to a growth of importance in the agencies, which still, however, were virtually agents of the Press, or at most intermediaries. Gradually, and with increasing emphasis from the 1880s, the agencies began to change their functions, offering advice and service to manufacturers, though still having space to sell for the newspapers. By the turn of the century, the modern system had emerged: newspapers had their own advertising managers, who advanced quite rapidly in status from junior employees to important executives, while the agencies stopped selling space, and went over to serving and advising manufacturers, and booking space after a campaign had been agreed. In 1900 the Advertisers Protection Society,

later the Incorporated Society of British Advertisers, was formed: partly
to defend advertising against such attacks as those of SCAPA, partly to
bring pressure on newspapers to publish their sales figures, so that campaigns might be properly planned. Northcliffe, after initial hesitations
about advertising (he had wanted to run *Answers* without it), came to
realize its possibilities as a new basis for financing newspapers. He
published his sales figures, challenged his rivals to do the same, and in
effect created the modern structure of the Press as an industry, in close
relation to the new advertising. In 1917 the Association of British
Advertising Agents was founded, and in 1931, with the founding of the
Audit Bureau of Circulations, publishing audited net sales, the basic
structure was complete.

It is in this same period that we hear first, with any emphasis, of
advertising as a profession, a public service, and a necessary part of the
economy. A further aspect of the reorganization was a more conscious
and more serious attention to the 'psychology of advertising'. As it neared
the centre of the economy, it began staking its claims to be not only a profession, but an art and a science.

The half-century between 1880 and 1930, then, saw the full development of an organized system of commercial information and persuasion,
as part of the modern distributive system in conditions of large-scale
capitalism. Although extended to new kinds of product, advertising
drew, in its methods, on its own history and experience. There is an
obvious continuity between the methods used to sell pills and washballs
in the eighteenth century ('promise, large promise, a quality truly
wonderful') and the methods used in the twentieth century to sell anything from a drink to a political party. In this sense, it is true to say that all
commerce has followed the quack. But if we look at advertising before,
say, 1914, its comparative crudeness is immediately evident. The 'most
costly, colossal and convincing advertisement' of 1901 shows two badly-
drawn men in tails, clinking port-glasses between announcements that
the cigarettes are five a penny, and the slogan ('The Englishman's
Toast—Don't be gulled by Yankee bluff, support John Bull with every
puff') is in minute type by comparison with 'Most Costly' and
'Advertisement'. Play on fear of illness was of course normal, as it had
been throughout quack advertising, and there were simple promises of
attractiveness and reputation if particular products were used. But true
'psychological' advertising is very little in evidence before the First War,

and where it is its techniques, both in appeal and in draughtsmanship and layout, are crude. Appropriately enough, perhaps, it was in the war itself, when now not a market but a nation had to be controlled and organized, yet in democratic conditions and without some of the older compulsions, that new kinds of persuasion were developed and applied. Where the badly-drawn men with their port and gaspers belong to an old world, such a poster as 'Daddy, what did YOU do in the Great War' belongs to the new. The drawing is careful and detailed: the curtains, the armchair, the grim numb face of the father, the little girl on his knee pointing to her open picture-book, the boy at his feet intent on his toy-soldiers. Alongside the traditional appeals to patriotism lay this kind of entry into basic personal relationships and anxieties. Another poster managed to suggest that a man who would let down his country would also let down his sweetheart or his wife.

The pressures, of course, were immense: the needs of the war, the needs of the economic system. We shall not understand advertising if we keep the argument at the level of appeals to taste and decency, which advertisers should respect. The need to control nominally free men, like the need to control nominally free customers, lay very deep in the new kind of society. Kitchener, demanding an Army, was as startled by the new methods as many a traditional manufacturer by the whole idea of advertising, which he associated with dubious products. In both cases, the needs of the system dictated the methods, and traditional standards and reticences were steadily abandoned when ruin seemed the only alternative.

Slowly, after the war, advertising turned from the simple proclamation and reiteration, with simple associations, of the earlier respectable trade, and prepared to develop, for all kinds of product, the old methods of the quack and the new methods of psychological warfare. The turn was not even yet complete, but the tendencies, from the twenties, were evident. Another method of organizing the market, through consumer credit, had to be popularized, and in the process changed from the 'never-never', which was not at all respectable, to the primly respectable 'hire-purchase' and the positively respectable 'consumer credit'. By 1933, a husband had lost his wife because he had failed to take this 'easy way' of providing a home for her. Meanwhile Body Odour, Iron Starvation, Night Starvation, Listlessness and similar disabilities menaced not only personal health, but jobs, marriages and social success.

These developments, of course, produced a renewed wave of criticism of advertising, and, in particular, ridicule of its confident absurdities. In part this was met by a now standard formula: 'one still hears criticism of advertising, but it is not realized how much has been done, within the profession, to improve it' (for example, a code of ethics, in 1924, pledging the industry, *inter alia* 'to tell the advertising story simply and without exaggeration and to avoid even a tendency to mislead'. If advertisers write such pledges, who then writes the advertisements?). The 'super-sensitive faddists' were rediscovered, and the 'enemies of free enterprise'. Proposals by Huxley, Russell, Leavis, Thompson and others, that children should be trained to study advertisements critically, were described, in a book called *The Ethics of Advertising*, as amounting to 'cynical manipulation of the infant mind'.

But the most significant reply to the mood of critical scepticism was in the advertisements themselves: the development of a knowing, sophisticated, humorous advertising, which acknowledged the scepticism and made claims either casual and offhand or so ludicrously exaggerated as to include the critical response (for example, the Guinness advertisements, written by Dorothy Sayers, later a critic of advertising). Thus it became possible to 'know all the arguments' against advertising, and yet accept or write pieces of charming or amusing copy.

One sustained special attack, on an obviously vulnerable point, was in the field of patent medicines. A vast amount of misleading and dangerous advertising of this kind had been repeatedly exposed, and eventually, by Acts of 1939 and 1941, and by a Code of Standards in 1950, the advertisement of cures for certain specified diseases, and a range of misleading devices, was banned. This was a considerable step forward, in a limited field, and the Advertising Association was among its sponsors. If we remember the history of advertising, and how the sellers of ordinary products learned from the quack methods that are still used in less obviously dangerous fields, the change is significant. It is like nothing so much as the newly-crowned Henry the Fifth dismissing Falstaff with contempt. Advertising had come to power, at the centre of the economy, and it had to get rid of the disreputable friends of its youth: it now both wanted and needed to be respectable.

4. *Advertising in Power*

Of the coming to power there was now no question. Estimates of expenditure in the inter-war years vary considerably, but the lowest figure, for direct advertising in a single year, is £85,000,000 and the highest £200,000,000. Newspapers derived half their income from advertising, and almost every industry and service, outside the old professions, advertised extensively. With this kind of weight behind it, advertising was and knew itself to be a solid sector of the establishment.

Some figures from 1935 are interesting, showing advertising expenditure as a proportion of sales:

Proprietary medicines	29.4%
Toilet goods	21.3%
Soaps, polishes etc	14.1%
Tobacco	9.3%
Petrol and oil	8.2%
Cereals, jams, biscuits	5.9%
Sweets	3.2%
Beer	1.8%
Boots and Shoes	1.0%
Flour	0.5%

The industry's connections with its origins are evident: the three leading categories are those which pioneered advertising of the modern k ind. But more significant, perhaps, is that such ordinary things as boots, shoes and flour should be in the table at all. This, indeed, is the new economy, deriving not so much from the factory system and the growth of communications, as from an advanced system of capitalist production, distribution and market control.

Alongside the development of new kinds of appeal came new media. Apart from such frills as sky-writing, there was commercial radio, not yet established in Britain (though the pressure was there) but begun elsewhere in the 1920s and beamed to Britain from the 1930s. Commercial television, in the 1950s, got through fairly easily. Among new methods, in this growth, are the product jingle, begun in commercial radio and now reaching classic status, and the open alliance between advertisers and apparently independent journalists and broadcasters. To build a reputation as an honest reporter, and then use it either openly to recommend a product or to write or speak about it alongside an advertisement for it, as in the evening-paper 'special supplements', became commonplace. And what was wrong? After all, the crowned heads of Europe, and many of our own Ladies, had been selling pills and soaps for years. The extension to political advertising, either direct or by pressure-groups, also belongs, in its extensive phase, to this period of establishment; in the 1950s it has been running at a very high rate indeed.

The only check, in fact, to this rapidly expanding industry was during the last war, though this was only partial and temporary, and the years since the war, and especially the 1950s, have brought a further spectacular extension. It is ironic to look back at a book published in wartime, by one of the best writers on advertising, Denys Thompson, and read this:

> A second reason for these extensive extracts is that advertising as we know it may be dispensed with, after the war. We are getting on very well with a greatly diminished volume of commercial advertising in wartime, and it is difficult to envisage a return to the 1919-1939 conditions in which publicity proliferated.

Mr Thompson, like Dr Johnson two centuries earlier, is a sane man, but it is never safe to conclude that puffing has reached its maximum distension. The history, rightly read, points to a further major growth, and to more new methods. The highly organized field of market study, motivation research, and retained sociologists and psychologists, is extremely formidable, and no doubt has many surprises in store for us. Talent of quite new kinds is hired with increasing ease. And there is one significant development which must be noted in conclusion: the extension of organized publicity.

'Public Relations'

Advertising was developed to sell goods, in a particular kind of economy. Publicity has been developed to sell persons, in a particular kind of culture. The methods are often basically similar: the arranged incident, the 'mention', the advice on branding, packaging and a good 'selling line'. I remember being told by a man I knew at university (he had previously explained how useful, to his profession as an advertiser, had been his training in the practical criticism of advertisements) that advertisements you booked and paid for were really old stuff; the real thing was what got through as ordinary news. This seems to happen now with goods: 'product centenaries', for example. But with persons it is even more extensive. It began in entertainment, particularly with film actors, and it is still in this field that it does most of its work. It is very difficult to pin down, because the borderline between the item or photograph picked up in the ordinary course of journalism and broadcasting, and the similar item or photograph that has been arranged and paid for, either directly or through special hospitality by a publicity agent, is obviously difficult to draw. Enough stories get through, and are even boasted about, to indicate that the paid practice is extensive, though payment, except to the agent, is usually in hospitality (if that word can be used) or in kind. Certainly, readers of newspapers should be aware that the 'personality' items, presented as ordinary news stories or gossip, will often have been paid for, in one way or another, in a system that makes straightforward advertising, by comparison, look respectable. Nor is this confined to what is called 'show business'; it has certainly entered literature, and it has probably entered politics.

The extension is natural, in a society where selling, by any effective means, has become a primary ethic. The spectacular growth of advertising, and then its extension to apparently independent reporting, has behind it not a mere pressure-group, as in the days of the quacks, but the whole impetus of a society. It can then be agreed that we have come a long way from the papyrus of the runaway slave and the shouts of the town-crier: that what we have to look at is an organized and extending system, at the centre of our national life.

5. The System

In the last hundred years, then, advertising has developed from the simple announcements of shopkeepers and the persuasive arts of a few marginal dealers into a major part of capitalist business organization. This is important enough, but the place of advertising in society goes far beyond this commercial context. It is increasingly the source of finance for a whole range of general communication, to the extent that in 1960 our majority television service and almost all our newspapers and periodicals could not exist without it. Further, in the last forty years and now at an increasing rate, it has passed the frontier of the selling of goods and services and has become involved with the teaching of social and personal values; it is also rapidly entering the world of politics. Advertising is also, in a sense, the official art of modern capitalist society: it is what 'we' put up in 'our' streets and use to fill up to half of 'our' newspapers and magazines: and it commands the services of perhaps the largest organized body of writers and artists, with their attendant managers and advisers, in the whole society. Since this is the actual social status of advertising, we shall only understand it with any adequacy if we can develop a kind of total analysis in which the economic, social and cultural facts are visibly related. We may then also find, taking advertising as a major form of modern social communication, that we can understand our society itself in new ways.

It is often said that our society is too materialist, and that advertising reflects this. We are in the phase of a relatively rapid distribution of what are called 'consumer goods', and advertising, with its emphasis on 'bringing the good things of life', is taken as central for this reason. But it seems to me that in this respect our society is quite evidently not materialist enough, and that this, paradoxically, is the result of a failure in social meanings, values and ideals.

It is impossible to look at modern advertising without realising that the material object being sold is never enough: this indeed is the crucial cultural quality of its modern forms. If we were sensibly materialist, in that part of our living in which we use things, we should find most advertising to be of an insane irrelevance. Beer would be enough for us, without the additional promise that in drinking it we show ourselves to be manly, young in heart, or neighbourly. A washing-machine would be a useful machine to wash clothes, rather than an indication that we are forward-looking or an object of envy to our neighbours. But if these associations sell beer and washing-machines, as some of the evidence suggests, it is clear that we have a cultural pattern in which the objects are not enough but must be validated, if only in fantasy, by association with social and personal meanings which in a different cultural pattern might be more directly available. The short description of the pattern we have is *magic*: a highly organized and professional system of magical inducements and satisfactions, functionally very similar to magical systems in simpler societies, but rather strangely coexistent with a highly developed scientific technology.

This contradiction is of the greatest importance in any analysis of modern capitalist society. The coming of large-scale industrial production necessarily raised critical problems of social organization, which in many fields we are still only struggling to solve. In the production of goods for personal use, the critical problem posed by the factory of advanced machines was that of the organization of the market. The modern factory requires not only smooth and steady distributive channels (without which it would suffocate under its own product) but also definite indications of demand without which the expensive processes of capitalization and equipment would be too great a risk. The historical choice posed by the development of industrial production is between different forms of organization and planning in the society to which it is central. In our own century, the choice has been and remains between some form of socialism and a new form of capitalism. In Britain, since the 1890s and with rapidly continuing emphasis, we have had the new capitalism, based on a series of devices for organizing and ensuring the market. Modern advertising, taking on its distinctive features in just this economic phase, is one of the most important of these devices, and it is perfectly true to say that modern capitalism could not function without it.

Yet the essence of capitalism is that the basic means of production are not socially but privately owned, and that decisions about production are therefore in the hands of a group occupying a minority position in the society and in no direct way responsible to it. Obviously, since the capitalist wishes to be successful, he is influenced in his decisions about production by what other members of the society need. But he is influenced also by considerations of industrial convenience and likely profit, and his decisions tend to be a balance of these varying factors. The challenge of socialism, still very powerful elsewhere but in Britain deeply confused by political immaturities and errors, is essentially that decisions about production should be in the hands of the society as a whole, in the sense that control of the means of production is made part of the general system of decision which the society as a whole creates. The conflict between capitalism and socialism is now commonly seen in terms of a competition in productive efficiency, and we need not doubt that much of our future history, on a world scale, will be determined by the results of this competition. Yet the conflict is really much deeper than this, and is also a conflict between different approaches to and forms of socialism. The fundamental choice that emerges, in the problems set to us by modern industrial production, is between man as consumer and man as user. The system of organized magic which is modern advertising is primarily important as a functional obscuring of this choice.

'Consumers'

The popularity of 'consumer', as a way of describing the ordinary member of modern capitalist society in a main part of his economic capacity, is very significant. The description is spreading very rapidly, and is now habitually used by people to whom it ought, logically, to be repugnant. It is not only that, at a simple level, 'consumption' is a very strange description of our ordinary use of goods and services. This metaphor drawn from the stomach or the furnace is only partially relevant even to our use of things. Yet we say 'consumer', rather than 'user', because in the form of society we now have, and in the forms of thinking which it almost imperceptibly fosters, it is as consumers that the majority of people are seen. We are the market, which the system of industrial production has organized. We are the channels along which the product flows and disappears. In every aspect of social communication, and in every version of what we are as a community, the pressure of a system of industrial production is towards these impersonal forms.

Yet it is by no means necessary that these versions should prevail, just because we use advanced productive techniques. It is simply that once these have entered a society, new questions of structure and purpose in social organization are inevitably posed. One set of answers is the development of genuine democracy, in which the human needs of all the people in the society are taken as the central purpose of all social activity, so that politics is not a system of government but of self-government, and the systems of production and communication are rooted in the satisfaction of human needs and the development of human capacities. Another set of answers, of which we have had more experience, retains, often in very subtle forms, a more limited social purpose. In the first phase, loyal subjects, as they were previously seen, became the labour market of industrial 'hands'. Later, as the 'hands' reject this version of themselves, and claim a higher human status, the emphasis is changed. Any real concession of higher status would mean the end of class-society and the coming of socialist democracy. But intermediate concessions are possible, including material concessions. The 'subjects' become the 'electorate', and 'the mob' becomes 'public opinion'.

Decision is still a function of the minority, but a new system of decision, in which the majority can be organized to this end, has to be devised. The majority are seen as 'the masses', whose opinion, *as masses* but not as real individuals or groups, is a factor in the business of governing. In practical terms, this version can succeed for a long time, but it then becomes increasingly difficult to state the nature of the society, since there is a real gap between profession and fact. Moreover, as the governing minority changes in character, and increasingly rests for real power on a modern economic system, older social purposes become vestigial, and whether expressed or implied, the maintenance of the economic system becomes the main factual purpose of all social activity. Politics and culture become deeply affected by this dominant pattern, and ways of thinking derived from the economic market—political parties considering how to sell themselves to the electorate, to create a favourable brand image; education being primarily organized in terms of a graded supply of labour; culture being organized and even evaluated in terms of commercial profit—become increasingly evident.

Still, however, the purposes of the society have to be declared in terms that will command the effort of a majority of its people. It is here that the idea of the 'consumer' has proved so useful. Since consumption is within its limits a satisfactory activity, it can be plausibly offered as a commanding social purpose. At the same time, its ambiguity is such that it ratifies the subjection of society to the operations of the existing economic system. An irresponsible economic system can supply the 'consumption' market, whereas it could only meet the criterion of human use by becoming genuinely responsible: that is to say, shaped in its use of human labour and resources by general social decisions. The consumer asks for an adequate supply of personal 'consumer goods' at a tolerable price: over the last ten years, this has been the primary aim of British government. But users ask for more than this, necessarily. They ask for the satisfaction of human needs which consumption, as such, can never really supply. Since many of these needs are social—roads, hospitals, schools, quiet—they are not only not covered by the consumer ideal: they are even denied by it, because consumption tends always to materialize as an individual activity. And to satisfy this range of needs would involve questioning the autonomy of the economic system, in its actual setting of priorities. This is where the consumption ideal is not only misleading, as a form of defence of the system, but ultimately destructive to the broad general purposes of the society.

Advertising, in its modern forms, then operates to preserve the consumption ideal from the criticism inexorably made of it by experience. If the consumption of individual goods leaves that whole area of human need unsatisfied, the attempt is made, by magic, to associate this consumption with human desires to which it has no real reference. You do not only buy an object: you buy social respect, discrimination, health, beauty, success, power to control your environment. The magic obscures the real sources of general satisfaction because their discovery would involve radical change in the whole common way of life.

Of course, when a magical pattern has become established in a society, it is capable of some real if limited success. Many people will indeed look twice at you, upgrade you, upmarket you, respond to your displayed signals, if you have made the right purchases within a system of meanings to which you are all trained. Thus the fantasy seems to be validated, at a personal level, but only at the cost of preserving the general unreality which it obscures: the real failures of the society which however are not easily traced to this pattern.

It must not be assumed that magicians—in this case, advertising agents—disbelieve their own magic. They may have a limited professional cynicism about it, from knowing how some of the tricks are done. But fundamentally they are involved, with the rest of the society, in the confusion to which the magical gestures are a response. Magic is always an unsuccessful attempt to provide meanings and values, but it is often very difficult to distinguish magic from genuine knowledge and from art. The belief that high consumption is a high standard of living is a general belief of the society. The conversion of numerous objects into sources of sexual or pre-sexual satisfaction is evidently not only a process in the minds of advertisers, but also a deep and general confusion in which much energy is locked.

At one level, the advertisers are people using certain skills and knowledge, created by real art and science, against the public for commercial advantage. This hostile stance is rarely confessed in general propaganda for advertising, where the normal emphasis is the blind consumption ethic ('Advertising brings you the good things of life'), but it is common in advertisers' propaganda to their clients. 'Hunt with the mind of the hunter', one recent announcement begins, and another, under the heading 'Getting any honey from the hive industry?', is rich in the language of attack:

> One of the most important weapons used in successful marketing is advertising.

> Commando Sales Limited, steeped to the nerve ends in the skills of unarmed combat, are ready to move into battle on any sales front at the crack of an accepted estimate. These are the front line troops to call in when your own sales force is hopelessly outnumbered by the forces of sales resistance...

This is the structure of feeling in which 'impact' has become the normal description of the effect of successful communication, and 'impact' like 'consumer' is now habitually used by people to whom it ought to be repugnant. What sort of person really wants to 'make an impact' or create a 'smash hit', and what state is a society in when this can be its normal cultural language?

It is indeed monstrous that human advances in psychology, sociology and communication should be used or thought of as powerful techniques *against* people, just as it is rotten to try to reduce the faculty of human choice to 'sales resistance'. In these respects, the claim of advertising to be a service is not particularly plausible. But equally, much of this talk of weapons and impact is the jejune bravado of deeply confused men. It is in the end the language of frustration rather than of power. Most advertising is not the cool creation of skilled professionals, but the confused creation of bad thinkers and artists. If we look at the petrol with the huge clenched fist, the cigarette against loneliness in the deserted street, the puppet facing death with a life-insurance policy (the modern protection, unlike the magical symbols painstakingly listed from earlier societies), or the man in the cradle which is an aeroplane, we are looking at attempts to express and resolve real human tensions which may be crude but which also involve deep feelings of a personal and social kind.

The structural similarity between much advertising and much modern art is not simply copying by the advertisers. It is the result of comparable responses to the contemporary human condition, and the only distinction that matters is between the clarification achieved by some art and the displacement normal in bad art and most advertising. The skilled magicians, the masters of the masses, must be seen as ultimately involved in the general weakness which they not only exploit but are exploited by. If the meanings and values generally operative in the society give no answers to, no means of negotiating, problems of death, loneliness, frustration, the need for identity and respect, then the magical system must come, mixing its charms and expedients with reality in easily available forms, and binding the weakness to the condition which has created it.

Advertising is then no longer merely a way of selling goods, it is a true part of the culture of a confused society.

Afterword (1969): Advertising and Communications

A main characteristic of our society is a willed coexistence of very new technology and very old social forms. Advertising is the most visible expression of just this combination. In its main contemporary forms it is the result of a failure to find means of social decision, in matters of production and distribution, relevant to a large-scale and increasingly integrated economy. Classical liberalism ceased to have anything to say about these problems from the period of depression and consequent reorganization of the market in the late nineteenth century. What we now know as advertising takes its origins from that period, in direct relation to the new capitalist corporations. That the same liberalism had produced the idea of a free press, and of a general social policy of public education and enlightenment, is a cŏntinuing irony. Before the corporate reorganization, the social ideas of liberalism had been to an important extent compatible with its commercial ideas. Widespread ownership of the means of communication had been sustained by comparable kinds of ownership in the economy as a whole. When the standing enemy of free expression was the state, this diverse commercial world found certain important means to freedom, notably in the newspapers.

What was then called advertising was directly comparable in method and scale. It was mainly specific and local, and though it was often absurd—and had long been recognized as such in its description as puff—it remained a secondary and subordinate activity at the critical point where commercial pressure interacted with free public communication. That early phase is now more than half a century in the past. From the 1890s advertising began to be a major factor in newspaper publishing, and from the same period control began to pass from families and small firms to the new corporations. Ever since that time, and with mounting pressure in each decade, the old institutions of commercial liberalism have been beaten back by the corporations. These sought not so much to supply the market as to organize it.

The consequent crisis has been most visible in newspapers, which have been very sharply reduced in number and variety through a period of expanding readership and the increasing importance of public opinion.

But while some of the other liberal ideas seemed to hold, and were even protected as such, as in broadcasting, by the state, it was always possible to believe that the general situation could be held too. Commercial priorities were extending in scale and range, but an entire set of liberal ideas, which in practice the priorities were steadily contradicting, seemed to stay firm in the mind: indeed, so firm that it was often difficult to describe reality, because the evidence of practice was met so regularly by the complacent response of the ideas.

What is now happening, I believe, is that just enough people, at just enough of the points of decision, are with a certain sadness and bewilderment, and with many backward looks, giving that kind of liberalism up. What used to be an uneasy compromise between commercial pressures and public policy is now seen as at worst a bargain, at best a division of labour. The coexistence of commercial and public-service television, which was planned by nobody but was the result of intense pressure to let in the commercial interest, is now rationalized, after the fact, as a kind of conscious policy of pluralism. The new name for compromise is 'mixed economy', or there is an even grander name: a 'planned diversity of structures'.

What has really happened is that a majority of those formerly dedicated to public policy have decided that the opposing forces are simply too strong. They will fight some delaying actions, they will make reservations, but a political situation, long prepared and anticipated, is coming through with such a force that these are mainly gestures. Public money raised in public ways and subject to public control has been made desperately (but deliberately) short. Public money raised in the margin of other transactions and consequently subject to no public control is at the same time continually on offer. Practical men, puzzling over the accounts in committees, think they have at last glimpsed reality. Either they must join the commercial interests, or they must behave like them as a condition of their temporary survival. And so a mood is created in which all decisions seem inevitable and in which people speaking of different solutions seem remote and impractical. It is a mood of submission, under the pressures of an effectively occupying power.

What must then, of course, be most desperately denied is that anything so crude as submission is in fact occurring. Some people are always ready with talk of a new forward-looking order. But the central sign of this sort of submission is a reluctance, in public, to call the enemy by its real name.

I see the form of the enemy as advertising, but what I mean by advertising is rather different from some other versions. Plenty of people still criticize advertising in secondary ways: that it is vulgar or superficial, that it is unreliable, that it is intrusive. Much of this is true, but it is the kind of criticism advertising can learn to take in its stride. Does it not now employ many talented people, does it not set up rules and bodies to control and improve standards, is it not limited to natural breaks? While criticism is discrete in these ways, it has only marginal effects.

So I repeat my own central criticism. Advertising is the consequence of a social failure to find means of public information and decision over a wide range of everyday economic life. This failure, of course, is not abstract. It is the result of allowing control of the means of production and distribution to remain in minority hands, and one might add, for it is of increasing importance in the British economy, into foreign hands, so that some of the minority decisions are not even taken inside the society which they affect.

The most evident contradiction of late capitalism is between this controlling minority and a widely expectant majority. What will eventually happen, if we are very lucky, is that majority expectations will surpass the minority controls. In a number of areas this is beginning to happen, in small and temporary ways, and it is called, stupidly, indiscipline or greed or perversity or disruption. But the more evident fact, in the years we are living through, is the emergence and elaboration of a social and cultural form—advertising—which responds to the gap between expectation and control by a kind of organized fantasy.

In economic terms this fantasy operates to project the production decisions of the major corporations as 'your' choice, the 'consumer's' selection of priorities, methods and style. Professional and amateur actors, locally directed by people who in a different culture might be writing and producing plays or films, are hired to mime the forms of the only available choices, to display satisfaction and the achievement of their expectations, or to pretend to a linkage of values between quite mundane products and the now generally unattached values of love, respect, significance or fulfilment. What was once the local absurdity of puffing is now a system of mimed celebration of other people's decisions. As such, of course, advertising is very closely related to a whole system of styles in official politics. Indeed some of its adepts have a direct hand in propaganda, in the competition of the parties and in the formation of public opinion.

Seen from any distance—of time, space or intelligence—the system is so obvious, in its fundamental procedures, that one might reasonably expect to be able to break it by describing it. But this is now very doubtful. If advertising is the consequence of a failure to achieve new forms of social information and decision, this failure has been compounded by the development of the Labour government, which in submitting to the organized market of the corporations has paved the way to a more open and more total submission in the seventies. Historically, this may be seen as the last attempt to solve our crisis in liberal terms, but the consequences of the failure go beyond simple political history. For it has led to habits of resignation and deference to the new power: not only among decision-makers but much more widely, I think, among people who now need the system of fantasy to confirm the forms of their immediate satisfaction or to cover the illusion that they are shaping their own lives.

It is in this atmosphere that the crucial decisions about communications are now being taken. Some of them could have been worse. Pressure on the BBC to take advertising money has been held off, though there is still a lobby, of an elitist kind, prepared to admit it to Radio 1, where all things vulgar may lie down together. On the contrary, this is just where it must not be admitted, for the pressure to tie the cultural preferences of a young generation to the open exploitation of a 'young market' is the most intense and destructive of them all. Again, the emphasis on the licence, as a means of revenue, is welcome, as a way of preserving the principle of open public money. The fee is still comparatively low in Britain, and could easily be graduated for pensioners and in some cases abolished. In the BBC and in the government, some local stands are being made.

But it is not only that other people are already adjusting to the altered political climate of the seventies, in which the commercial interests expect to take full control. It is also that the decisions possible to this sort of government, or to a public corporation, are marginal to the continuing trend of economic concentration. A newspaper with two and a half million readers is now likely to shut down: not because such a readership is in a general way uneconomic, but because within a structure determined by competitive advertising revenue it is a relative loser. That process of cutting down choices will continue unless met by the most vigorous public intervention. Commercial radio would rapidly accelerate it.

And what then happens, apart from the long-term hedges and options, is that new figures for viability are accepted for almost all communications services. It is absurd that a sale of a million should be too low for a newspaper. But think of other figures. What is called a vast throng—a hundred thousand people—in Wembley Stadium or Hyde Park is called a tiny minority, a negligible percentage, in a radio programme. Content is then increasingly determined, even in a public service, by the law of quick numbers, which advertising revenue has forced on the communications system.

Submission is not always overt. One of its most popular forms is to change as the conqueror appears on the horizon, so that by the time he arrives you are so like him that you may hope to get by. I don't believe we have yet lost but the position is very critical. What was originally a manageable support cost, in the necessary freedom of communications, has been allowed to turn the world upside down, until all other services are dependent, or likely to be dependent, on its quite local, narrow and temporary needs. An out-dated and inefficient kind of information about goods and services has been surpassed by the competitive needs of the corporations, and these increasingly demand not a sector but a world, not a reservation but a whole society, not a break or a column but whole newspapers and broadcasting services in which to operate. Unless they are driven back now, there will be no easy second chance.

Utopia and Science Fiction

There are many close and evident connections between science fiction and utopian fiction, yet neither, in deeper examination, is a simple mode, and the relationships between them are exceptionally complex. Thus if we analyse the fictions that have been grouped as utopian we can distinguish four types: (a) *the paradise*, in which a happier life is described as simply existing elsewhere; (b) *the externally altered world*, in which a new kind of life has been made possible by an unlooked for natural event; (c) *the willed transformation*, in which a new kind of life has been achieved by human effort; (d) *the technological transformation*, in which a new kind of life has been made possible by a technical discovery.

It will of course be clear that these types often overlap. Indeed the overlap and often the confusion between (c) and (d) are exceptionally significant. One kind of clarification is possible by considering the negative of each type: the negative which is now commonly expressed as 'dystopia'. We then get: (a) *the hell*, in which a more wretched kind of life is described as existing elsewhere; (b) *the externally altered world*, in which a new but less happy kind of life has been brought about by an unlooked for or uncontrollable natural event; (c) *the willed transformation*, in which a new but less happy kind of life has been brought about by social degeneration, by the emergence or re-emergence of harmful kinds of social order, or by the unforeseen yet disastrous consequences of an effort at social improvement; (d) *the technological transformation*, in which the conditions of life have been worsened by technical development.

Since there can be no *a priori* definition of the utopian mode, we cannot at first exclude any of these dystopian functions, though it is clear that they are strongest in (c) and (d), perceptible in (b), and barely evident in (a), where the negative response to utopia would normally have given way to a relatively autonomous fatalism or pessimism. These indications bear with some accuracy on the positive definitions, suggesting that the element of transformation rather than the more general element of otherness, may be crucial. In the extension to the general category of science fiction we find:

(a) *The paradise or the hell* can be discovered or reached by new forms of travel dependent on scientific and technological (space-travel) or quasi-scientific (time-travel) development. But this is an instrumental function; the mode of travel does not commonly affect the place discovered. The type of fiction is little affected whether the discovery is made by a space voyage or a sea voyage. The place, rather than the journey, is dominant.

(b) *The externally altered world* can be related, construed, foretold in a context of increased scientific understanding of natural events. This also may be an instrumental function only; a new name for an old deluge. But the element of increased scientific understanding may become significant or even dominant in the fiction, for example in the emphasis of natural laws in human history, which can decisively (often catastrophically) alter normal human perspectives.

(c) *The willed transformation* can be conceived as inspired by the scientific spirit, either in its most general terms as secularity and rationality, or in a combination of these with applied science which makes possible and sustains the transformation. Alternatively the same impulses can be negatively valued: the 'modern scientific' ant-heap or tyranny. Either mode leaves open the question of the social agency of the scientific spirit and the applied science, though it is the inclusion of some social agency, explicit or implicit (such as the overthrow of one class by another), that distinguishes this type from type (d). We must note also that there are important examples of type (c) in which the scientific spirit and applied science are subordinate to or simply associated with a dominant emphasis on social and political (including revolutionary) transformation; or in which they are neutral with respect to the social and political transformation, which proceeds in its own terms, or, which is of crucial diagnostic significance, where the applied science, though less often the scientific spirit, is positively controlled, modified, or in effect suppressed, in a willing return to a 'simpler', 'more natural' way of life. In this last mode there are some pretty combinations of very advanced 'non-material' science and a 'primitive' economy.

(d) *The technological transformation* has a direct relation to applied science. It is the new technology which, for good or ill, has made the new life. As more generally in technological determinism, this has little or no social agency, though it is commonly described as having certain 'inevitable' social consequences.

We can now more clearly describe some significant relations between utopian fiction and science fiction, as a preliminary to a discussion of some modern utopian and dystopian writing. It is tempting to extend both categories until they are loosely identical, and it is true that the presentation of *otherness* appears to link them, as modes of desire or of warning in which a crucial emphasis is obtained by the element of discontinuity from ordinary 'realism'. But this element of discontinuity is itself fundamentally variable. Indeed, what has most to be looked at, in properly utopian or dystopian fiction, is the continuity, the implied connection, which the form is intended to embody. Thus, looking again at the four types, we can make some crucial distinctions which appear to define utopian and dystopian writing (some of these bear also on the separate question of the distinction of science fiction from older and now residual modes which are simply organizationally grouped with it):

(a) *The paradise and the hell* are only rarely utopian or dystopian. They are ordinarily the projections of a magical or a religious consciousness, inherently universal and timeless, thus commonly beyond the conditions of any imaginable ordinary human or worldly life. Thus the Earthly Paradise and the Blessed Islands are neither utopian nor science-fictional. The pre-lapsarian Garden of Eden is latently utopian, in some Christian tendencies; it can be attained by redemption. The medieval *Land of Cokaygne* is latently utopian; it can be, and was, imagined as a possible human and worldly condition. The paradisal and hellish planets and cultures of science fiction are at times simple magic and fantasy: deliberate, often sensational presentations of *alien* forms. In other cases they are latently utopian or dystopian, in the measure of degrees of connection with, extrapolation from, known or imaginable human and social elements.

(b) *The externally altered world* is typically a form which either falls short of or goes beyond the utopian or dystopian mode. Whether the event is magically or scientifically interpreted does not normally affect this. The common emphasis is on human limitation or indeed human powerlessness:

the event saves or destroys us, and we are its objects. In Wells's *In the Days of the Comet* the result *resembles* a utopian transformation, but the displacement of agency is significant. Most other examples, of a science-fiction kind, are explicitly or latently dystopian: the natural world deploys forces beyond human control, thus setting limits to or annulling all human achievement.

(c) *The willed transformation* is the characteristic utopian or dystopian mode, in the strict sense.

(d) *The technological transformation* is the utopian or dystopian mode narrowed from agency to instrumentality; indeed it only becomes utopian or dystopian, in strict senses, when it is used as an image of *consequence* to function, socially, as conscious desire or conscious warning.

'Scientific' and 'Utopian'

No contrast has been more influential, in modern thought, than Engels's distinction between 'utopian' and 'scientific' socialism. If it is now more critically regarded, this is not only because the scientific character of the 'laws of historical development' is cautiously questioned or sceptically rejected; to the point, indeed, where the notion of such a science can be regarded as utopian. It is also because the importance of utopian thought is itself being revalued, so that some now see it as the crucial vector of desire, without which even the laws are, in one version, imperfect, and, in another version, mechanical, needing desire to give them direction and substance. This reaction is understandable but it makes the utopian impulse more simple, more singular, than in the history of utopias it is. Indeed the variability of the utopian situation, the utopian impulse, and the utopian result is crucial to the understanding of utopian fiction.

This can be seen from one of the classical contrasts, between More's *Utopia* and Bacon's *New Atlantis*. It is usual to say that these show, respectively, a humanist and a scientific utopia:

> that excellent perfection of all good fashions, humanitye and civile gentilnesse [More—first English translation, 1551];

> the end of our foundation is the knowledge of causes and secret motions of things and the enlarging of the bounds of human empire, to the effecting of all things possible [Bacon, 1627].

It can be agreed that the two fictions exemplify the difference between a willed general transformation and a technological transformation; that More projects a commonwealth, in which men live and feel differently, while Bacon projects a highly specialized, unequal but affluent and efficient social order. But a full contrast has other levels. Thus they stand near the opposite poles of the utopia of free consumption and the utopia of free production. More's island is a cooperative subsistence economy; Bacon's a specialized industrial economy. These can be seen as permanent alternative images, and the swing towards one or another, in socialist ideology as in progressive utopianism, is historically very significant. One might indeed write a history of modern socialist thought in terms of the swing between a Morean cooperative simplicity and a Baconian mastery of nature, except that the most revealing trend has been their unconscious fusion. Yet what we can now perceive as permanent alternative images was rooted, in each case, in a precise social and class situation. More's humanism is deeply qualified: his indignation is directed as much against importunate and prodigal craftsmen and labourers as against the exploiting and engrossing landlords; his social identification is with the small owners; his laws regulate and protect but also compel labour. It is qualified also because it is static: a wise and entrenched regulation by the elders. It is then socially the projection of a declining class, generalized to a relatively humane but permanent *balance*. Bacon's scientism is similarly qualified: the scientific revolution of experiment and discovery becomes research and development in an instrumental social perspective. Enlarging the bounds of human empire is not only the mastery of nature; it is also, as a social projection, an aggressive, autocratic, imperialist enterprise; the projection of a rising class.

Nineteenth-Century Utopias

We cannot abstract desire. It is always desire for something specific, in specifically impelling circumstances. Consider three utopian fictions of the late nineteenth century: Bulwer-Lytton's *The Coming Race* (1871); Edward Bellamy's *Looking Backward* (1888); William Morris's *News from Nowhere* (1890).

The Coming Race is at one level an obvious example of the mode of technological transformation. What makes the Vril-ya, who live under our

Earth, civilized is their possession of Vril, that all-purpose energy source which lies beyond electricity and magnetism. Outlying underground peoples who do not possess Vril are barbarians; indeed the technology is the civilization, and the improvement of manners and of social relations is firmly based on it alone. The changes thus brought about are the transformation of work into play, the dissolution of the State and in effect the outlawing of competitive and aggressive social relations. Yet it is not, for all the obvious traces of influence, either a socialist or an anarchist utopia. It is a projection of the idealized social attitudes of an aristocracy, now generalized and distanced from the realities of rent and production by the technological determinism of Vril. In its complementary liberation of sexual and family relations (in fact qualified, though apparently emphasized, by the simple reversal of the relative size and roles of women and men) it can be sharply contrasted with the rigidities of these relations within More's humanism. But this is of a piece with the aristocratic projection. It is (as in some later fantasies, with similarly privileged assumptions) a separation of personal and sexual relations from those problems of care, protection, maintenance, and security which Vril has superseded. Affluence delivers liberation. By contrast the greed, the aggression, the dominativeness, the coarseness, the vulgarity of the surface world—the world, significantly, both of capitalism and of democracy—are easily placed. They are what are to be expected in a world without Vril and therefore Vril-ya. Indeed there are moments when Vril can almost be compared with Culture, in Matthew Arnold's virtually contemporary *Culture and Anarchy*. Arnold's spiritual aristocracy, his spiritual force beyond all actual classes, has been magically achieved, without the prolonged effort that Arnold described, by the properties of Vril. It is in each case desire, but desire for what? A civilizing transformation, beyond the terms of a restless, struggling society of classes.

What has also to be said, though, about *The Coming Race* is that its desire is tinged with awe and indeed with fear. The title introduces that evolutionary dimension which from this period on is newly available in utopian fiction. When the Vril-ya come to the surface they will simply replace men, as in effect a higher and more powerful species. And it is not only in his unVril humanity that the hero fears this. Towards the end he sounds the note that we shall hear so clearly later in Huxley's *Brave New World*: that something valuable and even decisive—initiative and creativity are the hovering words—has been lost in the displacement of human industry to Vril. This was a question that was to haunt the technological utopia. (Meanwhile, back in nineteenth century society, an entrepreneur took his own short-cut. Inspired by Lytton he made a fortune from a beef extract called Bovril.)

Bellamy's *Looking Backward* is unquestionably a utopia, in the central sense of a transformed social life of the future, but it is in a significant way a work without desire; its impulse is different, an overriding rationalism, a determining total organization, which finds its proper institutional counterparts in the State-monopoly capitalism which is seen as the inevitable 'next stage in the industrial and social development of humanity' (the order of adjectives there is decisive.) That this forecast, rather than vision, was widely taken as an advocacy of socialism is indicative of a major tendency in Bellamy's period, which can be related to Fabianism but has also now to be related to a major current in orthodox Marxism: socialism as the next higher stage of economic organization, a proposition which is taken as overriding, except in their most general terms, questions of substantially different social relations and human motives. Morris's critique of Bellamy repeated almost exactly what is called the Romantic but is more properly the radical critique of utilitarian social models—that 'the underlying vice ... is that the author cannot conceive ... anything else than the *machinery* of society': the central point made in this tradition, from Carlyle's *Signs of the Times* onward. Morris's fuller response was his *News from Nowhere*, but before we look at this we should include a crucial point about the history of utopian writing, recently put forward by Miguel Abensour in his Paris dissertation 'Formes de l'utopie Socialiste-Communiste'.

Systematic and Heuristic Futures

Abensour establishes a crucial periodization in the utopian mode, according to which there is, after 1850, a change from the *systematic* building of alternative organizational models to a more open and *heuristic* discourse of alternative values. E.P. Thompson, discussing Abensour in *New Left Review*, 99 (1976), has interpreted this latter mode as the 'education of desire'. It is an important emphasis, since it allows us to see more clearly by contrast, how some examples of the mode of 'willed social transformation' can be shifted, in their essence, to the mode of 'technological transformation', where the technology need not be only a marvellous new energy source, or some industrial resource of that kind, but can be also a new set of laws, new abstract property relations, indeed precisely new *social machinery*. But then, when we have said this, and recognized the contrasting value of that more heuristic mode in which the substance of new values and relations is projected, with comparatively little attention to institutions, we have to relate the change to the historical situation within which it occurred. For the shift from one mode to another can be negative as well as positive. To imagine a whole alternative society is not mere model-building, any more than the projection of new feelings and relationships is necessarily a transforming response. The whole alternative society rests, paradoxically, on two quite different social situations: either that of social confidence, the mood of a rising class, which knows, down to detail, that it can replace the existing order; or that of social despair, the mood of a declining class or fraction of a class, which has to create a new heaven because its Earth is a hell. The basis of the more open but also the vaguer mode is different from either. It is a society in which change is happening, but primarily under the direction and in the terms of the dominant social order itself. This is always a fertile moment for what is, in effect, an anarchism: positive in its fierce rejection of domination, repression, and manipulation; negative in its willed neglect of structures, of continuity and of material constraints. The systematic mode is, then, often a response to tyranny or disintegration; the heuristic mode, by contrast, seems often to be primarily a response to a constrained reformism.

It is then not a question of asking which is better or stronger. The heuristic utopia offers a strength of vision against the prevailing grain; the systematic utopia a strength of conviction that the world really can be different. The heuristic utopia, at the same time, has the weakness that it can settle into isolated and in the end sentimental 'desire', a mode of living with alienation, while the systematic utopia has the weakness that, in its insistent organization, it seems to offer little room for any recognizable life. These strengths and weaknesses vary, of course, in individual examples of each mode, but they vary most decisively, not only in the periods in which they are written but in the periods in which they are read. The mixed character of each mode then has much to do with the character of the twentieth-century dystopias which have succeeded them. For the central contemporary question about the utopian modes is why there is a progression, within their structures, to the specific reversals of a

Zamyatin, a Huxley, an Orwell—and of a generation of science-fiction writers.

'News From Nowhere'

It is in this perspective that we have now to read *News from Nowhere*. It is commonly diagnosed and criticized as a generous but sentimental heuristic transformation. And this is substantially right, of the parts that are made ordinarily to stick in the mind. The medievalism of visual detail and the beautiful people in the summer along the river are indeed inextricable from the convincing openness and friendliness and relaxed cooperation. But these are residual elements in the form: the Utopians, the Houyhnhnms, the Vril-ya would have found Morris's people cousins at least, though the dimensions of universal mutuality have made a significant difference. But what is emergent in Morris's work, and what seems to me increasingly the strongest part of *News from Nowhere*, is the crucial insertion of the *transition* to utopia, which is not discovered, come across, or projected—not even, except at the simplest conventional level, dreamed—but fought for. Between writer or reader and this new condition is chaos, civil war, painful and slow reconstruction. The sweet little world at the end of all this is at once a result and a promise; an offered assurance of 'days of peace and rest', after the battle has been won.

Morris was strong enough, even his imagined world is at times strong enough, to face this process, this necessary order of events. But when utopia is not merely the alternative world, throwing its light on the darkness of the intolerable present, but lies at the far end of generations of struggle and of fierce and destructive conflict, its perspective, necessarily, is altered. The post-religious imagining of a harmonious community and the enlightened rational projection of an order of peace and plenty have been replaced, or at least qualified, by the light at the end of the tunnel, the sweet promise which sustains effort and principle and hope through the long years of revolutionary preparation and organization. This is a genuine turning-point. Where the path to utopia was moral redemption or rational declaration—that light on a higher order which illuminates an always present possibility—the mode itself was radically different from the modern mode of unavoidable conflict and resolution.

Morris's chapters 'How the Change Came' and 'The Beginning of the New Life' are strong and convincing. 'Thus at last and by slow degrees we get pleasure into our work'. This is not the perspective of reformism, which in spirit, in its evasion of fundamental conflicts and sticking points, is much nearer the older utopian mode. It is the perspective of revolution—not only the armed struggle but the long and uneven development of new social relations and human feelings. That they have been developed, that the long and difficult enterprise has succeeded, is crucial; it is the transition from dream to vision. But it is then reasonable to ask whether the achieved new condition is not at least as much rest after struggle—the relaxed and quiet evening after a long, hard day—as any kind of released new energy and life. The air of late Victorian holiday is made to override the complexities, the divergences, the everyday materialities of any working society. When the time-dreamer finds himself fading, as he looks in on the feast at the old church, the emotions are very complex: the comforting recall of a medieval precedent—'the church-ales of the Middle Ages'; the wrench of regret that he cannot belong to this new life; and then also, perhaps, for all the convinced assent to the sight of the burdens having been lifted, the impulse—and is it only unregenerate?—of an active, engaged, deeply vigorous mind to register the impression, though it is put into a voice from the future, 'that our happiness even would weary you.' It is the fused and confused moment of different desires and impulses: the longing for communism, the longing for rest and the commitment to urgent, complex, vigorous activity.

Conflict and Dystopia

When utopia is no longer an island or a newly discovered place, but our familiar country transformed by specific historical change, the mode of imagined transformation has fundamentally changed. But the historical agency was not only, as in Morris, revolution. It was also, as in Wells, some kind of modernizing, rationalizing force: the vanguard of Samurai, of scientists, of engineers, of technical innovators. Early rationalist utopias had, in the manner of Owen, only to be declared to be adopted; reason had that inevitability. Wells, though refusing popular revolution, belonged to his time in seeing agency as necessary, and there is a convincing match between the kind of agency he selected—a type of social engineering plus a rapidly developing technology—and the point of arrival: a clean, orderly, efficient and planned (controlled) society. It is easy to see this now as an affluent state capitalism or monopoly socialism; indeed many of the images have been literally built. But we can also, holding Morris and Wells together in our minds, see a fundamental tension within the socialist movement itself—indeed in practice within even revolutionary socialism. For there are other vanguards than those of Wells, and the Stalinist version of the bureaucratic Party, engineering a future which is primarily defined as technology and production, not only has its connections to Wells but has to be radically distinguished from the revolutionary socialism of Morris and of Marx, in which new social and human relations, transcending the deep divisions of industrial capitalist specialization, of town and country, of rulers and ruled, administrators and administered, are from the beginning the central and primary objective. It is within a complex of contemporary tendencies—of efficient and affluent capitalism set against an earlier capitalist poverty and disorder; of socialism against capitalism in either phase; and of the deep divisions, within socialism itself, between the reformist free-riders with capitalism, the centralizing social engineers, and the revolutionary democrats—that we have to consider the mode of dystopia, which is both written and read within this extreme theoretical and practical complexity.

Thus Huxley's *Brave New World* (1932) projects a black amalgam of Wellsian rationality and the names and phrases of revolutionary socialism in a specific context of mobile and affluent corporate capitalism. This sounds and is confused, but the confusion is significant; it is the authentic confusion of two generations of science fiction itself, in its powerful dystopian mode. 'Community, Identity, Stability': this is the motto of the *Brave New World* State. It is interesting to track these ideals back into the utopian mode. Stability, undoubtedly, has a strong bearing; most of the types of utopia have strongly emphasized it, as an achieved perfection or a self-adjusting harmony. Huxley adds the specific agencies of repression, manipulation, pre-natal conditioning, and drugged distraction. Western science fiction has been prolific in its elaboration of all these agencies: the models, after all, have been close to hand. Stability blurs to Identity: the manufacture of human types to fit the stabilized model; but this, crucially, was never an explicit utopian mode, though in some examples it is assumed or implied. Variability and autonomy, within the generally harmonious condition, are indeed among the primary utopian features. But now, under the pressures of consumer capitalism and of monopoly socialism, the mode has broken. As in the later stages of realist fiction, self-realization and self-fulfilment are not to be found in relationship or in society, but in breakaway, in escape: the path the Savage takes, like a thousand heroes of late-realist fiction, getting out from under the old place, the old people, the old family, or like a thousand science-fiction heroes, running to the wastes to escape the machine, the city, the system.

But then the last and most questionable irony: the first word of the motto of this repressive, dominating, controlling system is Community: the keyword, centrally, of the entire utopian mode. It is at this point that the damage is done or, to put it another way, is admitted. It is in the name of Community, the utopian impulse, and in the names of communism (Bernard Marx and Lenina) that the system is seen as realized, though the actual tendencies—from the degradation of labour through an ultimate division and specialization to the organized mobility and muzak of planned consumption—rely for their recognition on a contemporary capitalist world. In his 1946 foreword Huxley continued his running together of historically contrary impulses but then, interestingly, returned to utopia, offering a third way beyond the incubator society and the primitive reservation: a self-governing and balanced community, little different in spirit from Morris's future society except that it is limited to 'exiles and refugees', people escaping from a dominant system which they have no chance or hope of changing collectively. Utopia then lies at the far end of dystopia, but only a few will enter it; the few who get out from under. This is the path travelled, in the same period, by bourgeois cultural theory: from the universal liberation, in bourgeois terms, through the phase in which the minority first educates and then regenerates the majority, to the last sour period in which what is now called 'minority culture' has to find its reservation, its hiding-place, beyond both the system and the fight against the system.

But then what is so strange is that this last phase, in some writing, returns to the utopian mode, throwing strange questions back to the whole prior tradition: questions which disturb the apparently simple grammar of desire—that desire for another place and another time which, instead of being idealized, can be seen as always and everywhere a displacement, but which can itself be transformed when a history is moving.

> Not in Utopia—subterranean fields—
> Or in some secret island, Heaven knows where!
> But in the very world, which is the world
> Of all of us—the place where in the end
> We find our happiness, or not at all!

Wordsworth's emphasis, it is true, can go either way: into revolutionary effort, when history is moving; into a resigned settlement when it goes wrong or gets stuck. The utopian mode has to be read, always, within that changing context, which itself determines whether its defining subjunctive mood is part of a grammar which includes a true indicative and a true future, or whether it has seized every paradigm and become exclusive, in assent and dissent alike.

For the same consideration puts hard questions to the now dominant mode of dystopia. Orwell's 1984 is no more plausible than Morris's 2003, but its naturalized subjunctive is more profoundly exclusive, more dogmatically repressive of struggle and possibility, than anything within the utopian tradition. It is also, more sourly and more fiercely than in Huxley, a collusion, in that the state warned against and satirized—the repression of autonomy, the cancellation of variations and alternatives— is built into the fictional form which is nominally its opponent, converting all opposition into agencies of the repression, imposing, within its excluding totality, the inevitability and the hopelessness which it assumes as a result. No more but perhaps no less plausible than Morris's 2003; but then, in the more open form, there is also Morris's 1952 (the date of the revolution), and the years following it: years in which the subjunctive is a true subjunctive, rather than a displaced indicative, because its energy flows both ways, forward and back, and because in its issue, in the struggle, it can go either way.

New Heavens and Hells

The projection of new heavens and new hells has been a commonplace in science fiction. Yet perhaps a majority of them, just because they are so often literally out of this world, are functions of fundamental alteration: not merely the intervention of altered circumstance, which in the type of the externally altered world is a minor mode of the utopian, but a basic recasting of the physical conditions of life and thence of its life forms. And then in most stories this is a simple exoticism, generically tied to the supernatural or magical romance. There is a range from casual to calculated fantasy, which is at the opposite pole from the hypothesized 'science' of science fiction. Yet, perhaps inextricable from this genre, though bearing different emphases, there is a mode which is truly the result of a dimension of modern science: in natural history, with its radical linkages between life-forms and life-space; and in scientific anthropology, with its methodological assumption of distinct and alternative cultures. The interrelation between these is often significant. The materialist tendency of the former is often annulled by an idealist projection at the last, mental phase of the speculation; the beast or the vegetable, at the top of its mind, is still a human variation. The differential tendency of the latter, by contrast, is often an overriding of material form and condition: an overriding related to idealist anthropology, in which alternatives are in effect wholly voluntary. Yet it is part of the power of science fiction that it is always potentially a mode of authentic shift: a crisis of exposure which produces a crisis of possibility; a reworking, in imagination, of *all* forms and conditions.

In this at once liberating and promiscuous mode, science fiction as a whole has moved beyond the utopian; in a majority of cases, it is true, because it has also fallen short of it. Most direct extrapolation of our own conditions and forms—social and political but also immanently material—has been in effect or in intention dystopian: atomic war, famine, overpopulation, electronic surveillance have written 1984 into millennia of possible dates. To live otherwise, commonly, is to be other and elsewhere: a desire displaced by alienation and in this sense cousin to phases of the utopian, but without the specific of a connected or potentially connecting transformation and then again without the ties of a known condition and form. So that while the utopian transformation is social and moral, the science-fiction transformation, in its dominant Western modes, is at once beyond and beneath: not social and moral but natural; in effect, as so widely in Western thought since the late nineteenth century, a mutation at the point of otherwise intolerable exposure and crisis: not so much a new life as a new species, a new nature.

It is then interesting, within this largely alternative mode, to find a clear example of an evidently deliberate return to the utopian tradition, in Ursula K. Le Guin's *The Dispossessed* (1974). It is a return within some of the specific conditions of science fiction. The alternative society is on the moon of a far planet, and space-travel and electronic communication—to say nothing of the possibilities of the 'ansible', that device for instantaneous space-wide communication developed from the theory of simultaneity—permit interaction between the alternative and the original society, within a wider interaction of other galactic civilizations. At one level the spaceship and the ansible can do no more, technically, than the sea voyage, the cleft in the underground cavern or, crucially, the dream. But they permit, instrumentally, what is also necessary for another and more serious reason: the sustained comparison of the utopian and the non-utopian options.

The form of the novel, with its alternating chapters on Anarres and Urras, is designed for this exploratory comparison. And the reason is the historical moment of this looking again at utopia: the moment of renewed social and political hope, of a renewed alternative social and political morality, in a context which has one variable from the ordinary origins of the utopian mode, that within the world in which the hope is being interestedly if warily examined there is not, or apparently not, the overwhelming incentive of war, poverty, and disease. When Morris's dreamer goes back from twenty-first to nineteenth century London the questions are not only moral; they are directly physical, in the evidently avoidable burdens of poverty and squalor. But when Le Guin's Shevek goes from Anarres to Urras he finds, within the place provided for him, an abundance, an affluence, a vitality, which are sensually overwhelming in comparison with his own moral but arid world. It is true that when he steps out of his privileged place and discovers the class underside of this dominant prosperity the comparison is qualified, but that need only mean that the exuberant affluence depends on that class relationship and that the alternative is still a shared and equal relative poverty. It is true also that the comparison is qualified, in the novel as a whole, by what is in effect a note that our own civilization—that of Earth, which in its North American sector Urras so closely and deliberately resembles—has been long destroyed: 'appetite' and 'violence' destroyed it; we did not 'adapt' in time; some survivors live under the ultimate controls of 'life in the ruins'. But this, strictly, is by the way. Urras, it appears, is not in such danger; Anarres remains a social and moral option, a human alternative to a society that is, in its extended dominant forms, successful. Yet it is among its still repressed and rejected that the impulse stirs, renewing itself, after a long interval, to follow the breakaway revolution, anarchist and socialist, which took the Odonians from Urras to a new life on Anarres. Shevek's journey is the way back and the way forward: a dissatisfaction with what has happened in the alternative society but then a strengthened renewal of the original impulse to build it. In two evident ways, then, *The Dispossessed* has the marks of its period: the wary questioning of the utopian impulse itself, even within its basic acceptance;

the uneasy consciousness that the superficies of utopia—affluence and abundance—can be achieved, at least for many, by non-utopian and even anti-utopian means.

The shift is significant, after so long a dystopian interval. It belongs to a general renewal of a form of utopian thinking—not the education but the learning of desire—which has been significant among Western radicals since the struggles and also since the defeats of the 1960s. Its structures are highly specific. It is a mode within which a privileged affluence is at once assumed and rejected: assumed and in its own ways enjoyed, yet known, from inside, as lying and corrupt; rejected, from in close, because of its successful corruption; rejected, further out, by learning and imagining the condition of the excluded *others*. There is then the move to drop out and join the excluded; a move to get away, to get out from under, to take the poorer material option for a clear moral advantage. For nothing is more significant, in Le Guin's contrasted worlds, than that Anarres, the utopia, is bleak and arid; the prosperous vitality of the classical utopia is not there but in the existing society that is being rejected. This is a split of a major kind. It is not that Anarres is primitivist: 'they knew that their anarchism was the product of a very high civilization, of a complex diversified culture, of a stable economy and a highly industrialized technology.' In this sense, the modification of Morris˙is important; it is clearly a future and not a past, a technically advanced rather than a simplified form. But it is significantly only available in what is in effect a waste land; the good land is in the grip of the Urrasti dominance. It is then in effect the movement that Huxley imagined, in his 1946 foreword. It is not the transformation, it is the getaway.

Yet it is a generous and open getaway, within the limited conditions of its waste-land destination. The people of Anarres live as well, in all human terms, as Morris's cooperators; mutuality is shown to be viable, in a way all the more so because there is no abundance to make it easy. The social and ethical norms are thus at the highest point of the utopian imagination. But then there is a wary questioning beyond them: not the corrosive cynicism of the dystopian mode, but a reaching beyond basic mutuality to new kinds of individual responsibility and, with them, choice, dissent, and conflict. For this, again of its period, is an open utopia: forced open, after the congealing of ideals, the degeneration of mutuality into conservatism; shifted, deliberately, from its achieved harmonious condition, the stasis in which the classical utopian mode culminates, to restless, open, risk-taking experiment. This is a significant and welcome adaptation, depriving utopia of its classical end of struggle, its image of perpetual harmony and rest. This deprivation, like the waste land, may be seen as daunting, as the cutting-in of elements of a dominant dystopia. But whereas the waste land is voluntary deprivation, by the author—the product of a defeatist assessment of the possibilities of transformation in good and fertile country—the openness is in fact a strengthening. Indeed it is probably only to such a utopia that those who have known affluence and known with it social injustice and moral corruption can be summoned. It is not the last journey. In particular it is not the journey which all those still subject to extreme exploitation, to avoidable poverty and disease, will imagine themselves making: a transformed this-world, of course with all the imagined and undertaken and fought-for modes of transformation. But it is where, within a capitalist dominance, and within the crisis of power and affluence which is also the crisis of war and waste, the utopian impulse now warily, self-questioningly, and setting its own limits, renews itself.

The Welsh Industrial Novel

Walking from Swansea to Neath on a 'dull and gloomy afternoon' in
November 1854, George Borrow had 'surmounted a hill' when

> an extraordinary scene presented itself to my eyes. Somewhat to the
> south rose immense stacks of chimneys surrounded by grimy diaboli-
> cal-looking buildings, in the neighbourhood of which were huge
> heaps of cinders and black rubbish. From the chimneys, notwith-
> standing it was Sunday, smoke was proceeding in volumes, choking
> the atmosphere all around. From this pandemonium, at the distance
> of about a quarter of a mile to the south-west, upon a green meadow,
> stood, looking darkly grey, a ruin of vast size with window holes,
> towers, spires and arches. Between it and the accursed pandemon-
> ium, lay a horrid filthy place, part of which was swamp and part
> pool: the pool black as soot, and the swamp of a disgusting leaden
> colour. Across this place of filth stretched a tramway leading seem-
> ingly from the abominable mansions to the ruin. So strange a scene I
> had never beheld in nature. Had it been on canvas, with the addition
> of a number of diabolical figures, proceeding along the tramway, it
> might have stood for Sabbath in Hell—devils proceeding to
> afternoon worship, and would have formed a picture worthy of the
> powerful but insane painter Jerome Bos.[1]

The painter, presumably, is Old Hieronymo. Borrow turned to him
again when he arrived at Merthyr, which

> can show several remarkable edifices though of a gloomy horrid
> Satanic character. There is the hall of the Iron, with its arches, from
> whence proceeds incessantly a thundering noise of hammers. Then
> there is an edifice at the foot of a mountain, halfway up the side of
> which is a blasted forest and on the top an enormous crag. A truly
> wonderful edifice it is, such as Bos would have imagined had he
> wanted to paint the palace of Satan.[2]

[1] *Wild Wales*, 1862, ch. 102.
[2] Ibid., ch. 104.

That is one way of seeing what is now, more politely, called industrial development. So conscious a view of a sketch for Hell is one of the ways of seeing which led to the industrial novel. It was not confined to vagrant, romantic, literary men. Consider this from the inventor of the steam hammer, James Nasmyth, in his autobiography as edited by Samuel Smiles:

> The Black Country is anything but picturesque. The earth seems to have been turned inside out. Its entrails are strewn about; nearly the entire surface of the ground is covered with cinder-heaps and mounds of scoriae. The coal, which has been drawn from below ground, is blazing on the surface. The district is crowded with iron furnaces, puddling furnaces, and coal-pit engine furnaces. By day and by night the country is glowing with fire, and the smoke of the ironworks hovers over it. There is a rumbling and clanking of iron forges and rolling mills. Workmen covered with smut, and with fierce white eyes, are seen moving about amongst the glowing iron and the dull thud of forge-hammers.
>
> Amidst these flaming, smoky, clanging works, I beheld the remains of what had once been happy farmhouses, now ruined and deserted. The ground underneath them had sunk by the working out of the coal, and they were falling to pieces. They had in former times been surrounded by clumps of trees; but only the skeletons of them remained, dilapidated, black, and lifeless. The grass had been parched and killed by the vapours of sulphureous acid thrown out by the chimneys; and every herbaceous object was of a ghastly gray—the emblem of vegetable death in its saddest aspect. Vulcan had driven out Ceres.[3]

What we can observe, in each case, is an authentic sense of shock at the unaccustomed sight of an industrial landscape, and the mediation of this shock through received conventional images: the panorama of Hell, as painted by Bosch, or the irruption of the classical Vulcan. There is much writing of this kind in the nineteenth century, but it is only a step towards a new kind of novel. For within the panorama there are as yet no men, or men are there only as figures attendant on this landscape. The apparent chaos of their labour has within this perspective obliterated or incorporated them. The movement towards the industrial novel is then, in this phase, a movement towards describing what it is like to live in hell, and slowly, as the disorder becomes an habitual order, what it is like to get used to it, to grow up in it, to see it as home.

[3] James Nasmyth, *An Autobiography*, ed. Samuel Smiles, 1883.

But that full movement is not yet. The first phase of the industrial novel is a particular crystallization within English culture, from the mid-1840s to the mid-1850s, when a group of middle-class novelists, for the most part not themselves living in the industrial areas, began to explore this turbulent human world. Charles Dickens visited Preston, and his first response to it, in the Coketown of *Hard Times*, is in the panoramic manner:

> a town of red brick, or of brick that would have been red if the smoke and ashes had allowed it; but as matters stood it was a town of unnatural red and black, like the painted face of a savage.[4]

In this first general view Coketown

> contained several large streets all very like one another, and many small streets still more like one another;

an accurate enough observation, but then

> inhabited by people equally like one another;

the external, incorporating perspective, which, characteristically, Dickens did not sustain or try to sustain for a moment, once he touched other springs and made his always variable people—Dickensian people very unlike one another—move and relate. And that second look is the significant transition. Not only are you not a devil if you live in this new sketch of Hell; you are not an automaton if you are a secular Vulcan; you are not a savage if you live in this savage-looking landscape. But you are still, perhaps, a labouring man and only a labouring man. Certainly that external, representative and as a matter of fact highly class-conscious perspective is the method of other novelists in this group; of Disraeli, in *Sybil*; of Kingsley, in *Alton Locke*; even of Dickens among the workers in *Hard Times*. But the true second look came from the one novelist who lived in her landscape; Elizabeth Gaskell, especially in *Mary Barton*, and even more, if we could get back to it, in the abandoned first version of that novel, *John Barton*, when the crisis was not to be observed but experienced, internalized; the world of industrial conflict seen from the point of view of a militant who is at the same time

> my hero, *the* person with whom all my sympathies went.

[4] London 1854, Book I, ch. 5.

Under pressure she drew back from that transforming identification, but still what she wrote was the best of these early English industrial novels: a story of these changes happening to people who were, are and remain individual human beings through all the fierce and dynamic trajectories of social and economic transformation and conflict. All these English middle-class novelists observed the industrial landscape under the pressure of industrial and political crisis: specifically the crisis of Chartism. All shaped what they saw and show with images and narratives of the reconciliation of conflict. That part of their ideology is easily recognized. But all to some extent, and Elizabeth Gaskell to a remarkable extent, succeeded in peopling this strange, fierce world; succeeded, that is, in the crucial transition from the industrial panorama to the industrial novel.

It was a remarkable crystallization, but what is also remarkable is that it did not last. As the social crisis faded, as it assumed new forms, other forms of fiction succeeded it. There is a brief and altered example in the 1860s, in George Eliot's *Felix Holt*, shaped by the crisis of the suffrage. There is a specific new form, in the 1880s, in the novels of George Gissing, *The Nether World* and *Demos*, but these, as more simply in the Cockney School of the 1890s, are primarily novels of the crisis of the city—of course the industrial city which London's East End had become, but also that East End against a West End; an area of darkness—'Darkest London'—physically contiguous but socially in another world from the luxurious and powerful Imperial capital. These novels again coincide with a period of open crisis: the new class struggles of London's East End. There is also a new ideology: not now of reconciliation, and not only of shattered hopelessness; rather a sour distancing, as between East and West, and specifically, as Gissing goes on, a distancing between the lives of working people and the values of literature: a distance which has become institutional in that dominant fraction of English writing. Lawrence, of course, was to come, but we can understand some of his difficulties as well as part of his development if we remember that characteristic comment by Katharine Mansfield, on one of his plays, that it was 'black with miners'.

Black with miners, meanwhile, were the valleys of South Wales. There, indeed, was to be a new crystallization, a new form of the industrial novel. But knowing what we do of the history, this coming of the Welsh industrial novel is, at first sight, surprisingly late. It is the lateness as well as the significant emergence that we have now to try to understand.

In certain respects, and notably in ironworking and in mining, the Industrial Revolution came almost as early to Wales as to England. By the middle of the nineteenth century three workers out of five in Wales were in jobs not connected with farming. One in three were in mines, quarries and industrial enterprises. But then in the second half of the nineteenth century there was a further major transformation: the intense development of valleys like the Rhondda, in the independent coal trade; the very rapid expansion of Cardiff as a coal port. But still, through almost the whole of the nineteenth century, the Welsh industrial novels did not come. There is perhaps one quite general reason for this, which would be relevant also in England. The English industrial novelists, when you look more closely, touched mainly the textile districts, the new mills, or as in Kingsley the sweatshops of London. George Eliot, in the next generation, is in touch mainly with craftsmen, though she is aware, as in *Felix Holt*, of a mining district, of which she is clearly imaginatively (and perhaps otherwise) nervous. There may be complex differentials, here, in the kinds of working-class life and community which are accessible to this kind of observing fiction. It may be significant that the first internal English working-class novel—Tressell's *Ragged-Trousered Philanthropists*—is set in the small-scale provincial building trade: a social location which has important effects on its tone; the small, relatively unorganized group as distinct from the major collectives of large-scale industry. Thus it is not, even in English, until the second decade of the twentieth century, with Lawrence, that fiction effectively touches the kinds of industry and community which have been most important in Wales. So in that sense, for these kinds of work, there is perhaps no specifically Welsh delay. But there is nevertheless, I believe, a distinguishably Welsh reason for lateness, and this has to do, above all, with the central problems of language and the literary tradition. These are still very difficult to analyze, but you have only to look at the English-language and Welsh-language literary traditions, at any point in the nineteenth century, to see how much more central, in English, was the tradition of prose fiction. Moreover, in just that century, and closely involved with the social and economic consequences of industrialism, the relations between Welsh and English, within the country, were decisively changing. It is difficult to be certain, but one might risk the hypothesis that Welsh industrial working-class life was relatively inaccessible to the new kind of fiction because of the combined influence of the types of working-class community (which were also still inaccessible in English), of the relative lack of motivated and competent middle-class observers, and, perhaps prepotently, because of the problems of the two languages and the relative unfamiliarity, in Welsh, of the appropriate realist form.

Those may be the reasons for delay, but they are also, in the twentieth century, reasons for the special character of the Welsh industrial novels when they at last appear. For, unlike the English nineteenth-century examples, when they come they are, in majority, written from *inside* the industrial communities; they are working-class novels in the new and distinctive twentieth-century sense. Thus, for all their problems—and these, as we shall see, are many—they compose, when they come, a distinctive and special contribution.

The decisive decade was to be the nineteen-thirties, but it is necessary to pick up a few scattered earlier examples. In Welsh there is John Thomas's *Arthur Llwyd* (1879; 1892), which includes an account of the opening of a mine in farming country, but this is really a scene within a different kind of fiction: a temperance novel. T. Gwynn Jones's *Gwilym Bevan* (1900) has the life of a quarryman. Then, in writing in English, there is one significant moment of emergence or perhaps, more strictly, pre-emergence. It can be traced to 1871, in what the writer concerned described as the 'charming, pastoral village' of Mountain Ash.

Joseph Keating was the son of an immigrant Irish Catholic, and grew up in The Barracks, the Catholic settlement, very aware of his family's difference from the West Country immigrants in Newtown and of course from the native Welsh, in just the years when the pits there were opening. He went down the pit at the age of twelve and worked there until he was sixteen. Then he moved out to clerical work and eventually to journalism, on the *Western Mail* in Cardiff and then to London. He was writing novels—among them *Gwen Lloyd*, *Maurice*, and *Son of Judith*—from the late 1890s, and he published an interesting autobiography, *My Struggle for Life*, in 1916. Keating—Kating as he liked it to be pronounced—is significant as an example of a much wider cultural history. From the beginning of the formation of the industrial working class—as indeed earlier, among rural labourers, craftsmen and shepherds—there were always individuals with the zeal and capacity to write, but their characteristic problem was the relation of their intentions and experience to the dominant literary forms, shaped primarily as these were by another and dominant class. Within a relatively coherent religious culture, the difficulties were less formidable; the modes of witness, confession and praise were more generally accessible. But within a culture and especially a literature in which contemporary social experience had become important and even central, as is clearly the case in English after the bourgeois consolidation of the eighteenth century, the situation of the working-class writer is exceptionally difficult. In verse he may have the support of traditional popular forms, and these produced, in fact, an important body of street ballads and work songs. But in prose the forms which are nearest to him are the autobiography and the novel, and it is significant that for several generations it was the autobiography that proved most accessible. These writers, after all, although very conscious of their class situations, were at the same time, within it, exceptional men, and there are central formal features of the autobiography which correspond to this situation: at once the representative and the exceptional account. The formal features of the novel, on the other hand, had no such correspondence. The received conventional plots—the propertied marriage and settlement; the intricacies of inheritance; the exotic adventure; the abstracted romance—are all, for obvious reasons, at a distance from working-class life. It is then hardly surprising that for several generations the most powerful writing of working-class experience is in autobiographies. Indeed this situation has lasted so long that one might still say that the most effective writing about mining life in South Wales is in the autobiographical work of B.L. Coombes, and especially in *These Poor Hands*.

But there is of course another and at first sight plausible tactic: to accept one of the dominant forms and to insert, to graft on to it, these other experiences, of work and struggle. There is a considerable history of such attempts, but Keating is significant because he illustrates the consequent problems so graphically. I will take as an example *The Flower of the Dark*, published in 1917: a novel which contains, in separation, several remarkable elements, but which taken as it comes, as it essentially presents itself, has quite specific significant difficulties.

The first difficulty is to get past the second page:

> The mountains under her small feet had made her a rich young woman, owing to the fact that dark workings of collieries, in which she held the largest share of proprietorship, ran beneath her lawn and increased her

wealth while she amused herself or slept in gentle happiness. Whether she had ten thousand or twenty thousand pounds a year she had never tried to discover. Before she had come into the world, Richard Parry, her father, had bought a few fields, knowing that there was coal under them. Her mother had died while her father was struggling to get rich. Mr Parry had become rich. Then he died, and the fruit of the golden tree he had planted dropped into his daughter's red mouth.

It is so high a romantic strain, not to know whether you have ten or twenty thousand a year, that even the 'orange aigrette' in Aeronwy's hair and her 'brocaded shoes with emerald heels and buckles of emeralds' may not quite pull you through.

Yet this is the real problem, for in less than thirty pages you are in another world:

> Tomos, in his stall far down and in under the mountains, with his lamp swinging at his belt, was testing the coal with his mandrel. He had stripped himself to the waist, as the place was warm. A forest of posts held up the roof, which was so low that he was bent almost in double beneath it. He had worked in the Cragwyn mine since he was a boy of seven and knew every subtle characteristic of coal, as far as getting it out of its bed was concerned. Each swing of his pick was the stroke of a master craftsman. His mandrel was the inspired tool of an artist achieving the complete expression of an idea. He cut skilfully. Yet when the big slip came down, it crumbled as if it were only black flour. Tomos, coughing in the cloud of dust, swore at the heap of rottenness. He wanted big lumps for his tram, but could only see two or three bits like pickled walnuts in the dust on the ground. He tried again at another slip. His task was troublesome, owing to the impossibility of cutting out any large pieces, and he frequently paused to gaze in sorrow at the seam, with his lamp held close to it. The face did not shine under the rays as good coal would have done. It looked dull and dismal. It had all the jointures and sections of coal formation. But when the sharp points of the mandrel touched it, it shuddered and broke as if it were nothing but solidified mud veined with slag and bast that stretched across it like rows of old wounds on a black man's cheek.
>
> 'Is it worth while trying to earn a living in the Cragwyn pit?' Tomos was asking himself seriously, as all pay for his work depended on the number of tons of solid coal he sent out.

What Keating is writing here, of work in which he had shared, is an unusually early and an exceptionally strong realization of the shift that most mattered: the shift to work as a primary kind of consciousness: that shift which is still so rare even in the most social, most industrial of novels, and which is held at a fictive distance in the overwhelming majority of fictions. Here, but of course only fragmentarily—as I said, inserted, temporarily allowed—is a working man's consciousness: his consciousness as working man.

Yet no such consciousness determines the form of the novel. In its place, corresponding no doubt to Keating's own trajectory but also and more decisively to his period and its dominant ideology, interfused as it was with a dominant and popular fictional form, the shaping element is that of the romantic heroine's choice between a good and a bad man, and the good man, significantly, is a hardworking manager, while the bad man—but there the ideology and the date are decisive—the bad man, Cragwen, is selling his coal to the German Navy, while all the good people are producing it for the British Navy. Within this direct presentation of the patriotic romance, the other elements—all potential elements of a quite different kind of novel; realistic accounts of strikes, of blackleg colliers, of conscription, of a slide of a slagtip—are not only diluted; they are fundamentally displaced; incidentally substantial, like the account of Tomos at the coalface, but then formally instrumental to the structure which overrides them, of which the only real outcome, after all, is that Aeronwy marries her Osla.

That is as late as 1917, just a few years before the decisive events that shaped a new phase of Welsh history and culture, and with it a new generation of writers. What we can now see, from those years between the wars—years of profound depression and of intense struggle—is the emergence of what is, I believe, within the general category of the industrial novel, a specifically Welsh structure of feeling, but a structure still facing quite radical problems of form.

What basically informs the industrial novel, as distinct from other kinds of fiction? Both the realist and the naturalist novel, more generally, had been predicated on the distinctive assumption—I say assumption, though if I were not being academic I would say, more shortly, the distinctive truth—that the lives of individuals, however intensely and personally realized, are not just influenced but in certain crucial ways formed by general social relations. Thus industrial work, and its characteristic places and communities, are not just a new background: a new 'setting' for a story. In the true industrial novel they are seen as formative. Social relations are not assumed, are not static, are not conventions within which the tale of a marriage or an inheritance or an adventure can go its own way. The working society—actual work, actual relations, an actual and visibly altered place—is in the industrial novel central: not because, or not necessarily because, the writer is 'more interested in sociology than in people'—which is what a degraded establishment criticism would have us believe—but because in these working communities it is a trivial fantasy to suppose that these general and pressing conditions are for long or even at all separable from the immediate and the personal. The abstracted categories of 'social' and 'personal' are here, in these specific human conditions—the conditions, moreover, of the great majority of human beings—interfused and inextricable though not always indistinguishable. The privileged distances of another kind of fiction, where people can 'live simply as human beings', beyond the pressures and interruptions and accidents of society, are in another world or more specifically in another class. Here, in the world of the industrial novel—as indeed in the best rural fiction; in Hardy for example—work is pressing and formative, and the most general social relations are directly experienced within the most personal.

So then, if we have learned to look in this way, it is no surprise to find at the centre of so many of the Welsh industrial novels of this period one decisive experience: the General Strike of 1926 in its specifically Welsh form; that is to say the General Strike followed by the long months of the miners' lockout, by the long years of depression, and, very deeply, by the pervasive sense of defeat. The defeat becomes fused with the more general sadness of a ravaged, subordinated and depressed Wales, but also, and from both these sources, there is the intense consciousness of struggle—of militancy and fidelity and of the real human costs these exact; the conflicts within the conflict; the losses and frustrations; the ache of depression and that more local and acute pain which comes only to those who have known the exhilaration of struggle and who also come to know, having given everything, that they have still not given enough; not enough in the terms of this world, which has not been changed, which has even, in the Depression, got worse.

But then also, beyond this, and very specific to this particular community, there is a structure of feeling which has one of its origins in the very distinctive physical character of the Welsh industrial areas, and beyond that in the distinctive physical character of Wales as a whole. The immediate landscape, the physical presence of industrial development, in the era of steam and coal, is almost invariably dark, smoke-ridden, huddled. These are its true physical bearings. In the mines these general qualities are intensified: the sense of darkness, of running grime, of a huddled enclosure. Yet not only in coming back up from the pit, to a general daylight, but also at any time in any Welsh mining valley, there is the profoundly different yet immediately accessible landscape of open hills and the sky above them, of a rising light and of a clear expansion, into which it is possible, both physically and figuratively, to move. These familiar experiences of the hills above us are profoundly effective, even when they are commonplaces, in so much Welsh feeling and thought. But in this specific environment they have a further particular effect. There are sheep on the hills, often straying down into the streets of the settlements. The pastoral life, which had been Welsh history, is still another Welsh present, and in its visible presence—not as an ideal contrast but as the slope, the skyline, to be seen immediately from the streets and from the pit-tops—it is a shape which manifests not only a consciousness of history but a consciousness of alternatives, and then, in a modern form, a consciousness of aspirations and possibilities. The traditional basic contrasts of darkness and light, of being trapped and of getting clear, are here on the ground in the most specific ways, and are the deepest basic movement of all this writing.

Yet there are problems in interlocking this basic rhythm—the adequate basis of so many poems—with the close and absorbing human relations of any industrial novel. As imagery it can run, but there are still acute compositional difficulties between these essentially general feelings and any accessible human formations. I want now to look briefly at some of the local forms through which these shared general feelings were in fact articulated, and at this level, inevitably, it is a story of some losses as well as some gains, of limitations as well as of achievements.

The most accessible immediate form, in this kind of novel, is the story of a family. This gives the writer his focus on primary relationships but of course with the difficulty that what is really being written, through it, is the story of a class; indeed effectively, given the local historical circumstances, of a people. The family has then to be typical, carrying the central common experiences, but in relationships, in a *bonding*, which are in the whole experience much wider. And there is then a further problem. The immediate family can be seen, from much attested experience, as the local bonding, of love and care, against the general hardship. But then, in one powerful form, what happens to this family, as not only industrial development, and not only industrial conflict, but now industrial depression, at once unites it in a common condition and then pulls it this way and that, dividing or even breaking it, in the struggle for survival. Gwyn Jones's *Times Like These*, published in 1936, is a memorable example of this form. Its deliberately general social and historical placing, signalled by its title, interacts with this at once real and formal emphasis on a family: the immediate nuclear relationships but within them the spread of alternatives, the pressures to go different ways, including going away altogether, solving their problems differently. There is then a characteristic tension of this generation of Welsh writing: that the family is being pulled in one direction after another and yet that the family persists, but persists in a sense of defeat and loss. The bitter experience of that period—of the massive emigrations to England and yet of the intense and persistent family feeling of those who stay and those who remember—are then powerfully but always temporarily articulated: the moment of a very local sadness:

> Do without—that's what we always been doing, Luke told himself, back in his old bed. Always doing without something or other. What did Olive ever have out of life? Or mam? Mary was a lucky un, she was. Poor old Olive! I do miss that bad, look, Olive. His eyes filled with tears, and he was very conscious that the bed was unshared. 'Never mind,' he could hear his father saying: 'We can manage, ay. We'll manage, mam.' P'raps they would.
>
> At last he slept, not lonely in sleep, until towards morning he awoke to hear the clatter and tramp of the depleted night shift returning over the hill to Camden. That was life, that was: sleeping and waking to one empty day after another. No need to get up yet, for there was nothing a fellow could do. It passed a bit of time to stay in bed. 'Indeed to God,' he said quietly, and without profanity, 'what are we in the world for? Everything do seem useless, somehow.'

THE END

Another memorable example of this same basic form—of the immediate family but of that family under pressure—is the later *Chwalfa* (1946) of T. Rowland Hughes: in the different environment of the North Wales slate quarries, and in the earlier historical crisis of the struggle over the contract system, the long strike and its repression, and then what happened to a community but now in formal immediacy to a family: the dispersal (*Chwalfa*)—to the waterworks at Rhayader, to the Liverpool docks, to America, to coal and copper mining. The old simple nucleus, in which there are organically extending links between family, village, place and class—and in and through all these, of course, the specific link of Welshness—is at once affirmed and seen in dispersal. The very form of the affirmation, of the family carrying these general meanings, is then in effect an elegy: what is affirmed is also lost. Or, as more generally in this period of Welsh writing, loss and dispersal are what are most closely affirmed.

Of course this is not the only way in which the family can be used as an immediate compositional form. In Lewis Jones's novels—*Cwmardy* (1937) and *We Live* (1939) a related but different general orientation is evident. The family, now, is an epitome of political struggle, and the conflicting versions and affiliations of that struggle are represented not only generally—in the events of the lockout and the struggles in the Miners' Federation and between parties—but inside the family, between Len and Mary and Ezra—and the movement in the end, for all the loss that is attested, is beyond the family, in a kind of willing break: the transfer of affiliation to a cause and to a party.

We can now easily see the problems, in this as in the earlier form. The deep and unmediated dispersal, breaking, of the family can end in a sense of enclosed loss. The political projection of a family can move out from this, but the move only retains its validity—a validity of substance—while the form of the affiliation remains unproblematic. Yet how problematic it was—in a serious sense, beyond the details of immediate and divisive controversies—we can see if we turn to a quite different form, that of Jack Jones's *Rhondda Roundabout* (1934), which some people say is not really a novel at all. The difficulty with the insertion of a complex political struggle into a local family form is that it can quickly become too selectively exemplary, and then too early limited by exemplary consonances of personal quality and political correctness. The episodic randomness which the very title of *Rhondda Roundabout* so directly signals is indeed a kind of loss; an affective loss. But it is an attempt, very similar in some ways to *The Ragged-Trousered Philanthropists*, which it partly resembles also in tone, to write to the variety, the complexity and—crucially—the *disconnections* of a wide political and cultural life. Certainly Tressell found a unity, at another thematic level, which Jack Jones did not, but the point is really how this episodic form moves, if jerkily and unrelatedly, towards the wider shape of the actual society, a shape which characteristically the family form had compressed. Moves towards but does not arrive. What comes through, as so often in working-class writers, when for understandable reasons the received forms are unavailable or are refused, is a series of sketches, at most a panorama. It is not a new whole form, but it can include elements which older whole forms could not.

In his later work Jack Jones moved, with others, to a particular form which is one of the available extensions of the family novel: the family as history, not the years of one generation but of several generations. *Black Parade* (1935) was originally three times as long as its published version, and this raises a general point. There are many internal problems of form in the twentieth-century novel, but there are some outstanding external problems, and notable among them this problem of length. By our own day the commercially preferred, and often imposed, length of a novel is some eighty thousand words; and indeed that is long enough for some kinds of fiction. But for one important kind of fiction, and especially for the extending realist novel, it is absurdly restrictive. A dominant mode in English fiction has in any case moved away from these themes as well as this form. But for Welsh writers, less willing than those English to restrict or cancel their sense of community and of history, it is a special kind of obstacle. A contemporary writer, in this extended realist mode, is expected or required to make a whole work at a length which is less than a quarter or a sixth of earlier works of this kind. Every writer can cut, and almost always with advantage, but this basic pressure on length remains a major limitation of this otherwise attractive and experienced form.

Black Parade, nevertheless, shows what can be gained by a sense of historical movement. The black despair of locality can, paradoxically, be surpassed in the run of the years. In the run from the rough years of immigration into the coalfield, down to the thirties and emigration, there is a strong perspective, and it is interesting that increasingly it is this historical perspective, as a formal element, that novelists have sought. But historical perspective is not the only sense of history, even in *Black Parade*. Waiting seductively for this form is another, the historical romance.

It is always difficult to make any categorical distinction between the historical novel and the historical romance. Except at the extremes of the simpler form, which are really not even romance but costume fiction, the same apparent elements enter the composition, and, in the case of Welsh industrial fiction, it could even be said that more history—both the wider process and the critical details—can be found in the romances than in the novels. Actually one of the possible distinctions is closely related to this fact, since the mode of realist fiction both allows and requires its characters to exist at moments other than those of manifest and colourful historical crisis, whereas the mode of romance enacts a kind of absolute convergence between selected familiar persons and the best known events. It is indeed in this respect that we must remind ourselves that there is no necessary generic superiority of the realist mode: some kinds of convergence enact a deeper movement than the more bystanding and incidental versions of realism.

Black Parade is strong because, in its earliest periods at least, it includes the many-sided turbulence, the incoherence and contradictions, which the more available stereotypes of the history exclude. It can be properly contrasted with Richard Llewellyn's *How Green Was My Valley* (1939) on just this point, and the contrast indicates one of the terms in which the more general contrast of forms can be described. It is not that the realist mode excludes either sentiment or rhetoric. It is rather that the romance is wholly organized by a single, central, sentimental or rhetorical figuration, which is at once its simple and particular coherence, its readily indeed instantly communicable potency, and of course, at any second look, its form of excluding limitation or reduction. But *How Green Was My Valley*, widely and properly seen as the export version of the Welsh industrial experience, is not the most difficult case to understand. Its sentimental figuration is of its period, but perhaps that is not its only difference from the rhetorical figurations of Alexander Cordell. For what remains remarkable in Cordell is the scale of the admission, to be sure within this mode, of a history at once wide and intense: a history that writers closer to its specific consequences, less able to stand back and read the general history of a place and a people, had not, at least at first, been eager or even willing to include. At the same time this work can be no more than transitional. Its rhetorical figuration, boldly announced and resolutely executed in *The Rape of the Fair Country* (1959) and similar so-to-say headline novels, was perhaps understandably inaccessible, from deep inside the culture, in a period of close-up contemporary depression and militancy. The will to a wider perspective, always more readily accessible to a fascinated observer than to the sons and daughters of the history who had its defeats, its settlements, its local rhythms and local fractures in their bones, has now increasingly more pull, more weight, in a different phase of the national culture. It is at any rate in this direction that much contemporary writing is moving.

Yet in fact, at a turning point from the one period to the other, and from inside the culture, there was one major achievement which in effect stands quite alone, although its general connections with the underlying structure of feeling, and with the more particular elements so far described, are very close. Gwyn Thomas's *All Things Betray Thee* (1949) is a remarkable creative achievement. Its mode is surprising, in retrospect, both in its deliberate distance from the close identifications of the realist manner, and in its effective distance from the simple figurations of romance. It has evident historical origins, not too far from the crises of nineteenth-century Merthyr. But it is not only that in place names and in style it is deliberately distanced—moving, indeed, in character and action, to an effectively legendary distance. It is also that in mode it is less representation—the common currency of fiction—than rehearsal and performance: a composition primarily governed by the rhythms of speech and song, in an action centred, at once traditionally and with a significant contemporary emphasis, on the harpist. Its inner movement is then the possibility of writing—singing, playing—this general experience: the first movement of art away from a turbulent involvement; the succeeding movement towards its deepest and most inevitable fidelities and commitments. There is then at once a wariness about the literary and ideological small change of the history, and yet the passion of discovery of what really lies beyond this and is more profoundly general. The deep structure of the novel is indeed very general: that awareness of light, of song, of human liberty, which are there close enough to grasp, yet seemingly always just out of reach, in the harsh close-up world of deprivation and struggle. It is for a people and not for a separated observer that one of its characters declares:

> Some of us are cursed with the urge to be making assertions that are either too big or too deep to fit into the box of current relations.

'Cursed', you notice; that deep ambiguity of a subordinated people, a subordinated class, whose visions are larger not only than those of the alien system by which they are dominated but larger also than is tolerable, when you are that far down and still seeing that far up. It is an extraordinarily difficult feeling to sustain. Follow the movement in this passage:

> 'Men like John Simon Adams and myself, we are not much more than leaves in the wind, bits of painful feeling that gripe the guts of

the masses. From the cottages, the hovels, the drink-shops and sweat-mills, anger rises and we are moved. No choice, Mr Connor, save perhaps the last-minute privilege of adjusting the key of the scream we utter.'

The voices are indeed of that kind: anger rising, painfully, fragmentarily, as the decisive alternative to 'a replete and sodden silence'. But the movement is so precarious that the voice literally hesitates in the throat. Just beyond that consciousness is another tone: the relieving irrelevance, the bitter displacing joke, the distracting or reductive idiosyncrasy which not only keeps the pain at a distance but in time can be sure of its on-cue and relieving, exportable, laugh. Not here, however. Against every difficulty—and the weight is shown to be crushing—the accents of a fidelity at once visionary and historical are precisely achieved. It is a novel of voices and of a voice, and that voice is not only the history, it is the contemporary consciousness of the history.

At a point of transition; and every element of the transition is still, we do not need reminding, very bitterly contested. What is happening now, in a new kind of crisis, is a wider movement than that of the industrial experience alone, and if that movement ('nationalism') is sometimes evasive—for the body of the industrial experience is still here and still decisive— it is also, at its best, a reaching for new perspectives and new forms.

Meanwhile it is right to look back and to honour—honour because we know the difficulties; indeed know them too well, having so closely inherited them—that effective generation, that brotherhood of fiction writers; adapting, as we can, these words from *All Things Betray Thee*:

'We state the facts,' said Jameson. 'We state them now softly, now loudly. The next time it will be softly for our best voices will have ceased to speak. The silence and the softness will ripen. The lost blood will be made again. The chorus will shuffle out of its filthy aching corners and return. The world is full of voices, harpist, practising for the great anthem but hardly ever heard. We've been privileged. We've had our ears full of the singing. Silence will never be absolute for us again.'

5

Notes on Marxism in Britain Since 1945

'The neo-Marxist Left which now dominates the Labour Party', said a speaker at this year's Conservative Party conference.[1] Or it may have been 'near-Marxist Left', given the difficulty of ruling-class English with the consonant 'r'. In other speeches neither qualification was entered: the 'Marxist Left' now 'dominates the Labour Party'. Everything goes fuzzy as these terms circulate. What a triumph it would be if the main governing party of the last fifteen years were indeed now guided by a system of political thought which until 1960 and beyond was very generally regarded as un-English, irrelevant and irremediably out-of-date. To unpick the rhetoric which would induce such a fantasy is a complicated task, but looking back to 1945 one point can be made immediately. 'Marxist', in these years, has changed its meaning—or, more strictly, has taken on additional meanings. What would have been said in 1945, in the same kind of speech, was that the Labour Party was dominated, or at least heavily influenced, by 'Communists and fellow-travellers'. Of course, we still hear about 'Communists', or about 'Communists and Trotskyites', in the unions and elsewhere. But what is new is this all-purpose term 'Marxist' to describe—what? The whole Left in Britain, it usually seems, from *Tribune* to out of sight. And it is certainly a problem that this use co-exists with the phrases of polemic within the socialist culture, in which almost everyone can inform almost everyone else, in snappy and putting-down ways, that 'this position has nothing in common with Marxism', or that 'measured against Marxism this position reveals itself as . . .', and then comes the deluge.

What are the reasons for the shift in general use? And when did it

[1] 1976, but the description is so commonplace that it could be any recent year.

occur? These are the first questions about Marxism in Britain since 1945. Some of the reasons are not hard to find. Until 1956, though minor variants existed and were known to specialists, there was a simple general equation between Marxism and the ideological positions of the Communist Party, representing a body of Communist Parties led by that of the Soviet Union. From 1957 onwards, there was a rapid proliferation of other organizations and groups which claimed, if in different ways, the significant inheritance of revolutionary socialist practice and Marxist theory. It was reasonable, in this situation, to begin to speak more generally of 'the Marxist Left'. Then, from the early 1960s, there was the open ideological split between the Soviet Union and China, each with its ruling Communist Party and its competitive version of Marxist theory and practice. Variations extended from Cuba to Vietnam; Yugoslavia was remembered. 'Marxist' co-existed with 'Communist', but by the mid-1970s the liberation movements of Mozambique and Angola were known, in general English description, as 'Marxist guerrillas'. If it was a long way from FRELIMO and the MPLA to the Left of the Labour Party, still the general term was used, to cover a multitude of sinners.

But there is then, beyond this accessible history, an immediate problem. If Marxism is not only a theory but a theory of practice, it becomes very difficult to use the same general term to describe such evident variations of practice, and especially in Britain where (at least on the mainland) all known Marxist groups are taking part in an open and legal political process. This can be explained by referring to the specific conditions of British and other West European societies, but what then follows is the disappearance of any obvious dividing line between Marxists and other socialists. Certain extraordinary contortions around 'socialist' and 'social democrat', and around the (American) classifications of 'extremist' and 'moderate', have been attempted in order to redraw the line. But these have only further confused the general use of 'Marxist', since (and this is especially true in Britain) socialists who are not, do not claim to be, or positively deny that they are Marxists are nevertheless swept, by their 'socialist' or 'extremist' views, into the general 'Marxist' classification.

A Terminological Shift to the Right

This point has immediate relevance to the diagnosis that the 'Marxist Left' now dominates, or significantly influences, the Labour Party.

Looking back to 1945, it seems to me evident that there is a decisive continuity, over three decades, of what can be specifically identified as the
Labour Left. It is true that this is not easy to identify within any more
general range of theoretical positions, but this is because it is an amalgam
of theories within a specific practice, in specific social and historical conditions. Elements of Marxism, indeed, are part of the amalgam: the
general analysis of capitalist society, and the consequent policy of seizing
by nationalization at least the 'commanding heights'—the leading corporations, the banks, the insurance companies—of the economy. But
there are also significant elements of other systems: of Keynesianism, in
the generalized form of public intervention in a still mainly capitalist
('mixed') economy; of Fabianism, in a more extended public intervention, through planning agreements, in a still basically capitalist industry,
to expand production and to maintain full employment, and in the
specifically Fabian policy of appointed public boards and experts to
manage 'nationalized' (as distinct from 'socialized') industries and
services; of Liberalism—especially in its Lib-Lab phase—and again of
Fabianism, in its theory of the social services as the 'Welfare State'; of a
liberal anti-imperialism—*political* freedom for colonial peoples; and of a
non-Marxist, anti-capitalist critique of industrial capitalism and of militarism. We can identify this amalgam, now, as the Labour *Left*, but we
could once identify it (and can often still when it is in opposition) as the
Labour *Party*. In strictly Marxist terms, as I understand them, this is
precisely Social Democracy, in its post-1917 sense. It is also, in earlier
terms, a Parliamentary version of economism. For nothing is more significant, in the continuing formation of the Labour Left, than the centrality
of Parliament as the main—indeed often the only—agency for such
changes. In this it can generally be distinguished from the central modern
Marxist theories of the nature of a capitalist order and of state power. But
it is now *called*, flatly, Marxist. The whole spectrum of the political
vocabulary has then been moved to the right. For these relatively
orthodox and traditional Social Democrats are distinguished from others,
in the centre and right of the Labour Party, who retain only elements of
the amalgam, mainly Fabian, Keynesian and Lib-Lab, who have settled
permanently for the 'mixed economy' (capitalism sustained and made
more efficient by state intervention), for 'welfare' programmes financed
out of profits and out of growth, and—decisively—for military alliance
against socialist and national-liberation movements, but who are still

after this, after all this, *called* democratic socialists. Perhaps the time will soon come when they can complete, formally, their actual evolution, and become a frankly centrist (Democratic, Radical or Liberal) party. That would at least open some distance between them and the parliamentary socialists (Social Democrats) of the Labour Left.

If then, from these necessary distinctions, we identify the Labour Left as the real social democrats, we may have cleared the ground for a more accurate definition of Marxism and Marxists in Britain since 1945. But there is again an immediate difficulty. A majority of groups which would directly define themselves as Marxist have, throughout this period, identified themselves in practice, and in locally supporting theory, with just this version of Social Democracy. There have been extra emphases here and there: on workers' control of industry; on democratization of the social services; on solidarity with liberation movements; on withdrawal from the military alliances; on opposition to neo-colonialism. But all these emphases have been made also within the Labour Left. Until 1957, the only major and practical dividing line between the Labour Left and most Marxists was in attitudes to the Soviet Union. But while that still holds for the Communist Party, it does not hold in many other Marxist groupings. A majority of Marxist groups, meanwhile, support (as is said, critically) the election and continuation of a monopoly Labour Government. There are serious political reasons for all these connections and alliances, but there is the obvious danger, again, of sweeping the whole Left into the description 'Marxist' or, just as seriously, of sweeping all (or almost all) British Marxism into this amalgam of Left theory and practice.

The Three Strands of Theory

One way out of this confusion, which has been widely taken since the early 1960s, has been a concentration on Marxist theory. If political practice could be only occasionally and temporarily distinguished from a much broader spectrum of the Left, then at least in theoretical positions a distinctive Marxism could be maintained. But there are at least three strands within this 'theoretical' option, and it is important to distinguish them, even where in practice they have overlapped or coexisted within the same persons and groups. The earliest strand to appear, notably from 1957 but with isolated examples from the late forties, can be called 'legitimating' theory. Closely or exclusively connected with arguments about the character of Soviet society (and above all with this as reflected in the conflict between Stalin and Trotsky) this kind of work led to distinctions of theoretical and then often organized position in terms of the unfinished struggle within the world Communist movement. As world Communist divisions and variations became more open, theoretical and organizational reflections of all the major positions—Soviet, Fourth International, Chinese, Cuban, Yugoslav and eventually Euro-communist (Italian)—were adopted and asserted or reasoned in British theoretical work. What was at issue, in these cases, was the legitimate inheritance of an authentic Marxism—including the identification of an authentic Marxist Marx—and thus, hopefully, an authentic revolutionary tradition.

Then, secondly, there was a decisive insertion or re-insertion of Marxism into a range of strictly academic work. Again there had been earlier examples, but in the academic expansion of the sixties and early seventies there was a qualitative difference, quite evident to anyone who had also experienced the academic world of the forties and fifties. The strongest work was, significantly, in English history, which already had a strong base in the work of the Communist Party historians. But there were also significant contributions in economics, sociology, political and cultural theory, literary studies, and, most remarkably, in the history and scholarship of Marxist thought itself. This important body of academic work is, incidentally, yet another reason for the change in the usage of 'Marxist' and its common replacement of 'Communist'. For what was evident in most of this work was that it was academically professional history or economics or some other 'subject', which had also a set of distinctive theoretical assumptions or methodological procedures. It was, therefore, in an increasingly reputable and respectable sense, the work of Marxist academics: the question of 'communism' or one of its variants did not *necessarily* arise.

Thirdly, however—in some cases inextricable from work of the first or second kinds, in other cases quite clearly distinguishable—there was an attempt to build 'operative' theory: theoretical analysis of late capitalist society; theoretical analysis of the specificities of British late capitalist society; theoretical analysis of the consequent situations and agencies of socialist practice.

It is important to distinguish these three kinds of work—legitimating, academic and operative—because their varying proportions seem to me to determine the character of Marxism in Britain in different parts of this period (the leading period for operative theory, for example, was 1957-71, whereas we have since been, and still perhaps are, in a predominantly academic period). Each kind of work has had to be done. But while legitimating theory, at its best, leads to clearer orientations within an inescapably international political process, it can lead, at its worst, to a series of self-alienating options, in which our real political presence is as bystanders, historians or critics of the immense conflicts of other generations and other places, with only marginal or rhetorical connections to the confused and frustrating politics of our own time and place. Again while academic theory, at its best, gives us the necessary foundations for any operative theory, it can, at its worst, be quite quickly incorporated—the unlooked-for recognition of the untouchable becoming, rather smoothly, the invitation to stay—within the fluid eclecticism now characteristic of academic institutions, until even Marxism becomes a 'subject'.

Moreover, through the conflicts of legitimating theory, and in the very amplitude of academic theory (in its establishment of several clear and alternative Marxist traditions, and its critique of particular selective traditions), it has become more and more difficult to use 'Marxism' as the crucial definition of alignment which, in the late forties, it ordinarily was. It has become, that is to say, less and less an adherence to any significant kind of operative theory—a theory carrying practice—to announce, flatly, that one is a Marxist and (which follows in polemic as night follows day) that someone else is not, or is not yet, or might yet be, or could well be if he tried. Is or is not what?, any serious inquirer is bound to ask, as he sees the significant and important variations of operative Marxist theory (leaving aside the even wider variations of legitimating and academic theories) on such central questions as class, culture, the democratic process, the capitalist state, productive forces, the division of labour, industrial growth and political organization.

I do not mean that a significant affiliation to the Marxist tradition is not now possible, in good faith. On the contrary, I believe that in operative theory it is crucial, in the crisis we have now entered. But as it is made, in what may in many of its elements be unfamiliar ways, in the genuinely unprecedented social and economic crisis now so rapidly developing, it will be necessary to have continual discussion and contestation, and this will be only impeded if the polemical habit of measuring everything against a pure (and therefore often undefined) essence called Marxism is revived, as if this were 1948 or for that matter (in the persistent intellectual habits of a transposed Catholicism) 1483. It will indeed be necessary to move beyond the eclecticism of the 'New Left' of 1957-63, but only by identifying the altered social relations to which that mixed movement was a response, and by developing and completing theories of those altered social relations—rather than by reverting to the orthodoxies which then had to be *broken* (and not only by-passed) or, as irrelevantly, by resolving the confusions of political experience in an academically congenial formalism. It will be even more necessary, as a matter of direct practice, to move beyond the eclecticism—which has been brave and generous as well as limited and self-limited—of the Labour Left, but this will again be only impeded by the (on the evidence, quite unwarranted) assumption that, as practice rather than as study and critique, there is already a thing called Marxism which has simply to be announced and applied.

This may be seen more specifically if we look at three issues which have been important in Britain throughout the post-war period, and which are currently identified, at least in polemic, as populism, culturalism and reformism.

Populism

It is only in formalist or categorical criticism that we can speak of 'populism' as if it were some constant position. In radical history, from the bourgeois revolutions through to many parts of the labour movement, and in socialist history, in its significant and now crucial connection with national liberation movements, the habitual assumptions and strategies of populism—a mobilization of the existing resources of 'the people' against a native or alien ruling class—have an honourable record. At the same time we have seen, in the twentieth century, a 'populism' of the Right, superficially similar, in which a version of 'the people' is effectively mobilized, in periods of social crisis, as a way of altering the character of class rule or of foreclosing socialist solutions. If we note that both the assumptions and the rhetoric of 'populism' survived into much modern Marxism, even though the crucial redefinition into classes had been its major and distinctive theoretical contribution, we become aware of two problems: first, that most 'Marxist' movements, as distinct from some Marxist theories, grew out of and inherited and often depended on radical movements of other kinds; secondly, that the relation between 'class' and 'nation' ('people') proved to be exceptionally complex, and indeed is still complex.

In Britain since 1945, a form of populist proposition—the category 'the people'—has been very common in Marxism. It has also of course become common in the political rhetoric of every electoral party, including the most privileged and authoritarian (the similar evolution of 'democracy', as an electorally necessary article, is pertinent). Thinking now only of Marxism, I remember my 1939 induction, in literary studies, into topics and titles such as 'The Novel and the People', 'Poetry and the People', 'A People's Theatre'. I had initial sympathy with them; my own class and for that matter my own people had little representation in the orthodox cultural world that was offered to me. In that sense, and in the work which has been done within English Marxism, with notable fullness and authority in the decades since 1955, the impulse which some now characterize as 'populism' is strong and indispensable. And I still prefer the productive popular formations of the Left of the thirties, and their successors today in popular and community publishing and drama, to the largely critical milieu of one kind of later Marxism.

At the same time, I remember reading an article in *Modern Quarterly* in Autumn 1951 (it was in the same issue as the continuing Caudwell discussion, which shows many of the limits of pre-1956 Marxist cultural argument—flat assumptions of 'not Marxist' and so on—but shows also a divergence of fundamental positions which is not usually, in retrospect, acknowledged). The date is significant, for this was a turning-point in the whole post-war period, when the Labour Government was just being defeated (though on its highest ever electoral vote) and the outlines of a successful post-war capitalism—the credit and consumer society—were beginning to form. I then read with what was doubtless an excessive incredulity one of the ordinary propositions of what I and everyone else knew as English Marxism. It was on the Festival of Britain: 'Most of these Exhibition artists are lost, are pitifully out of touch and behind the people in 1951. The people have grown in stature, their aspirations are nearer to fulfilment. Until the artists turn their way with all their sight and all their capacity, the source from which their work should flow is dead and dry and will become more so. It shows. The people see it. The artist's only place for his life and strength is theirs, is with the people's struggle.'

'The people see it.' But that is as may be. As one of the people I did not see it then, but I brought some other things together: the powerful new pull of that public-relations and advertising Festival style; the glossy futurism against the hard, rationed, sharing world of the war; and then the options, under pressure, of so many actual people; the immanent probability of the stylish consumer society which would be the new form of capitalism. From then till now I have never been a populist, in the sense of that residual rhetoric. But because I saw the process as options under pressure, and knew where the pressure was coming from, I could not move either to the other most generally available position: that contempt of people, of their hopelessly corrupted state, of their vulgarity and credulity by comparison with an educated minority, which was the staple of cultural criticism of a non-Marxist kind and which seems to have survived intact, through the appropriate alterations of vocabulary, into one fashionable form of Marxism which makes the whole people, including the whole working class, mere carriers of the structures of a corrupt ideology.

Through 1955 and 1959, with a majority of English people (though not necessarily of Scots or Welsh) opting, in politics fairly clearly, in everyday practice more substantially, for consumer capitalism, it was hard to hang on, but it was still not true that the existing resources of the people were so depleted or corrupted that there was no option but to retreat to a residual minority or a futurist vanguard. It was a case (as the early New Left most notably emphasized) of a people both changing and being changed, but always differentially: the political geography and sociology but even more the political culture of Britain needed quite new kinds of exploration. There were still, and still powerful, existing resources. There were observable new forces which, taking consumer-credit capitalism at its word, made demands on it which eventually threw it into prolonged crisis. There were new resources, in a healthier and better-educated generation. There were also continuities, some of them crucial. When the South Wales miners in 1973 carried a poster saying 'This time we shall win', only a few people outside them knew that it was a reference back to 1926.

What then of populism? To stay with the existing resources; to learn and perhaps to teach new resources; to live the contradictions and the options under pressure so that instead of denunciation or writing-off there was a chance of understanding them and tipping them the other way: if these things were populism, then it is as well that the British Left, including most Marxists, stayed with it. On the other hand, of course, to go on insisting that 'the people' were simply being betrayed or manipulated, and thus to ignore the changes that were being lived into the fibres: that was a kind of populism, and I suppose it reaches its ironic dead end when, with a theory of ideology substituted for both culture and experience, a hypothetical new people will be delivered at a stroke, or at a rupture.

One harsher note about the current use of 'populism' as a term of abuse of parts of the Left. I remember an extraordinary experience during the Cold War when the institution I worked in was almost evenly divided between Communist Party members (Marxists, we would now say) and Labour Party members. For internal reasons it became very bitter, and there was both intrigue and witch-hunting. It was a curious phenomenon (which I recall, not biographically, but as a necessary illustration of some remarkably persistent cross-currents in the British Left) that at the worst moments I was the only person to whom both sides spoke: the Communists because I shared their intellectual perspectives and most of their political positions; the non-Communists—but there's the rub—because I, like almost all of them, was from a working-class family and had the same tastes in food and drink and enjoyment, whereas most of the Communists (Marxists) were public school boys to whom much of our incidental behaviour was vulgar. I joined neither camp, but I remember the experience, and I remember it especially when any later generation, coming from where it will, starts using either form of the contradictory rhetoric: either 'these bloody Communist (Marxist) intellectuals' or, on the other hand, the more abstract diagnoses of vulgarism, corporatism, workerism or populism. What has been at issue, throughout, is a crisis of relationships, within a crisis of change. Certainly the assumption of 'the people' and, moreover, after so much change, of 'the working class' will have to be reworked in detail; are already in part being reworked. Simple projections of the common interests of 'the people' or 'a people' have been decisively broken down: in the vain rhetoric of 'Britain' during the Wilson governments; in the failures of the Scottish and Welsh referenda; and in the economic nationalism of the Labour Left, which paradoxically, to be serious, has to provoke an immediate class conflict within the national rhetoric. But it is often equally rhetorical to substitute 'class' for 'people', unless the full weight of changes in the labour process, in education and in the changing (increasingly paranational) character of capitalist employment is followed through to the evident fragmentation, particularism and confusion which it is the precise purpose of an adequate definition and organization of 'class' to resolve.

Culturalism

It is now widely conceded that what was known, at the beginning of this period, as Marxist cultural theory (which incidentally, for those of us then working it, came through not only as Engels and Plekhanov, or Fox and Caudwell and West, but as Zhdanov) needed radical revision. On the whole this has happened, in the Marxism of many different national traditions, of course with results that are still controversial. In Britain my own work has been centrally involved with this, and for this reason I have to run together a general and a personal argument.

It took me thirty years, in a very complex process, to move from that received Marxist theory (which in its most general form I began by accepting) through various transitional forms of theory and inquiry, to the position I now hold, which I define as 'cultural materialism'. The emphases of the transition—on the production (rather than only the reproduction) of meanings and values by specific social formations, on the centrality of language and communication as formative social forces, and on the complex interaction both of institutions and forms and of social relationships and formal conventions—may be defined, if any one wishes, as 'culturalism', and even the crude old (positivist) idealism/ materialism dichotomy may be applied if it helps anyone. What I would now claim to have reached, but necessarily by this route, is a theory of culture as a (social and material) productive process and of specific practices, of 'arts', as social uses of material means of production (from language as material 'practical consciousness' to the specific technologies of writing and forms of writing, through to mechanical and electronic communications systems). I can only mention this here; it is spelled out more fully in *Marxism and Literature* and in *New Sociology: Culture*. What bears on this note is that what turned out to be, when developed, a materialist (but non-positivist) theory of language, of communication and of consciousness was assigned, along the way, to 'idealism' just because, in received Marxist theory, these activities were *known* to be superstructural and dependent—so that any emphasis on their specific primacies (within the complex totality of other primary forms of the material social process, including those forms which had been abstracted as 'labour' or 'production') was known *a priori* to be 'idealist'.

On the other hand, it is certainly true, and for a significant reason, that the relations between this account of cultural process and the more general social and political process were and still are insufficiently explored, theoretically, though they were inquired into again and again, empirically. One particular confusion, on both sides of the argument, was on the question of 'struggle': what has been called the substitution of an 'extensive' for a 'conflict' theory. I thought I had indicated my own position clearly enough in calling the process a long *revolution*. Perhaps the trouble was that it was indeed long (as the seventies most bitterly reminded us) and that it was much easier to go to a desk or a meeting and say that it should be short. But then again I did, and still do, find extension, transfer, slow development at least as often as I find the transitional process, transformation, and as often, also, as explicit conflict and struggle. What I would still insist on is that this is not a shop-counter of theoretical options. It is, or it can become, a theory of the historical variations of cultural process, which then necessarily connects (has to be connected) with a more general social, historical and political theory.

The point that now most interests me, looking back at Marxism in Britain since 1945, is that though I was well aware of my struggle with what was current as Marxist cultural theory, I made the mistake of assuming that, in other areas of theory and therefore in other parts of the social process, Marxism *already possessed* adequate principles, procedures and positions, and that in some cases, at least, I could take them for granted. All through the forties and early fifties, I used to go to Marxist friends who were economists or political theorists to be *told*, to have *explained*, what was happening. It was only in the late fifties, when I could see that it was not, and that there were other available and possible socialist explanations, that I began to realize that what was needed was much more general theoretical revision.

Some part of that realization went, eventually, into the collaborative effort of the *May Day Manifesto*, which started out with a group of mainly Marxist socialists thinking that they could put together their various analyses—economic, political, international, cultural and so on—and present, however briefly, a general position. What we found, and would still find, is that they did not simply add up; in the politics (and especially political organization) most obviously. But by the end of the work, and of the complex political practice that followed from it, I was clear that there was indeed a danger of my accounts of cultural process being taken (including by me) as a general social theory or as a general practical option. It is true that they had some practical bearings and indeed some limited practical effects. But that they were not a general theory was as obvious as the further fact, still relevant to the prospect of continuing collaborative work, that nothing would be gained by a simple announcement of Marxism, or by going yet again, if to a different generation, to be *told*, to have *explained*, not now what was happening (that style had gone out) but what other concepts must be grasped, inserted, to bring the whole thing into line. This is not now, as it was not then, how theory happens.

For cultural theory was not reworked as a critique within a theoretical tradition, but as a response to radical changes in the social relations of cultural process within British and other comparable societies. The failure to grasp these changing relations was evident in the distance between Marxist and other theories of 'mass communications' and Marxist and other theories of 'imaginative expression', 'art'. The short-cut solution, in one powerful modern variant of Marxism, has been to unify these theories within a theory of Ideology; but the only thing right about this is the realization that the theoretically separated 'areas' have to be brought within a single discourse. The main error of this solution is that it substitutes Ideology (a general, coherent and monopolizing practical consciousness, with its operative functions in institutions, codes and texts), for the complex social relations within which a significant (including alternative and oppositional) range of activities, in a significant (including dominating and subordinated but also contesting) range of situations, were being at once expressed, produced and altered, in practice in contradictory as well as in coherent, directive ways. These could in any case not be seen as a superstructure, or as simple ideological manipulation, in a period in which the process involved quite large-scale primary production, in publishing and broadcasting, and in which, also, what was seen by capitalist institutions as a market often contradicted what was seen by bourgeois ideologists as a culture. Moreover, it was impossible, looking at the new forms of broadcasting (especially television) and at formal changes in advertising and the press, to see cultural questions as practically separable from political and economic questions, or to posit either second-order or dependent relations between them.

In the necessary struggle to establish the qualitative unity of the modern socio-cultural process, and to specify it as a process through which the political and economic processes could and must also be seen, it was always likely that one would be understood as saying—or in the effort of establishing an emphasis actually say—that one process could be substituted for the others, when what was really in question was a new emphasis of perspective. Much of the actual controversy was against the conservative criticism of 'mass civilization', against the technological determinism (mechanical production = mass society = mass communications) of McLuhan and of some Marxists, and later against formalism. None of this, as controversy, is yet over, but as a note on the development of Marxism in Britain, which in this field has not been an offshore island but a major contributor, it can be suggested that the practical connections between this kind of cultural theory and the Gramscian account of hegemony and the hegemonic are significant, not only as a theoretical phase but because they developed, in struggle, from such different preoccupations and sources. What 'Marxism' is at any time seems dependent, finally, less on the history of ideas, which is still among most Marxists the usual way of defining it, than on the complex developments of actual social being and consciousness.

Reformism

What is usually called 'reformism' has been a crucial issue in Western Marxism since 1945, and especially since 1948 and 1956. The theoretical and practical development of most Western Communist Parties, in this period, has been described as 'the new reformism', and it is as well to remember, when writing of the differences between 'Marxism' and 'reformism', that the major political movements claiming Marxist authority, in societies like our own, have in their present phase no *a priori* qualitative difference from what, in a self-hating rhetoric, is so often called 'the stifling reformism' of the British Left.

There are, evidently, two kinds of reformist theory. The first, which is not even exclusive to the Left, proposes that radical changes in social institutions and relationships—the simplest example is the growth of 'equality'—can be made without transforming or, in some versions, even greatly disturbing the existing social order. The second, which now lies on the borderline between social-democratic and majority Communist

Parties, in highly developed capitalist societies, denies theoretically that significant and central reforms can be made without transforming the social order, but claims practically that struggles for specific reforms are the most accessible means of political mobilization, and that these are not only worthwhile in themselves but are necessary—indeed often the only immediately accessible—stages in the transformation of the dominant order.

In Britain there has been great complexity in the relations between these theories and strategies. The Labour Left, for example, and during much of the period the Communist Party, while in general adhering to the theory of struggles for reform in a perspective of transformation (the term ordinarily substituted for revolution), have often in practice, with effects on theory, seen the reforms as ends in themselves and as sufficiently worthwhile to make necessary not only temporary but persistent compromises with political formations whose strategy, explicitly, has been reform as a condition of sustaining capitalism or of making it more efficient. The continued collaboration of the Labour Left with Labour Governments which, more and more openly, have become the agency of promoting capitalist transformation ('modernization') is, of course, a striking example. The 'historic compromise' which seemed a new development in Italian Communism has been a feature of the Labour Left, in conscious ways, since 1945 and especially 1963—and, of course, has much older roots.

Two things have then to be said. First, that a working-class political formation which does not respond to and represent the perceived, often short-term interests of the working class becomes impotent, except in theoretical argument or in a form of internal exile. Secondly, that in conditions of electoral democracy, the making of alliances and coalitions has seemed, overwhelmingly, to be a condition of this response and representation. It is in these terms that most political struggles of the period since 1945 have been conducted, and it is not enough to denounce them theoretically; it is necessary to discover realistic alternatives.

A theoretical alternative appears to be readily available, from the Marxist theoretical tradition and from the practice of other, in fact very different, societies. But any significant theoretical inquiry must begin from a more precise analysis of reformism, rather than from its rhetorical rejection. Thus we can come to see the contradiction, within the Labour Left and its allies, between reform as response, which is then necessarily a process of new popular mobilization and organization, and reform as representation, in which the political formation, in alliance and coalition with others, pursues its percentage within the system. This case is very evident in the nationalization programmes, where the Fabian procedure of the public board has been at best 'representative' reform, at worst a new form of incorporation. The workers' control movement, as distinct from 'worker participation', has been the most significant response, within both the social-democratic and Marxist traditions, to what is otherwise clearly a barren (because from the beginning subordinated and partial) reformism.

But suppose we put the problem the other way round. Suppose we say, frankly, that we are only interested in the politics of response, and indeed in the provocation of the politics of response. We have still to make a crucial theoretical distinction. There is a strategy of mobilizing need and demand, in existing and where necessary new organizations, to the point where one struggle connects with and implies another, and where there is then a process of putting the central system under strains which can lead to transformation, since the converging demands can be met by no less. There is also a strategy, superficially much like it, where the system is put under strains which lead to its open crisis and probable breakdown, but where there is no coherent strategy of the convergence of demands in the actual (as distinct from the theoretically assumed) organization of social forces. As I have followed the argument, the former strategy is lumped in as 'reformist' with the other quite different tendencies of non-socialist and 'representative' reformism, whereas the latter strategy is proclaimed as 'revolutionary'.

Of course the latter strategy at least theoretically includes the organization of social forces of a kind adequate to win the fierce and confused battles which would follow anything like actual breakdown of the existing system. In this it is different from the formalist proposition of systemic rupture, in which the breakdown of a structure releases the elements of a new structure. That kind of 'revolution' can be made with diagrams, but nowhere else. What is practically in question—and with special urgency in the years through which we are now living—is the political counterpart of the same formalism, with its figurative precedents in societies in which the *political and social* defences of the system were very much weaker, and with its consequent reliance on simple breakdown as the crisis of capitalism which makes possible the socialist transition. Nobody would wish to deny the possibility, but in all strictly comparable conditions the result has more often been fascism (in Italy and Germany before the war) or that more immediate and probable enemy, a constitutional (often populist) authoritarianism, of a kind now latent or actual in several West European societies, including, in Thatcherism, our own. There is now a real danger, in a kind of theoretical opportunism leading to political, economic and sub-military ('terrorist') opportunism, of using the rhetoric against 'reformism' to the point where isolated militant sectors enter battles in which a totalizing alternative is precipitated against them.

I write, of course, from my own generation, but I have seen in practice and at close range the repressive capacities, and the degree of willing violence when it comes to the point, of an endangered system. They are very different forces from the mediated practices of 'repressive tolerance'. They can indeed be defeated, usually at great cost, but only by forms of mobilization in which actual and potential social forces are deeply and persistently organized. To adopt a theoretical position from which, for example, the trade unions are seen as merely reformist, and the perceived political Left is dismissed as incurably reformist, is to go into a very dangerous kind of internal exile. I can agree with those who say that all these formations will have no choice but to change their deeply learned consensual perspectives or accept comprehensive defeat. Indeed, through these years in which we are now living, that situation has been reached. In exceptionally confused and contradictory local ways, but with certain very simple choices lying directly behind them, the organization of need and demand—virtually all of it, in detail, reformist or even incorporated—has thrown the system into prolonged crisis, preventing any continuation of the perspectives of 1948-73. I made my own final break from one kind of reformism—a strong and active reformism of the majority of the British Labour movement—in 1966, when the long-looked-for condition of a large Labour parliamentary majority, with five years of peacetime government ahead of it, was at last achieved and was turned, very rapidly, into the opposite of what had been generally foreseen: not into social democracy, or into reformism, but into an actual and necessary agency of the mutation of capitalism by the representative incorporation of the working class. This has been much more evident and open in the new period since 1973, but now in conditions where the price of full incorporation (the capitalist version of reformism) is increasingly too high for the system to pay, and where any new incorporation must include the substance of actual defeat of major sectors of the working class, in prolonged mass unemployment and in the restoration of the absolute prerogatives of capital. The development of even a Labour government, from 1976, into an identification of the trade unions as the main obstacle to a capitalist national regeneration, and into an insistence that the working class should pay the prime costs of a specifically capitalist crisis, foreshadowed, very clearly, the emergence of a determined right-wing government which need have no backward glances to social democracy but could deal directly, and for many disconcertingly, with what it now openly named as its enemies. As the Right thus breaks the consensus, the crisis of reformism becomes quite inescapable.

Conclusion

So the mood of a review of theoretical options, and that sense of a space in which, encouraged by events elsewhere, we could be mainly concerned, on the Left, with each other's errors, have been dramatically and it would seem suddenly changed. Indeed there is even a danger that what we have really learned about the nature and limits of some kinds of populism, culturalism and reformism, alongside the nature and limits of some kinds of 'revolutionary' theory and rhetoric, will be swept aside in this new sense of danger, as if what we had primarily to do was to reconstitute, unchanged, these earlier and more reliable—because in some cases apparently effective—alternatives. But this would be merely a lurch from an abstract over-confidence in various kinds of theoretical inquiry to an equally abstract setting aside of theory in the (in fact dispersed) urgency of immediate struggles.

Remembering the long years, since 1945, of struggle and argument, involving so many people, I do not find it any easier at the end of the period than at the beginning to suppose that there is already an authentic, accessible and adequate Marxism which, simply from some obstinacy or blindness or ideological subjection, active socialists have refused. But then this is even more true of the theories of orthodox social democracy and its liberal allies, which flourished precisely in the space which an expanding capitalist economy had cleared for them. Indeed what has happened, negatively, is a practical opening for the relevance of a distinctive Marxist analysis, as the consensus and its intellectual habits begin not only to break down but to be actively broken down.

Nevertheless this is so only negatively, since the problem for at least twenty years has been one of connection between such analysis and effective political practice. And however it may have seemed in the years of intellectual expansion, no Marxist can now reasonably claim that the various specific theories already cohere, even theoretically, into operative theory and practice. Then just because there will be powerful movements to recover the old ground, where battles might not exactly be won but were not decisively lost either, there is an urgent need to move on from what has been so widely discussed but as yet, at any operative level, so partially learned.

My final note must then be one of welcome to an observable if still small current tendency to move beyond the theoretical loud-hailing, the fiercely excluding and damning spirit of the late sixties and most of the seventies, into a more open and more actually rigorous re-examination and practical construction. For Marxism as history and analysis of ideas, and of social forces and movements through ideas—one of the most telling developments of the period since 1945 and especially since 1960—stands now to be tested in quite new ways, as immediate and possible and sustainable organization.

Beyond Actually Existing Socialism

'Communism is not only necessary, it is also possible.' The quiet words carry a major historical irony. For what has now to be proved, before an informed and sceptical audience, is indeed possibility. And this not only in the reckoning of strategic or tactical chances, which in these dangerous years carry as much fear as hope. Where the proof really matters is at another level, where intention and consequence, desire and necessity, possibility and practice, have already bloodily interacted. Thus we are no longer in any position to cry great names or announce necessary laws, and expect to be believed. The information and the scepticism are already too thoroughly lodged at the back of our own minds. Strategy and tactics can still be played from the front, but the greatest unknown quantity in any of their moves is again possibility. The condition of shifting any of it beyond the parameters of a desperate game is possibility in the hardest sense: not whether a new human order might, in struggle, come through, but whether, as a condition of that struggle, and as the entire condition of its success, enough of us can reasonably believe that a new human order is seriously possible.

It has, after all, been widely believed before. It has, nevertheless, been widely believed. We can choose either of these ways of putting it, without much effect. The tenses of past and of an implied present lead us only into known conditions and known difficulties. Yet with most future tenses now comes at best a familiar scepticism, at worst a conventional hopelessness. Possibility, seriously considered, is different. It is not what with luck might happen. It is what we can believe in enough to want, and then, by active wanting, make possible. Specifically, for socialists, after defeats and failures, and both within and after certain profound disillusions, it is not recovery or return but direct, practical possibility. Of course not practical or possible within the reduced terms of the existing order: possibility as a resignation to limits. Possibility, rather, as a different order, which no longer from simple assumptions, or from known discontents and negations, but on our own responsibility, in an actual world, we must prove.

Bahro's Alternative in Eastern Europe

The quiet words come at the end of Rudolph Bahro's important book, *The Alternative in Eastern Europe.*[1] Their full effect depends on their position, for what is most remarkable about Bahro's work is that while its first part covers familiar ground, in an analysis of 'the non-capitalist road to industrial society', and its second part important ground, in an 'anatomy of actually existing' socialist societies, its third part, over two hundred pages, begins from an insistence that 'today utopian thought has a new necessity' and yet proceeds to something very unlike utopianism, indeed to a relatively detailed outline of a practical and possible communist society.

It is a very significant moment in socialist thought. We can fall back on the irony that, within a nominally socialist or communist society, its author was at once put in prison. This is an irony which cannot be compounded by the success of the book in the West, in the spirit of that romantic notion which Brecht identified, with Galileo's *Discorsi* crossing the frontier in a closed coach. The fact is that either in Eastern or Western Europe, of course under different local conditions, the challenge which Bahro is making must immediately encounter and engage—for that is its whole purpose—the fixed institutional and ideological habits of 'actually existing socialism'. Bahro chose this awkward phrase, after much hesitation, to describe the non-capitalist societies of Eastern Europe. But it has also to be applied, again noting our different conditions, to the institutions, ideologies and programmes of majority West European socialism, including its Communist Parties. It makes an important difference that our comrades in Eastern Europe are not, like us, confronting an entrenched and still powerful capitalist order. It means that they can look, already, along a different road. Yet in practice, like us, only look. Any actual generation of effective possibility faces as many, if different,

---

[1] NLB, 1978, p. 453.

obstacles, on either side of the line. But then at the same time it is true that effective movement, anywhere, will assist every other struggle.

This possible community of purpose, through what is certain to be a long, difficult and uneven effort, is the most heartening effect of Bahro's work. It is already significant that it allows us to move beyond the defensive, qualified solidarity with what has been defined, in Eastern Europe, as dissidence; to move beyond it, moreover, by distancing ourselves, in a more specific solidarity, from the anti-communism which can so readily exploit more limited positions. In one sense Bahro's work joins what has been already, for a generation, a marginal dissidence within Western socialism, but then the fact that it was written from within a non-capitalist society, with close day-to-day experience of its actual workings, and moreover from within a profound attachment to Marxism and to communism, makes a crucial difference. What it prevents, above all, is any complacent continuation of those perspectives of majority Western socialism which still, over a range from social democrats to communists, share with the countries of Eastern Europe certain common definitions of the nature of a socialist economic order, adding only, but often rhetorically, that in addition to this there should be substantially greater civil and political liberties.

For that is the depth of the challenge, and of the call to possibility: 'Humanity must not only transform its relations of production, but must also fundamentally transform the overall character of its mode of production, i.e. *the productive forces as well* . . . it should consider its perspective as not bound to any one historically inherited *form* of development and satisfaction of needs, or to the world of products that is designed to serve these.'[2]

Thus a communist perspective of general emancipation has to be sharply distinguished from those governing perspectives, East and West, which in their primary emphasis on the 'organization of production', in the special form of growth of existing *kinds* of production, and in their consequent emphasis on social relations and social welfare as dependent on the stage this has reached, have made and are making of socialism a would-be higher form of capitalism. Against this, Bahro puts a communist emphasis: 'Not a growth in production,

[2] *The Alternative*, pp. 261-2.

but cultural revolution—as the present form of *economic* emancipation—is the means finally to dissolve the capitalist structure'.[3]

Meanings of Cultural Revolution

It is really only now, seeing Bahro's work written within an explicit and central Marxist perspective, that we can find ways of bringing together the apparently different emphases and concerns of those movements, in different parts of the world, which have identified themselves as working for 'cultural revolution'. I can remember, for example, the sneering use of the phrase to mark off the early New Left. Our use of 'culture' to designate a central process and area of social and political struggle was at best identified (as significantly, later, was the Prague Spring) as the emergence of a group of intellectuals with special interests in 'the superstructure', having nothing much or at all to say to the organized working class in its continuing material struggles at 'the base'. But then no sooner had this dismissive or marginalizing description got into general currency than, to everyone's surprise, the same phrase, 'cultural revolution', became known as a description of the most remarkable political movement of the twentieth century: the sustained (and of course confused) attempt, in People's China, to define new priorities and alter actual and foreseen political relations, trying to make new forms of popular power within and where necessary against the received shapes of a socialist economic order. Now again, as the phrases settle, and as those particular historical moments have passed, an East European communist, writing from inside his experience of actually existing socialism, chooses the same phrase, 'cultural revolution', to describe his central emphasis on the revolutionary way forward, for the achievement of communism.

Is this some accident of a phrase? There are differences, evidently, in these ideas and movements, but they are not necessarily greater than the radical differences of social conditions within which they were mounted. When these have been taken into account, what comes through is a line of division within Marxist theory and within socialist practice: a line which must now be more clearly drawn.

The central theoretical point is this. All Marxists share the belief that social being determines consciousness. The main conclusion that is

---

[3] *The Alternative*, pp. 265-5.

ordinarily drawn from this is that we cannot change social being by changing consciousness; we must, on the contrary, change consciousness by changing social being. This conclusion is then stabilized as a contrast and opposition between 'idealist' and 'materialist' theory and practice, and, typically, the proponents of 'cultural revolution' are assigned to the former: 'culture' is the 'sphere of consciousness'. But what has then happened is that consciousness has been separated from the 'sphere of social being', characteristically in the form of abstracting 'the superstructure' from 'the base'. Work in the latter is then materialist; in the former either idealist or at best 'voluntarist'.

'Conservatives in both systems raise a hue and cry about voluntarism. But this only gives it away how much they fear changes, or at the very least do not want to lead and take responsibility for them. We must bear in mind that it is a social body in its *subjective capacity* that has economic laws, and not the other way round.' 'Even mechanical materialists today have an inkling that the "growing role of the subjective factor" involves something quite different from the mere conscious execution of historical laws. Marxism has always claimed that being can determine consciousness precisely to determine being *anew*.'[4]

There is room for argument about the relation of either of these emphases to a single system called 'Marxism'. But Bahro's emphasis is the common factor in the propositions of 'cultural revolution'. Consciousness is no longer the mere product of social being but is at once a condition of its practical existence and, further, one of its central productive forces.

This theoretical distinction can be said to be permanent. It is and has been made and practised in widely different social formations. But at the centre of Bahro's argument is a specific interpretation of conditions in modern industrial societies, where the production and reproduction of ideas and of intellectual practices have become and are becoming, at a growing rate, inherent in wide areas of the basic labour processes and in the general social order. Thus a fundamental form of the division of labour, between mental and manual operations, is being at once practically eroded and yet, in the forms of a class-based social order or of an apparently new order which is continuous with this in its mode of production though in other respects discontinuous, is still being practically imposed.

To put the point again theoretically: change in a mode of production

[4] *The Alternative*, p. 256

can not occur only on the basis of a change in *relations* of production—as in the removal of capitalist owners of the means of production and their replacement by State planning authorities or public boards, where as a matter of fact even the relations of production have not necessarily been more than abstractly altered—but must also involve change in the *forces* of production, which are never only manual or mechanical but are also (and now increasingly) intellectual means. Thus a cultural revolution, by contrast with other social programmes, is directed towards the general appropriation of all the real forces of production, including now especially the intellectual forces of knowledge and conscious decision, as the necessary means of revolutionizing the social relations (determination of the use of resources; distribution and organization of work; distribution of products and services) which follow from variable forms of control of and access to all the productive forces. A cultural revolution is then always practically centred on the areas and processes of knowledge and decision, each ineffective without the other. In going beyond those changes in the relations of production which are practicable, especially at the distributive level, within persistent inequalities in control of and access to the underlying productive forces—changes which have been both partly achieved and programmatically projected in social-democratic and in 'actually existing socialist' formations—cultural revolution—but then, in effect, any full revolution—works for those more general (and necessarily connected) changes which, in changing the whole mode of production, would be at once the processes and the conditions of a general human emancipation.

'Mature Industrialism'

It may be relatively easy to accept such definitions, at their usual level of generality. But we are speaking, in our conditions, among informed and sceptical people. The factor of information, uneven and incomplete as in all cases it must be, is at once the problem and the opportunity of contemporary socialist argument. Indeed the scepticism and worse with which such argument is now widely met is the inevitable consequence of failure to recognize this qualitatively new level of information (a failure which those listening to the arguments can now, in the forms of rhetorical replication, local opportunism, large promise and practical evasiveness, so quickly identify). At the same time, and more fundamentally (for it is here that the refusal of socialism is generated) there is a self-protecting and eventually indulgent habit of resigned but knowing acquiescence in the central reality of the existing mode of production: a widespread conclusion that information and argument have little or no purchase on the range of actual decisions; that it is then 'all talk'. It is then not only against its declared enemies—the existing owners, controllers and distributors of privileged knowledge and decision—but also against the cultural consequences, in long experience and habituation, of this decisive element of the mode of production itself—sceptical subordination, compensatory marginal avoidances, in Bahro's terms, *subalternity*—that the cultural revolution sets out to act. That is why, always vulnerably but still deliberately, it sets *possibility* as its central challenge.

But 'possibility' can then acquire a utopian tinge. Indeed a familiar form of Marxism stands especially ready to confront it. Possibility is the future—the Sunday after next. Social democracy, in its late and most resigned forms, has of course settled to saying that 'when we have got the economy right' we can go on to 'the things we all want', but meanwhile . . . in this mode of production, produce. Yet in remarkably similar ways, many Marxist arguments, and the settled practices of 'actually existing socialism', offer the same message: 'when we have achieved plenty, which is a condition of communism'; 'when we have caught up with the West'. It is especially against such positions and practices, with their very serious social and political consequences in the relations between socialist formations and actual working people, that Bahro develops his arguments.

His central point applies equally in the East and in the West, though for historical reasons, of uneven development, it is not new in 'Western socialism' even if it has been effectively forgotten. Thus it is widely believed that communism, or full socialism, will be possible only when the productive forces have 'matured'. But, 'given the present structure of industrial societies in both formations, the productive forces will never become mature, despite and precisely on account of their technical dynamic. Yet even today those countries that first set out on the industrial-capitalist road are those materially closest to socialism. Nowhere is the *beginning* of the transformation more pressing than it is there. But it is also nowhere more hard. And neither the less developed nor the underdeveloped peoples can afford to wait for them.'[5]

[5] *The Alternative*, p. 125.

'The industrial-capitalist road', but we must then make distinctions. It is not new in Marxist thought, though it has not often been emphasized, that the *capitalist* mode of production, for deep internal reasons, can *never* become mature. Since it has become dominant, in one area after another, it has been uncontrollably disturbing and restless, reaching local stabilities only almost at once to move away from them, leaving every kind of social and technical debris, disrupting human continuities and settlements, moving on with brash confidence to its always novel enterprises. And the real reason for this is that it is not, finally, a mode of *production*, in any primary sense. In its developed forms it is centred not on social production but on the reproduction of capital and the maximization of profit, which impose quite different priorities.

But what then of the linkage with what is now commonly called 'industrialism'? For historical reasons the theoretically distinguishable types—'capitalism' and 'industrialism'—are virtually impossible to disentangle, in advanced capitalist societies. It is then very striking to find Bahro extending the point to an 'industrial society' in a non-capitalist order. The local reason he offers, in the fact of the 'technical dynamic', is not in itself convincing. Maturity, whatever that might be, or in more practical terms a non-disruptive continuity of production, ought certainly to be able to include a series of quite extensive technical changes, while these are governed by the needs of social production rather than by the priorities of capital. Bahro's later reason, that the non-capitalist and ex-colonial economies are in many ways determined by the forms and pressures of industrial capitalism elsewhere, is more convincing. But the most important eventual point of the analysis is to show that what has to be overcome, for any general emancipation, is not only 'capitalism', in the important but limited sense of minority ownership of the means of production, but that wider mode, in which the scale and complexity and technical redivisions of labour characteristic of modern industrial enterprises are central factors. And then the deep obstacles of this wider mode are the facts of the appropriation, expropriation, at many levels of general social and working processes, of skills, effective knowledge and powers of practical decision. It is against this expropriation that the cultural revolution, much wider than that against the more immediately recognizable features of capitalism, is directed.

But there are also other reasons for insisting that the capitalist mode of production, and its non-capitalist simulacra, can never become mature.

These reasons are historical. First, that the successful struggles against political and economic imperialism are already altering, and seem certain to alter further, the access to cheap raw materials and controlled markets on which the most successful phases of advanced capitalism depended. Second, that within the advanced capitalist societies, economic and technical solutions, of a rationalizing and modernizing kind, are already, in structural unemployment, in consequent market, credit and service difficulties, and in the political disruption of settled social (national and regional) formations, moving very rapidly *away from* rather than towards maturity. Third, and decisively, that the now evident crises of resources, and of the unwanted side-effects of several central productive processes, are combining to set *material* limits to what has been, not only in ideology but in its central dynamic, a limitless expansion. The combined effect of these reasons is what now makes communism necessary. But given the exceptional dangers and difficulties of any real alteration of priorities and of any effective alternative construction, the question is still: is it possible?

'Surplus Consciousness'

Bahro sees the way through in one of his most memorable but also arguable concepts: that of the contemporary production of 'surplus consciousness'. He defines this as 'an energetic mental capacity that is no longer absorbed by the *immediate* necessities and dangers of human existence and can thus orient itself to more distant problems.'[6]

There is obviously some truth in this, as in any local comparison of the lives of most workers between, say, the mid-nineteenth and the late twentieth centuries. Something very important is then being indicated. But on any wider historical scale it can be reasonably argued that this 'surplus consciousness' is at once a cultural and a material variable. There is no unilinear progression of 'free consciousness', but on the contrary a highly variable and always complex relation between this sphere of mental possibility and the local imperatives of specific modes and types of production. And because this is so we cannot rest on the essentially quantitative notion of a 'surplus'. For the consciousness and energy that are available beyond the immediately necessary tasks are not

[6] *The Alternative*, p. 257.

simple quanta; they are and must be related to the forms of consciousness and energy expended and generated in the primary tasks. Of course this correction must not be extended to the absurd point reached in an opposite tendency in Marxism, in which there is *no* free consciousness (except, ambiguously, at the level of theory) but only the labyrinthine monopoly of a totalized ideology. Yet there can be no simple reliance either on the mere fact of a 'surplus', and Bahro is much more convincing when he goes on to recognize this by distinguishing, usefully, between 'compensatory' and 'emancipatory' uses of this 'surplus': that is, between drives to possession, consumption and power, which can be seen as partial substitutes for any certain and equitable share in human needs, and those other non-exploitative orientations towards self-realization and the collective realization, recognition, of the essential qualities of others.

The cultural revolution is then for *the conditions of* the emancipatory and against *the need for* the compensatory activities. (This distinguishes Bahro, as a Marxist theorist, from the strictly 'moralist' version of a comparable argument, in which the shift is seen only as internal and suasive). But then this is not really the appropriation of a surplus. Indeed the very sharp rise in every kind of 'compensatory' activity—a process now central to advanced capitalist production itself—not only reminds us of the obstacles but should force us to review, much more carefully than has been common in most branches of criticism of 'consumer' society, the relatively simple initial categories. It is not only that the argument (more commonly the sermon or the tirade) can slip very quickly into asceticism or into revived forms of cultural ethno-centrism. It is, more fundamentally, that human emancipation is intrinsically, and as a matter of principle, more diverse than *any* philosophical definition of emancipatory transformation. Utopia, that is to say, as a singular noun, is not an emancipatory concept; indeed it is often and at its best frankly compensatory.

A Long Revolution

In fact Bahro is not a utopian; that is the most important quality of his book. He thinks through, in unusually sustained detail, the processes of transformation of conditions and needs. This was for me a remarkable experience, in that it came through, quite personally, as another version of the project of *The Long Revolution*. When Bahro comes to summarize his 'perspectives for general emancipation' I find myself back in those years and the kinds of thinking that followed from them. A redivision of labour; unrestricted access to general education; a childhood centred on the capacity for development rather than geared to economic performance; a new communal life based on autonomous group activities; socialization (democratization) of the general process of knowledge and decision. Moreover 'there is neither the hope nor the danger that these goals . . . can be achieved "too quickly". A society cannot be taken by surprise or with a coup d'état. . . . The question is rather to create first of all the political and mental conditions . . . '[7]

It is then not at all a question of who said what when. The project is too widely shared and too essentially collaborative for any of that. But it remains remarkable that there should be this convergence, within such different conditions, and then the irreplaceable and quite novel merit of Bahro's work is that he has defined this project from close practical experience of an 'actually existing socialism'. What was then already outlined in communications, in education and in communal self-management is radically strengthened by proposals in economic planning, in factory organization and in the 'problem-solving collectives' of technical and scientific work. The problems of political organization, within such perspectives, are again convergently but in each case incompletely seen. What has then to be thought through (for the details of Bahro's arguments and proposals must simply be read) is an interlocking set of questions which, beyond the exhilaration of the realization of convergence, remain as real difficulties: the true difficulties of possibility.

Self-Management

The case for self-management, in every kind of social and economic activity, has often been made, and in some important cases has been endowed with practical detail. It is the indispensable objective of any movement to achieve (for it is not really to recover) the powers and faculties of effective knowledge and decision. Moreover, while Bahro is writing from an 'existing socialist' experience, in which, at least internally, there are not the implacable barriers of direct monopoly and

[7] *The Alternative*, p. 275.

finance capitalism, we have to notice that in our own blocked and bleak situation the most active social forces have already arrived at this point. In various kinds of community organization, and especially those around schools, housing, transport and hospitals, a vigorous if usually local collective activity is already widespread. Many kinds of 'voluntary' organization (the conventional description throws an ironic light on the true character of the dominant order) already engage kinds of collective activity and self-organization which offer repeated evidence of practical possibility. In work the growing practice of factory occupations is not always limited to protest but is producing some notable examples of counter-planning; this is also, if intermittently, widespread in education. In some strikes there have been remarkably vigorous instances of direct collective organization and—as in the flying pickets—initiative.

It remains true, of course, that all such examples compose only a minority experience, when set against the predominant experience of frustrated energy and initiative within blocked bureaucratic and hierarchical organizations. It has also to be said that most such actions are defensive protests, often at a very late stage, rather than fully constructive. But then it is not only that all such practices are the necessary means of learning the new and difficult skills of autonomous organization: something that is also happening, again vigorously, in the alternative and oppositional collectives. It is also that the limited character of the available and developing modes reminds us, sharply, of the next and decisive theoretical barrier that has to be crossed.

For if it is becoming clear that the best democratic and socialist way of running organizations is through regular and informed collective decision-making, it should be at once equally clear, and especially to socialists, that this principle cannot be limited to specific enterprises and communities. Indeed there is even some danger that the growing belief in existing and commonly foreseen forms of community politics and workers' control will actually hide from us the more difficult problems of the general framework within which, necessarily, they must be practised. It is here, with Bahro, that we arrive at the hitherto intractable concepts and realities of Party, State and Plan.

Party, State and Plan

There is a powerful socialist tradition, almost equally reinforced by both

Bolshevism and Fabianism, which whether or not it has been modified by ideas of local democracy arrives at the problems of the general framework with firm ideas of a unitary general authority. In modern 'communist' practice this authority has been the Party, as the projected will and interest of the working class. Bahro's analysis of this, in its actual development into monopoly and repression, can be debated, historically, since his reference to conditions of external pressure and deformation, and of immediate 'backwardness', is insufficient, as indeed he later argues, to account for its remarkable and ideologically defended persistence. And we can join the argument here from our own experience, since in relatively much more favourable conditions the dominant socialist perspective is again the unitary party and the state plan. It is true that in the West this is modified by the substantial practices of (relatively) open elections and of the 'mandate'. But what election and mandate are still intended to deliver is 'the party in government' with its central plan. When this in practice interlocks with the existing and relatively unaltered framework of the capitalist state it is already suspect and invariably deceptive. But then there is equally no reason to believe, from the experience of Eastern Europe, that any simple removal of capitalist property relations is sufficient to alter the realities of monopoly state power and the imposed authority of the plan; indeed it may lead directly to them. It is then on this common site, if under radically different conditions, that the cultural revolution must be waged, and as something more than a series of local options.

The first area to contest, as Bahro convincingly recognizes, is that of the plan. It is obviously necessary that within any effective political community (and in modern material conditions this is unlikely to be small) basic allocations of resources and conditions of distribution have to be affirmed. The concept of the socialist 'plan' competes, here, with the (always in practice qualified) imperatives of the capitalist market. It is commonly supported by the paired notions of 'public interest' and 'rationality', which together are held to compose 'socialism'. But then the whole point is that public interest and rationality, which are general human conditions and processes, have been theoretically and practically appropriated by a centrally directive mechanism. In any actual case of 'public interest' the reality (and not only in class societies) is only rarely unitary; it is almost always in practice a *relativity* of interests, variable from instance to instance and through time. The exercise of 'rationality' is then in its turn a more complex and variable process than any conceivable amalgam of 'expert' inquiries and directions. Yet at the same time it is clearly not possible in any complex society to make rational decisions without very advanced effective knowledge.

It is then a good test of where any socialist stands, in this matter of cultural revolution, to see how he reacts to the proposal that in any issue requiring general decision there should *never be less than two* independently prepared 'plans'. For this goes to the heart. It is not just the practical point that we have had more than enough experience of expert plans which turned out to be wrong (the switches from coal to oil, and from rail to road, are only the most obvious examples). It is, more fundamentally, that the preparation of at least two plans, while fulfilling the necessary conditions of effective and where necessary specialist knowledge, provides, in its practical alternatives, genuine conditions for the actual as distinct from the appropriated exercise of public interest and rationality. Moreover it is inherent in the requirement of detailed and practicable alternatives that decision is neither appropriated nor mandated but is each time actively and generally made.

We are only now beginning to learn, with notable assistance from Bahro, at once the genuine difficulties and the practical possibilities of so radically new a social order. And then nothing is to be gained by underestimating the complexity of such decision-making, or the long period of active learning and informed participation which would be necessary to make it effective. But it is not only, theoretically, that this is the way to cultural revolution: a way drawing on the only actual social forces which are capable of achieving general emancipation. It is also that the material means of such complex, informed and relatively rapid decision-making are becoming increasingly available in modern communications technology, which indeed it must be one of the first conditions of cultural revolution to direct for this rather than (as now mainly) for existing marketing uses. Practicable institutions and procedures, in many different areas of reference and at varying levels of formality, directly corresponding to the nature and effect of the decisions, are now indeed within our material capacity. The main thrust must then be towards political and educational practice of the many kinds necessary to give them substance; to make them *possible*.

It is then necessary to consider the relations between such new kinds of decision-making and our received notions of 'representation' and of 'party'. It might be said that in the West we already have such alternatives and procedures of choice, in competing parties and plans. Yet the combined practices of representation and of parties conceived in its terms radically limit—and often seem meant to limit—democratic procedures. It is not only that representatives, in such conditions, are not in theory or practice bound by the kinds of reporting back and *specific* instruction which would make general opinions and wishes regularly effective. It is much more that the theory of representation offers an all-purpose and generalized substitute for the specific, diverse and shifting interests of what are always diverse individuals and groups. Indeed in this it resembles, though under some qualifying controls, the explicit 'substitutionism' of the would-be monopoly party which 'represents' the working class, not by taking its instructions or even consulting it, but by the kinds of ideological appropriation which Bahro so vividly describes. It is customary to contrast such 'totalitarian' parties with the 'democratic' parties of the West, yet these are only different forms of appropriation of popular information and decision. The means of this appropriation, in the West, is the procedure of electoral mandate, on an unsortable bundle of plans and policies, which delivers some years of monopoly of power. This form of 'representation' inherently generalizes and preempts what is always in practice a sequence of specific, variable and often unforeseeable decisions, of which the direct *presentation* would be a wholly different political practice from all-purpose and appropriated *representation*.

Of course individuals and groups must combine and find resolutions as and where specific interests and decisions interact. But these, though they may at any time take the immediate form of parties, are properly alliances, blocs, coalitions, always specifically formed and necessarily open to change, rather than the fixed 'representative' parties which now appropriate these active processes. It is indeed at this level that we might be said to be already in the first phase of a cultural revolution. For it is evident that the traditional delivery of representative blocks of all-purpose votes, which then monopolize and exhaust the political process, is relatively rapidly breaking down. Yet the forms of movement beyond it, in what are called 'single-issue campaigns', are distrusted even by those who have moved into them, against the existing appropriations and exclusions. Out of habit, it would seem, they look to forms of influence which would in practice incorporate them into parties of an existing kind, when the real lesson of their experience is that they are early forms of a movement towards conditions of direct and specific public decision-making, to which, without mediation and beyond appropriation, their interests and campaigns can be directly and associatively addressed. For they are already, in embryo, those forms of 'collectives of associated individuals' which are rightly seen by Bahro as the fibres of a communist society. Their diversity and specificity, now experienced, within the dominant appropriation, as disadvantages, are in fact an early (if of course incomplete, indeed fragmentary) realization of that principle of 'the association of individuals into unions in which they pursue the various specific purposes that make up the process of their social life' which Bahro, following Marx, addresses as the only basis for general emancipation.[8]

What the cultural revolution is then really proposing is a radical recasting of the old problem of the relations between special interests and the general interest. It has of course to find means of negotiating such relations, but it starts from the position that all existing institutions and procedures of the 'general interest' are in fact falsifications, either in the arbitrary definitions of a dominant class, or in those more complex procedures of representation in which the 'general interest' is a negative appropriation deployed against each 'special interest' in turn, the only means of ascertaining the true general interest in relation to any actual special interest, by direct consultation and specific popular decision, having been systematically excluded. In these false systems, the lines of communication and of decision, which have been directly appropriated, flow from 'top' to 'bottom' as a matter of course. The cultural revolution, by contrast, seeks a system in which there are still indeed many levels of generality—including levels of elected delegate assemblies—and in which decisions and relevant information necessarily move from the more local and specific to the more general, extensive and indeed in these senses determining, but in which, because the lines of communication and decision now flow the other way, 'individuals are equally and simultaneously present at all levels of subjective interest'.[9]

[8] *The Alternative*, p. 440.
[9] *The Alternative*, p. 440.

What a Society Produces

Yet the scepticism and impatience which such proposals now commonly induce, even among those whose own definitions of a desirable form of society already lead them in such directions, have to be directly faced. For in both East and West, if in different ways, a potentially lethal combination of abstract desire and practical cynicism seems now to be overtaking actual majorities, as a consequence not only of repeated disappointments but of the (in itself correct) identification of their causes as systematic: an unbearable state of mind in itself, where no alternative is really believed in, and quickly convertible either to violent reaction or to projection of the systematic failure to the human species and order—a projection which even the waiting formulae of religion can only temporarily hold.

The urgency of cultural revolution then hardly needs to be argued. But though it has necessarily to be attempted in every area of social existence, there are good reasons for believing, with Bahro, that the decisive engagement will be with the problems of 'the economy'. Yet it is clear that the form of this engagement, as distinct from the now dominant and preoccupying 'programmes for economic survival', has to begin in some new and still unfamiliar ways. Thus when we speak of plans and programmes, which are undoubtedly necessary, we have first to challenge the alienated logic of a capitalist order and its non-capitalist derivatives. In his detailed discussions of economic planning and factory organization Bahro is at his best, not only because of his relevant experience, but because his central beliefs are then so directly connected.

The point reaches deeply back into theory, but of course emerges every day as practice. It is centred on the question of what a society needs to produce. Within the alienated logic this is necessarily defined, even by many socialists, in the quantitative terms of necessary objects. Plans and targets are then derived, and collective production is organized, throughout, in these habitually alienated terms. Consciousness, individuality, the social order itself, are then seen as by-products of this necessary production.

Against this logic, the cultural revolution insists, first, that what a society needs, before all, to produce, is as many as possible conscious individuals, capable of all necessary association. Thus not only is 'the plan' differently conceived from the beginning. It is in fact now the only developed response to the changed conditions of material production, in which quantitative results are relatively easily achieved, at the level of objects, but are still given their residual priorities over other general human interests and developments. Thus the material task which requires the work of sixty is developed, by capitalist logic, to the point where it requires the work of only six, and the other fifty-four become, in that deeply significant term of the current alienation, 'redundant'. In an alternative logic, there would be the choice, from the beginning, of associating more workers than are necessary, at any particular material stage, so that within the labour process itself there is room for other kinds of relationship and reflection, or of so redistributing necessary working time that other kinds of activity and relationship become the emancipatory centre rather than the compensatory margin of social life. It is of course clear that any such plan requires, absolutely, abolition of the current imperatives of capital, which exerts its quantitative dominance at just these points. And it is then deeply encouraging that, even within capitalist conditions, some trade unions are now moving strongly, if still in limited ways, towards these objectives, while at a more practical level (though still as often negative as positive) more and more people are actually treating work in such ways, as far as they can, of course to the outrage of all existing types of controller. What then urgently matters is the generalization, extension and where necessary conversion of these existing tendencies, with the now conscious rather than defensive or shamefaced purpose of remaking the working order. For, so far from being impractical, the positive and conscious pursuit of these aims is now the only practical alternative to a new stage of division of humanity into the engaged and the redundant.

What this really involves, as a central task of the cultural revolution, in its necessary alteration of the nature of the productive forces, is a practical redefinition of the nature of 'work'. For while, within the inevitable material limits and within the rational decisions of a society seeking genuine economic maturity, the necessary material tasks can undoubtedly be performed in less total time, any effective response to more general human needs, in care and relationships, and in knowledge and development, is in one sense genuinely limitless, and will make demands on our energies which are at the very opposite pole from a relaxed and unchallenging utopia. Indeed, these now equally basic needs, as we can already glimpse from their pressures at the end of the old logic—pressures which seem actually to be increasing in conditions of advanced commodity development—compose the necessary processes of a new kind of active (and, in that new sense, working) society.

Class

We have then to consider, finally, the relations between these definitions and perspectives of the cultural revolution and the most general received definitions and perspectives of revolutionary socialism. For many reasons, the problem of these relations is centred in the concept of class. Bahro scandalized many people, and not only the dogmatists against whom he was mainly arguing, with his vigorous assertion that 'the working class' is 'an inapplicable concept in proto-socialist society'.[10] Some distinctions have then to be made. In his analysis of a rhetoric of 'the working class' as a cover for practical appropriation and repression in Eastern Europe Bahro is on relatively firm ground. Clearly any adequate definition of the social situation of wage-workers in non-capitalist economies requires a whole new analysis. But then he both extends and has been taken by others to extend this specific problem to a very wide and (it must be said) very familiar critique of the Marxist idea of the proletariat and its revolutionary possibilities. The trouble with this part of his argument is that there is a recurrent slippage between consideration of the working class in non-capitalist and capitalist societies. As a result, while making some new points about a partly new situation, he drifts, not without some hesitations, into a familiar identification of the 'technical intelligentsia'—the most advanced sector of the 'collective worker'—as the leading edge of the cultural revolution. This conclusion is best understood within the specific difficulties of Eastern European societies, but, whatever may be its truth or plausibility there, it would be disastrous if in the West the idea of cultural revolution were given this kind of social location.

It is of course true that modern intellectual workers—no longer to be defined only by traditional intellectual occupations, but as very widely integrated into industrial, distributive and informational processes—are likely to be specially alerted to the facts of appropriation of effective knowledge and powers of decision by the existing social order. Precisely because in their own situations they have some real access to unmediated

[10] *The Alternative*, pp. 183-202.

knowledge, and are in a privileged position to observe and understand many of the actual processes of mediation and control and decision, they are potentially and often actually at the leading edge of effective (if usually localized) social criticism. And then it is not only that such groups can contribute (are already in some areas notably contributing) to the cultural revolution; it is also that the outcome of theoretical and practical struggles within such groups will have a major effect on the chances of effective socialist directions.

Yet it is obvious that at any time a significant proportion of such workers are, with whatever local dissatisfactions, elements of the very process of appropriation itself. Their practical enlistment into *new forms* of appropriation is then the most likely initial direction of any radical break. This is why, though necessarily on the basis of rigorous new analysis, socialists committed to the idea of cultural revolution have still to find common cause—and by learning as much as by teaching—with those who are *most* subject to appropriation, who alone have fully objective interests in its ending.

It can be readily shown that 'the working class' has changed, sometimes very radically, in modern productive and distributive conditions. Its mere invocation is indeed often, as Bahro argues, a protection against thought. But the major elements of these changes need not only be interpreted as the disintegration of the 'classical proletariat'; they can be interpreted also as a profound (and for the existing social order, dangerous) instability. It is not only, though it is crucially, the factual rise in expectations. It is also that the erosion of the old crude division between mental and manual labour has, partly through an extended educational system but at a rising rate within certain labour processes and their consequent problems of management, reached deep into the general class of wage-earners. The coexistence of such expectations and such erosion with the still firmly sustained imperatives of capital or of 'the plan' is then profoundly unstable, and incentives to challenge the existing appropriation of effective knowledge and decision-making are undoubtedly increasing, especially in conditions of structural industrial change. The practice of such challenges will require alliance with radical sectors of the 'technical intelligentsia', but the main social forces to identify, sustain and carry them through must, for both structural and ideal reasons, come from these working majorities.

Yet one of the advantages of the idea of cultural revolution, as it reaches beyond the area of immediate industrial property relations, is that it identifies wide groups who are subject to the appropriation of knowledge and effective decision but who are structurally different from the old or the new working class. The outstanding case is that of women, who as workers share one kind of subjection but who more generally, as women, are still profoundly subject to kinds of appropriation deeply rooted in the whole mode of production (and especially the appropriation of their full, as distinct from wage-earning productive forces). The cultural revolution, as distinct from incentives and reforms to permit their inclusion in 'the plan', will be deeply sited among women or it will not, in practice, occur at all.

The final major structural area is that of local communities, in their diverse and complex relations with the larger administrative units which increasingly appropriate even their local powers, and in their now critical relations with the large and brutal sweeps of capital relocation and the disruptive imposition of what, from the level of the appropriation, are seen as mere infrastructures. Nowhere now is there more active need and potential to challenge the fundamental appropriation of decision-making by the existing social order.

Conclusion

Thus, albeit in some new as well as some continuing forms, a socialist cultural revolution has still to be rooted in potential majorities which can, by their own organization and activity, become effective majorities. The principle of cultural revolution offers an outline of ways in which there can be both effective association and new forms of negotiation beyond specific associations. In this assertion of possibility, against all the learned habits of resignation and scepticism, it is already a definition of practical hope. Beyond that, it seems now to be the only way forward in a situation of very general and very dangerous unsettlement, where the taking of direct responsibility is not just an attractive idea but probably the only means of survival. We can agree that it will be long, hard, contentious and untidy—its criterion of success, for as far as we can see, being a possible majority of successes over its many failures. We can also be sure, in the West as certainly as in the East, that while many of its forms will be extensive and pervasive there will be certain decisive confrontations, with very powerful opposing forces, which will all too sharply remind us that we are attempting cultural *revolution* and not some unimpeded process of social growth. But what will get us through such confrontations, and in some important cases into them, is not only association and organization; it will be also what we can call, with Bahro, the 'material force of the idea': the production and the practice of possibility.

Index